Obstinate Education

Educational Futures

RETHINKING THEORY AND PRACTICE

VOLUME 72

The titles published in this series are listed at *brill.com/edfu*

Obstinate Education

Reconnecting School and Society

By

Gert Biesta

BRILL

SENSE

LEIDEN | BOSTON

All chapters in this book have undergone peer review.

The Library of Congress Cataloging-in-Publication Data is available online at http://catalog.loc.gov

Typeface for the Latin, Greek, and Cyrillic scripts: "Brill". See and download: brill.com/brill-typeface.

ISSN 2214-9864
ISBN 978-90-04-40108-2 (paperback)
ISBN 978-90-04-40109-9 (hardback)
ISBN 978-90-04-40110-5 (e-book)

This book is printed on acid-free paper and produced in a sustainable manner.

Printed by Printforce, the Netherlands

obstinate (adj.)

mid-14c., from Latin *obstinatus* "resolute, resolved, determined, inflexible, stubborn," past participle of *obstinare* "persist, stand stubbornly, set one's mind on," from *ob* "by" (see **ob-**) + *stinare* (related to *stare* "stand"), from PIE **ste-no-*, from root ***sta-** "to stand, make or be firm."[1]

Definition of obstinate

1: stubbornly adhering to an opinion, purpose, or course in spite of reason, arguments, or persuasion
2: not easily subdued, remedied, or removed[2]

∴

---

1   https://www.etymonline.com/word/obstinate [last accessed 25 April 2018].
2   https://www.merriam-webster.com/dictionary/obstinate [last accessed 25 April 2018].

Contents

Preface

I would like to thank Michael Peters for the invitation to publish a book in this series. Michael is not only an influential scholar and prolific writer, but may also turn out to be the most influential figure in the development of the global publication infrastructure of the philosophy of education at the end of the 20th and the beginning of the 21st century. His role as editor of a range of journals and book series, but also his role as initiator of a range of new publication initiatives and publication formats, has had a crucial impact on philosophy of education in the English-speaking world. In all this Michael displays a truly democratic generosity, constantly acting on the conviction that everyone has a right to a voice – which of course comes with a responsibility to use this voice well. I have personally benefitted from this in my own writing career, starting with Michael's kind invitation to publish my first monograph (*Beyond Learning: Democratic Education for a Human Future*) in a series he was editing at the time. I dedicate this book to Michael's unfaltering energy and enthusiasm.

Acknowledgements

I am grateful for the opportunity to use previously published work in this monograph. Chapter 1 is based on Biesta, G. J. J. (2013). Responsive or responsible? Education for the global networked society. *Policy Futures in Education, 11*(6), 734–745; Chapter 2 on Biesta, G. J. J. (2002). How general can *Bildung* be? Reflections on the future of a modern educational ideal. *British Journal of Philosophy of Education, 36*(3), 377–390; and Chapter 3 on Biesta, G. J. J. (2012). Becoming world-wise: An educational perspective on the rhetorical curriculum. *Journal of Curriculum Studies, 44*(6), 815–826. Chapter 4 is based on a paper co-authored with Geert-Jan Stams: Biesta, G. J. J. & Stams, G. J. J. M. (2001). Critical thinking and the question of critique. Some lessons from deconstruction. *Studies in Philosophy and Education 20*(1), 57–74, and Chapter 5 on Biesta, G. J. J. (2011). Philosophy, exposure and children: How to resist the instrumentalisation of philosophy in education. *Journal of Philosophy of Education, 45*(2), 305–319. A version of Chapter 6 was my presidential address for the Philosophy of Education Society of North America, subsequently published as: Biesta, G. J. J. (2012). No education without hesitation. Thinking differently about educational relations. In C. Ruitenberg et al. (Eds.), *Philosophy of education 2012* (pp. 1–13). Urbana-Champaign, IL: PES. Chapter 7 was written for this collection, incorporating material from Biesta, G. J. J. (2007). "Don't count me in." Democracy, education and the question of inclusion. *Nordisk Pedagogik, 27*(1), 18–31. Chapter 8 is based on ideas previously published as Biesta, G. J. J. (2010). "The most influential theory of the century." Dewey, democratic education and the limits of pragmatism. In D. Troehler, T. Schlag & F. Osterwalder (Eds.), *Pragmatism and modernities* (pp. 197–213). Rotterdam: Sense Publishers, whereas a version of Chapter 9 was published as Biesta, G. J. J. (2014). Making pedagogy public: For the public, of the public, or in the interest of publicness? In J. Burdick, J. A. Sandlinm, & M. P. O'Malley (Eds.), *Problematizing public pedagogy* (pp. 15–25). New York: Routledge. The Appendix was previously published as Biesta, G. J. J. (2014). From experimentalism to existentialism: Writing from the margins of philosophy of education. In L. Waks (Ed.), *Leaders in philosophy of education. Volume II* (pp. 13–30). Rotterdam: Sense Publishers. In all cases original texts have been checked and adjusted where needed.

Note on the Author

At the time of publication *Gert Biesta* (www.gertbiesta.com) works as (part-time) Professor for Public Education at Maynooth University Ireland, where he contributes to the work of the Centre for Public Education and Pedagogy. In addition, he is (part-time) NIVOZ Professor for Education at the University of Humanistic Studies, The Netherlands, and Visiting Professor (Professor II) at the University of Agder, working across the departments of education, art and fine arts, and psycho-social health. He is associate editor of the journal *Educational Theory* and co-editor of the *British Educational Research Journal*. From 2014 until 2018 he was a member of the Education Council of the Netherlands, the advisory body of the Dutch government and parliament. He has previously worked at universities in the Netherlands, England, Scotland, and Luxembourg, and has held Visiting Professorships in Sweden, Norway and Belgium. His work has so far appeared in 16 different languages. Recent books include: *The Beautiful Risk of Education* (Routledge, 2014) and *The Rediscovery of Teaching* (Routledge, 2017).

The Duty to Resist

C'est la marge qui tient la page. (It's the margin, that holds the page.)
JEAN-LUC GODARD

∴

This book brings together material from articles and chapters that were written and published over the past fifteen years. Unlike the monographs I have published since 2006 – *Beyond Learning* (Biesta, 2006a), *Good Education in an Age of Measurement* (Biesta, 2010a), *Learning Democracy in School and Society* (Biesta, 2011a), *The Beautiful Risk of Education* (Biesta, 2014a), and *The Rediscovery of Teaching* (2017) – the chapters in this book do not constitute a single line of argument, but are better seen as interconnected reflections on a number of key educational topics and themes that have to do with curriculum, pedagogy and democracy. What unites them, however, is the belief that education, as it takes place and is enacted in schools, colleges, universities, but also in other sites and settings, is never just an instrument for what individuals or groups desire from it. Education, in other words, is never just there to solve 'other people's problems,' but also has its *own* concern to take care of.

In the opening chapter of *The Rediscovery of Teaching* (Biesta, 2017) I have described this as a concern for the possibility for children and young people to exist in and with the world in a 'grown-up' manner. In doing so, I have sought to reconnect education with the question of human freedom, albeit not the freedom to do what one wants to do – which I have referred to as 'ego-logical' freedom or, in less philosophical terms, the neo-liberal 'freedom of shopping.' If such freedom is about simply pursuing one's desires, grown-up or *non*-ego-logical freedom is about ways of trying to lead one's life in which one always asks whether what one desires (or encounters 'in' oneself as a desire) is what one should be desiring in light of the challenge to live one's life well, with others, on a planet that has limited capacity for meeting all that is desired from it.

The work of educators here is not to tell children and young people what they should desire, but is about arousing an 'appetite' for living with this question, that is, for making it a living question in one's life. Also, it is about providing space, time and (curricular) forms for encountering and working 'through' one's desires, along the lines of Gayatri Spivak's definition of education as the "uncoercive rearrangement of desires" (Spivak, 2004, p. 526). The ambition, after all, is not to get rid of one's desires, as we need desires to sustain our existence with others in the world. The ambition rather is to identify which desires are going to 'help' and which desires are going to 'hinder.' This is not something that can be settled once and for all but is a fundamentally open and fundamentally ongoing question that requires fresh judgement in each new situation. In this regard, 'grown-up-ness' is not a state one can achieve but is better understood as a self-chosen *irritation*; an irritation one is willing to 'carry' throughout one's life.

Education's 'duty to resist' – to use the wonderful phrase introduced by Philippe Meirieu (2007) – therefore operates at two levels. First of all, it operates at the micro-level of educational interaction, where the work of the educator is never just to accept students and their desires but always should be oriented towards opportunities for bringing students into a relationship with their desires. From this angle the school is therefore not a place where students can *be free*, but rather a space where students can *encounter their freedom* and begin to see that freedom is not just a blessing but also a burden. At the very same time education has a duty to resist the desires society projects onto it. This is not in order to just say no to those desires, but in order to raise the question to what extent those desires are going to help or hinder the work education needs to take care of for its own sake, so to speak.

That is why, as the title of this book suggests, education should never just move smoothly and flexibly with what is wanted from it – by society, by parents, and by students themselves – but always needs a degree of obstinacy. This is not obstinacy for the sake of wanting to be difficult; it rather is informed or, to be more precise, *principled* obstinacy. And the key principle at stake here is the educational interest in the grown-up existence of children and young people, in the world and with the world, but never ego-logically in the centre of the world (for this phrase see Meirieu, 2007, p. 96).

The nine chapters that follow take up the theme of obstinacy in a number of different ways. The first three chapters focus on the relationships between education and society, with particular attention to the ways in which modern society has become a networked society and a society of networks. In Chapter 1, *Responsive or responsible? Democratic education for the global networked society*, I try to characterise the different networks that make up modern societies, and explore the question to what extent education should meet the demands of the global networked society and to what extent it should resist such demands and take its 'own' responsibility. The image I propose is that of a school that is closed towards society – a school that resists demands for just becoming functional – but that is open towards the world, precisely so that education can retain its connection with democracy, with living together in plurality and difference. Networks also play a role in Chapter 2, *How general can Bildung be? Reflections on the future of a modern educational ideal*, in which I explore three different ways in which the idea of *Bildung* as an encounter with something that goes 'beyond the present and particular' (Bailey, 1984) can be understood. In addition to an epistemological and a sociological understanding of the general character of *Bildung*, I propose a networked reading which, as I argue, provides a new impetus for education's duty to resist. In Chapter 3, *Becoming world-wise: An educational perspective on the rhetorical curriculum*, I continue these explorations through a discussion of the rhetorical 'turn' in education. Against the idea that the main task of education would be to make students 'symbol-wise,' I suggest that the more political and existential 'demand' is to help students to become 'world-wise.'

The idea that education is not just there to make students 'fit' existing ways of thinking, doing and being forms the main theme of the second set of three chapters. In Chapter 4, *Critical thinking and the question of critique: Some lesson from deconstruction*, I ask what the idea of critical thinking actually entails. This is important, so I argue, given the fact that critical thinking is often proposed as one of the ways in which students can become equipped to resist, or at least develop a perspective on, the world around them. Again, I move from a more technical towards a more political reading of critique and critical thinking, taking inspiration from the work of Derrida and his insistence that 'deconstruction *is* justice.' Chapter 5, *Philosophy, exposure and children: How to resist the instrumentalisation of philosophy in education?*, looks at the role philosophy might play in positioning students in the world. Rather than to think of philosophy as a strategy for thinking – thinking critically or thinking well – I highlight the importance of exposure, of being 'turned' towards the world so that we come in a position where the world, natural or social, may address us. This is also the point I work towards in Chapter 6, *No education without hesitation: Thinking differently about educational relations*, in which I argue that education, as relational 'work,' should be mindful of leaving a gap between teacher and student particularly so that something 'else,' to put it rather vaguely at this point, can 'enter.'

In the final three chapters I focus on the relationship – or perhaps we should say: relationships – between education and democracy. In Chapter 7, *Transclusion: Overcoming the tension between inclusion and exclusion in the discourse on democracy and democratisation*, I focus on the question what inclusion might mean in the context of democracy and democratic citizenship. Against the idea that democratisation can be understood as the ongoing inclusion of those who are 'outside' of democracy into the democratic 'order,' I suggest, in discussion with ideas from Iris Young and Jacques Rancière, that 'real' inclusion requires both the inclusion of those who are excluded and the reconfiguration of the very 'order' in which they are included. For this double process I propose the term 'transclusion.' In Chapter 8, *Democracy and education revisited: Dewey's democratic deficit*, I look in more detail at one of the most visible and in a sense more famous discussions of the relationship between education and democracy, namely John Dewey's 1916 book *Democracy and Education* (Dewey, 1966). Although the book is frequently referred to in discussions about democracy and education, I ask to what extent Dewey is really interested in democracy or, at least in this book, rather is interested in democracy because it allows for the most varied 'cultivation' of individuals. I argue that the latter seems to be the main 'logic' of Dewey's argument which, in my view, is a rather limited way to engage with the political project of democracy. In Chapter 9, *Making pedagogy public: For the public, of the public, or in the interest of publicness?*, I continue the discussion by asking how we might best understand the idea of public pedagogy and, more specifically, the public nature or character of pedagogy. I distinguish between three possible approaches to public pedagogy and argue that it is only in the third one – pedagogy with an interest in 'publicness' or 'public existence,' that a proper connection between education and democracy can be found.

The chapters brought together in this book contain ideas, arguments and lines of thought that may still be relevant for contemporary discussions, which is the reason why I have selected them for this volume. Nonetheless they also document the development of my own thinking, and there are aspects of what is presented in this book that I now see differently – mostly because over time I have become aware of further complexities of the discussions I have engaged in and have managed to gain a better understanding of the different traditions that I am in conversation with. In the brief concluding chapter, called *Looking back and going forward*, I reflect on some of these developments in order to provide my current perspective on the key themes and issues of this book. The chapter is brief, because I also hope – and this always remains my main ambition – that readers will draw their own conclusions, hopefully in conversation with what I have written. But I would also be entirely happy if readers resist some of the avenues in which I am trying to take them.

At the very end of this book I have included an autobiographical chapter in which I have tried to make some sense of my own development as writer and teacher. Some may find it helpful to engage with such a more personal account of on my work; others may see it as superfluous with regard to the content of my writing. I personally tend to veer towards the latter view, which is the reason why I have included it as an appendix and not as part of the main text. There may, however, be some wisdom in Jean-Luc Godard's observation, which I encountered in the work of Philippe Meirieu (2007, p. 125), that it is ultimately the margin that holds the page.

CHAPTER 1

Responsive or Responsible? Democratic Education for the Global Networked Society

Introduction[1]

The British sociologist Anthony Giddens has apparently once claimed that totalitarian regimes fall when in a given country a particular percentage of the population gains access to a telephone connection. While I do not remember the exact percentage (or even whether Giddens gave such a percentage), the interesting thing about this observation is what it suggests about the democratic potential of networks, particularly the 'flat' networks that have become part of the everyday lives of many people around the world. If, for a moment, we look at the statistics on mobile phones, the most ubiquitous networking devices around, we find that on a world population of close to 7 billion people there currently are more than 5 billion mobile phone connections (the 4 billion mark was passed in 2008 and the expectation in 2010 was that the 6 billion mark will be passed in 2012[2]). In 2010 Western Europe had a coverage of about 130% (i.e., 1.3 connections for every individual), and Eastern Europe of 123%. Other countries are catching up rapidly, with the expectation that China will have 1 billion connections in 2012 which amounts to a coverage of about 75%.[3] (This figure was apparently reached in May 2012.[4])

While of the 6 trillion or so text messages that were sent in 2010 (which is about 200,000 messages per second) many will have been entirely trivial – "I'm on the train," "I am not yet home," "LOL" – it seems reasonable to expect that this gigantic infrastructure is also being used in more meaningful ways. This already shows at a small scale that while network technology such as the mobile phone has the potential for meaningful use, it is in itself neither good nor bad, neither meaningful nor meaningless, neither democratic nor undemocratic. It all still depends on what people do with it. This was forcefully demonstrated in two recent events: the 'twitter revolutions' in Arab countries and the 'Facebook riots' in England in the summer of 2011. Two 'popular' events – and I use 'popular' here in the sense of 'events of the people' – that used the same network technology for very different aims and with very different outcomes. These events not only demonstrate the potential of 'flat' networks to mobilise people outside of the gaze of those in power – and in this respect we can say that such networks truly operate 'under the radar.' They also highlight

© KONINKLIJKE BRILL NV, LEIDEN, 2019 | DOI: 10.1163/9789004401105_002

the fact that anyone who nowadays wishes to control people, needs to control the flows of information and the modes of communication rather than, as Marx would have it, the modes of production.[5]

The idea that those who want to control other people, need to control information and communication is not a new idea. Educators actually know it quite well and have known it for a long time (see for example Apple, 2004). We could even say that the 'logic' of modern schooling is precisely based on the control of information – which, in the context of schooling, is called 'the curriculum' – and control of the modes of communication – which, in the context of schooling, is called teaching, instruction or pedagogy. While the control of information and communication in the school is often done with the best intentions and for good reasons, it is control nonetheless. If we want to look at this from a positive angle, we might say that the idea of the school as a controller of information made sense in a time when it was difficult to access information and, more importantly, to access *reliable* information. Here we have a rather traditional rationale for the school as an empowering institution, based on the idea that knowledge is power. There is of course also a darker side to this, because the very same educational infrastructure can also be used – and has been used and is still being used – for limiting the access to particular useful (or really useful; see Johnson, 1979) knowledge.

Yet we now live in a time in which information is abundant and knowledge comes cheap; a time in which old epistemological hierarchies are breaking down and where the centre can no longer hold. Is this a time in which the school as we know it, the school as a privileged provider of knowledge, has become obsolete? That, for me, would be too hasty a conclusion, one that would only follow from a very simplistic notion of what the school is but also – and that is where I want to start my argument – one which simply *accepts* the global networked society as a given and sees the task of educators and educationalists to figure out how the school can best adapt to this new reality.

For me the issue is neither to give up on the school altogether, nor to ask how the school can best adapt. The question for me rather is how the school should *respond* to this new reality, not by simply being responsive but by taking responsibility; a responsibility, so I wish to suggest, which needs to be both educational and democratic. What is at stake here, therefore, is the bigger theme of the relationship between school and world; a relationship that never can be one in which the school is just a function of and thus functional for society, but where, to a certain extent, the school also needs to be *dys*functional in relation to society because, as the French educationalist Philip Meirieu (2007) has argued, education always also comes with a 'duty to resist.'

Starting from here, my chapter consists of three parts. I will first explore the idea of the global networked society, raising some critical questions about its different manifestations. I will then focus on the question of education, where I will try to articulate what a responsible educational response to the phenomenon of the global networked society might be. In the final step I connect this with some brief observations about the question of democracy. I do not have the intention to solve all problems with regard to the relationships between networks, education and democracy, but hope to make some critical observations, provide tools for asking more precise questions, and hopefully will contribute some original and useful insights to the discussion.

The Global Networked Society: Fact or Fiction?

By asking whether the global networked society is fact or fiction, I do not wish to position myself as a global networked society denier, but do want to highlight two points. The first is that, to a large extent, the global networked society is not a new phenomenon, and by looking at its historical precursors we can begin to see where there is continuity and what might be really new about the current manifestation of the global networked society. The second point is that I do not want to see the global networked society simply as a *fact*, that is, as something that is just given and therefore inevitable. I rather want to approach it as a *choice*, a choice made by some and working in the interest of some. Let me begin with the first point.

Although the impression is sometimes given that the global networked society is a new phenomenon, any attempt to understand what is new about the contemporary manifestation of the global networked society has to start from the acknowledgement that networks with a large, if not global reach have been around for a pretty long time. Three impressive examples spring to mind: the Roman Empire; the Catholic Church; and the British Colonial Empire. What we know from history is that the Roman Empire was not only very well organised but also very well networked. It can thus be seen as one of the first examples of a networked society with a significant, albeit it not entirely 'global' reach (although we have to bear in mind that the conception of what constituted the 'globe' was of course different from our modern conception). The Catholic Church is another interesting example of a global network. While it cannot lay claim to being a society in the sense of a nation state, it is definitely another example of a very well connected and well networked structure with impressive global reach. This is also the case for the third example – the British Empire – which, at its height, was the largest empire in history covering, in

1922, not only one quarter of the then world population (it included about 450 million people) but also one quarter of the earth's total land area.

Centred Networks

There are lots of traces of these global networks still around – and the Catholic Church simply is still is around, making it one of the longest existing institutions in human history. For the Roman Empire there are not only many physical traces – not only the villa's and baths, but also extensive road networks and basic city plans – but also an ongoing influence of, for example Roman law and the Latin language on contemporary law and language. And while the British Empire no longer exists as an empire, many of its networks are still active and operational.

What unites these three examples of global networks is that they all operate on the centre-outpost model. Not only do all three networks have a clearly defined centre – Rome, the Vatican City and London – but the networks also existed because all outposts remained connected to the centre through lines of command and information. One could say that command flowed from the centre to the outposts and information flowed from the outposts to the centre so that the centre could keep an overview and remain in control. The decline of the Roman Empire can partly be explained by the erosion of the connection between centre and outposts – the Empire became too big and too complicated to maintain all its networks, also because outposts became self-sufficient and, subsequently, independent. The Catholic Church has been more successful in controlling its outposts. And, as mentioned, many of the networks of the British Empire still function in some shape or form.

Decentred Networks

What characterises centred networks is that they are based on the principle of asymmetry between centre and margins. Power, information and wealth are clearly located in the centre and the connection between centre and margins is one where the centre exerts power over the margins, where the centre is also in control – and perhaps we could even say in possession – of information, and where the centre is the location where wealth from the margins is collected and accumulated. Network-building according to the principles of this model is therefore as much a process of subjecting and incorporating new areas into the network as it is a process of translating and transforming such new areas into the 'logic' and principles of the centre.[6] This, then, is perhaps the main difference between the global networks that have been around for a long time and the networks that are currently emerging as a result of information and communication technology, particularly the internet and mobile phones. What characterises such networks – but with a proviso to which I will return below – is that they are to a much larger extent decentred networks, where there are multiple connections across the network but without a centre and without the need for a centre.[7]

Yet before we start celebrating the democratic potential of decentred networks there is one more dimension of the history of global networking that needs to be brought in the mix. This dimension is called capitalism. Capitalism, an economic system characterised by private ownership of the means of production and an orientation towards the generation of profit, usually through operation in competitive markets, is clearly a networking phenomenon, and perhaps it is the most influential network phenomenon of the modern age. The main reason for this has to do with the fact that capitalism, in order to sustain itself, needs to grow. While, up to a point, the expansion of capitalism could be contained within national markets, the rise of global capitalism, a mode of capitalism that is no longer bound by the nation state, is simply an effect of the need for capitalism to expand. It is here that we can see an interesting connection with colonialism which, in a sense started the capitalist cycle of wealth accumulation by using the colonies to source raw materials, but then turned around to use the same infrastructure for selling products thus opening up – sometimes forcefully (such as the 'opening up' of Japan in 1852–1854 by the US Navy; see Feifer, 2006) – ever new markets.

For a long time, capitalist expansion was predominantly a spatial phenomenon, both in terms of finding new resources and with regard to opening up new markets. Yet the limitations of this strategy have led to a shift in which capitalist expansion has increasingly become temporal. A prime example of this is the idea of fashion, which operates on the principle of constantly creating new demand and new desires.[8] We can thus see a constant 'speeding up' of capitalism or, stated in different terms, we can see an ongoing time-compression in order for capitalism to sustain itself. But just as it is becoming obvious that capitalism is running out of space – think for example about the statistics mentioned earlier about mobile phone contracts; but think also about the ecological crisis created by ever-expanding capitalism – capitalism is also running out of time.

Perhaps the starkest example of the latter is the recent banking crisis which exposed the ways in which the financial industry – and the phrase 'financial industry' is interesting in itself – tries to generate profit by making use of increasingly minimal temporal advantages. (The paradigm case for this is, of course, futures trading.) While capitalism thus generates global networks – and in this sense can be seen as one of the most influential drivers if not shapers of the contemporary global networked society – there is a real question about the sustainability of such networks. And what the banking crisis has shown is the fragility and vulnerability of the networks of global capitalism as they have created a situation in which everything hangs together so that when some part goes down there is a real danger that the whole system will collapse – which was one of the reasons why global capitalism needed to be propped up and saved by governments, a problem that is still ongoing.

Pseudo-Decentred Networks

For my analysis of the global networked society the important question is whether capitalism should be seen as generating centred or decentred networks. My suggestion would be to call them pseudo-decentred networks. What they share with centred networks is the fact that they both rely upon and are creators of asymmetries, particularly asymmetries in wealth, but also asymmetries in power. What they share with decentred networks is not only the fact that there is not one centre that aims to control the whole network – there are probably many centres – but also, and more importantly, the fact that those who are part of the network are in a real sense implicated in it. They have an interest in the survival of the network because if the network of global capitalism would collapse they would probably be worse of (and again this is a very real and ongoing problem).

It is because of these different historical and contemporary dimensions and manifestations of global networks and of the global networked society – and perhaps the word 'the' is actually quite misleading here – that I do not want to accept the global network society as a fact but rather want to see it as a choice; a choice that works in the interest of some and against the interest of others. While my use of the word 'choice' is not to suggest that it is easy or even possible to identify who have made a choice for a particular configuration of the global networked society, I use it to highlight that the global networked society in its current manifestation is not an inevitable reality without an alternative.

Unlike what politicians nowadays often tend to say about their policies – which, echoing Margaret Thatcher, is that 'there is no alternative' (something which Zygmunt Bauman has called the TINA-creed; see Bauman, 2000, p. 215) – the fact that the global networked society as it currently exist is the outcome of particular historical developments, means that it not only could have been different but that it still can be different, albeit – and this is again one of the ironies and complexities of the global networked society, particularly in its capitalist form – that it is quite difficult to disentangle oneself from its workings. It is very difficult, in other words, to go truly 'off grid' – but it is not impossible to do things differently as, for example, can be seen from a number of banks that were relatively unaffected by the recent banking crisis because they operate on significantly different principles than 'main stream' banks (for example, of co-operative banking, of building societies, and of different varieties of ethical banking).

If this begins to open up the idea of the global networked society, revealing both continuity and discontinuity and, perhaps most importantly, showing its connections with the logic of capitalism, we are now in a better position to ask the question of education, that is: "What kind of education might we need in 'the' global networked society?"

Education for the Global Networked Society: Responsive or Responsible?

I am, of course, not the first to engage with this question, although what I have been trying to do differently is not to start from the simple acceptance of 'the' global network society and ask how schools should adjust and adapt to it but raise some critical question first. What my brief exploration suggests, I think, is that we should be cautious and not simply embrace the global networked society. Although there are some potentially interesting aspects – and I will return to the question of the democratic potential below – I have indicated that the global networked society has a tendency to create and perpetuate inequalities, and I have indicated that the global networked society, at least in some of its manifestations, may result in networks that are extremely vulnerable and volatile, which not only raises the question how much we should 'invest' in such networks (and how much we should invest ourselves in such networks), but also whether there are more sustainable alternatives.

The Formalisation of the School Curriculum

When we look at the ways in which educators and educationalists have responded to the global networked society, we can discern a number of different approaches. Several of them start from a reading of the global networked society as a society where there is an abundance of information and where access to this information is generally free. This, as I have mentioned above, raises questions about the privileged role of the school in handing down knowledge to the next generation. Some have drawn the radical conclusion that this makes the school obsolete, but the more common response is one that argues for what I suggest calling the *formalisation* of the school curriculum (i.e., it becomes a matter of form, not of content or substance). Here the focus shifts from the acquisition of knowledge to the acquisition of the skills for acquiring knowledge, now and in the future. Notions such as 'learning to learn' or education as the preparation for lifelong learning fall in this category.

A potential problem with these approaches is that they are not only based on a rather narrow view about the function of schooling – I will return to this below – but also on a potentially uncritical view about knowledge, that is that knowledge is 'there' and either the school has the task to transmit this knowledge or, if knowledge is everywhere, it has the task to learn students to access knowledge themselves. I am therefore more interested in approaches that argue for the need for forms of *critical literacy*, particularly because the abundance of information raises the question how one can properly select from and make judgements about the information that is available to us. A critical literacy approach can also go one step further by making the very idea of the global networked society itself a topic for critical scrutiny – for example along the lines suggested above. The focus then shifts from a critical reading of knowledge and information to a critical reading of the world itself (see, for example, Freire & Macedo, 1987).

Such an approach, about which I will say a bit more below, stands in sharp contrast to approaches that uncritically embrace (a particular representation of) the global networked society and simply see the task of education as that of preparing students for this reality. One example of this is the idea of 21st century skills which is currently big in the USA and, if my observations are correct, is also gaining popularity in other countries. On the website of the 'Partnership for 21st Century Skills' (http://www.p21.org) we can read the following:

> The Partnership for 21st Century Skills is a national organization that advocates for 21st century readiness for every student. As the United States continues to compete in a global economy that demands innovation, P21 and its members provide tools and resources to help the U.S. education system keep up by fusing the three Rs and four Cs (critical thinking and problem solving, communication, collaboration, and creativity and innovation).[9]

What worries me about the idea of 21st century skills is not only the fact that it seems to suggest yet another one-size-fits-all educational solution for all problems, thus burdening teachers and schools again with unrealistic expectations about what they can and should achieve, but even more so the fact that the 'framework for 21st century learning' that 21st century skills purports to offer, takes the global competitive economy – i.e., global capitalism – as its unquestioned frame of reference. As a result, the purpose of education becomes (re)defined as making students ready for this 'reality,' and the phrasing even suggests that the global economy simply *demands* this. We can find the economic orientation of 21st century skills also in such claims as that the "P21's framework for learning in the 21st century is based on the essential skills that our children need to succeed as citizens and workers in the 21st century" and in highly rhetorical statements such as the following:

> Every child in America needs to be ready for today's and tomorrow's world. A profound gap exists between the knowledge and skills most students learn in school and the knowledge and skills they need for success in their communities and workplaces. To successfully face rigorous higher education coursework, career challenges and a globally competitive workforce, U.S. schools must align classroom environments with real world environments by fusing the three Rs and four Cs.[10]

While I do not wish to deny the importance of work, it is neither the be-all and end-all of education, nor the be-all and end-all of life. It is, therefore, not only rather narrow-minded to tie up education so strongly with the global economy. It is also ironic that while critical thinking is very prominently mentioned as a 21st century skill, the whole framework seems to rest on an uncritical acceptance of the reality of the global networked economy. For me this is therefore an example of a *responsive* – or perhaps we should say: *reactive* – *response* to the global networked society that, because it simply seems to accept the global networked society particular in its economic manifestation, runs the risk of becoming irresponsible. What then, would a more *responsible response* look like?

The Question of Educational Purpose(s)

In order to address this question, I would like to take on step back and say a few things about how I think we might productively engage with questions concerning the purpose – or as I will argue: purposes – of education. The problem is that when we ask the question how the school should respond to the global networked society or, even more precise, what kind of education we might need for the global networked society, the language we use can give the impression that education is monolithic, i.e., that it is one thing with only one aim. This continues to be the cause of a lot of confusion in discussions about what schools are for, and it is for this reason that in my own work I have argued that education not only *de facto* functions in relation to a number of different domains, but that it also *ought* to function in relation to a number of different domains. I have found it useful to make a distinction between three functions of education – qualification, socialisation and subjectification – which I also see as three domains of educational purpose. Let me briefly explain what I have in mind.[11]

One important function of education is that of *qualification*, that is, of the ways in which it qualifies children and young people to do certain things. Qualification is about the acquisition of knowledge, skills and dispositions, both those that allow children and students to do very specific things – such as in vocational education – and those that allow children and young people to function in modern society. While some people argue that this is the only thing that schools should focus on – the 'back to basics' phrase is often used in that context, and part of the rationale for 21st century skills is probably based here as well – there has, over the years, been increased attention for a second function of education, that of *socialisation*. Socialisation can be understood as the way in which through education children and young people become part of particular traditions and practices, that is, of particular cultural, social, historical, political, religious, and so on 'orders.'

Again, there is a narrow dimension to this which we can find in professional socialisation – that is, picking up the ways of doing and being of a particular job or profession – and a much wider way of thinking about socialisation, for example becoming a good citizen, picking up the values of 'Britishness' (or for that matter of any other culture or nation), and so on. Socialisation is, in other words, about becoming part of certain ways of doing, both informal and formal and institutionalised. Qualification and socialisation can, on the one hand, help to make clear what it is that education actually 'does' – which means that the research on the hidden curriculum has a place in looking at education through the lens of socialisation. But qualification and socialisation are also two views of what it is that education ought to be doing. They not only describe functions of education but also domains of educational purpose.

While some again would argue that schools should focus only on qualification and that socialisation is a task of parents and society, others argue that schools have a role to play both with regard to qualification and socialisation – and this is perhaps most explicit in a range of topics and issues that in recent years have been added to the curriculum, such as citizenship education, environmental education, global education, and so on. In addition to these two functions I wish to suggest that there is a third function and dimension of education that has to do with the ways in which education contributions to the formation of the person.

In my own work I have called this dimension the *subjectification* dimension of education, and the reason for that is that I wish to focus on the ways in which education contributes to the ways in which children and young people can become subjects of action and responsibility, to put it briefly. Subjectification thus has to do with notions like independence and autonomy, that is, with being the agent of one's own actions – albeit that my phrase 'subject of action and responsibility' tries to capture a conception of human subjectivity that is not selfish or self-centred but always understood as being-in-responsible-relation with other human beings and, by extension, with the natural world more generally.[12]

To make the main point one more time: these three functions of education both describe what education *actually does* – i.e., that it always in some way operates in these three domains – but at the same time it also gives us a framework to ask much more precise questions about what education *ought to do*; it gives us a framework, therefore, to engage with the question of the purposes of education. I don't see the three dimensions as separate, and I also don't think that we can organise education in such a way that it only would focus on one of the three functions – after all, even if one were only to focus on knowledge and skills one would, through this, also socialise one's students into a particular view about what matters in the world and would always also in some way impact on the formation of the person. That is why I think that any educational rationale always needs to have to say something about each of the dimensions. In practice they are difficult to disentangle, which is why I tend to depict all this in the form of a Venn diagram with three overlapping areas of educational function and purpose.

A Responsible Response?

When we look at the question as to what kind of education we might need for the global networked society through this lens, we can not only begin to locate some of the responses, but also see their limitations and work towards what I would wish to propose as a more *responsible* alternative. If we go back to some of the responses I have mentioned, it can now be made clear that those who say that the school as a transmitter of knowledge has become obsolete in the global networked society and who therefore argue for a formal curriculum – i.e., a curriculum focusing on skills for knowledge acquisition rather than a curriculum organised around content – see the function of the school mainly in terms of qualification.

That was behind my remark that these views run the risk of being based on a rather simplistic notion of what the school is and what the school is *for*. An approach like 21st century skills in my view combines qualification and sociali-sation. The qualification agenda is clear in the claim that children and young people should be made 'ready' for the 21st century and for the demands of the global economy. The socialisation agenda that comes with this is that it depicts education as the server of the global economy – despite, as I have shown, its emphasis on critical thinking. (And a more negative evaluation here would be to say that by giving critical thinking such a prominent position it actually works ideologically, that is, hiding the very power structures through which it operates.)

Approaches that argue for forms of critical literacy are, in my view, more interesting, more relevant and also more responsible, particularly if the aim is not only to make children and young people literate with regard to the content of the curriculum but also with regard to the wider socio-political context. Here one could say that education for the global networked society obtains an explicit political dimension – the literacy, in other words, is not only technical or cognitive, but explicitly political. This means that a critical literacy approach is not confined to the domain of qualification – although it clearly aims to qualify children and students in a particular way – but operates at the intersection between the qualification domain and something else. But the important and difficult question is what this 'something else' is. Is critical literacy located in the intersection between qualification and socialisation? Is it located in the intersection between qualification and subjectification? Is it perhaps located at the very centre of the diagram, that is, at the intersection of the three domains?

The quick way to see what is at stake here is that while proponents of a critical literacy approach might locate this in the intersection between qualification and subjectification on the assumption that to make people literate in reading how power operates behind the scenes, so to speak, can contribute to their independence from the workings of power. This is the classical argument from critical theory and critical pedagogy (see Biesta, 2010b; Galloway, 2012). But the classical critique of this approach is to claim that critical literacy provides students with a very particular perspective on the world that is based on a very particular set of values, and thus is at most a form of political socialisation – and strong critics of critical pedagogy and critical theory would probably claim that it is a form of political indoctrination. There is no easy way out here, but what at least distinguishes a critical literacy approach from other approaches is that it explicitly aims to engage with the subjectification dimension of education; it explicitly aims to support students in developing a stance in relation to phenomena such as the global networked society. It is an educational response, in other words, that aims to support the subjectivity, the becoming-subject, of the student (see also Meirieu, 2007).

My own position in relation to the question about the kind of education we might need for the global networked society starts even more explicitly in the subjectification domain. While I do think that it is legitimate to ask the question how education can help students to be ready for the realities of the global networked society – I am, after all, not denying that these realities are there; what I am denying is the line of argument that says that because they are there they are good and desirable and we should just adapt to them; I am denying, in other words, any suggestion that there would not be an alternative – this can only be done if, *analytically*, we try to understand how manifestations of the global networked society impact on processes of subjectification, processes of becoming-subject and, *programmatically*, if we try to articulate how we might support the becoming-subject of children and young people in light of the different manifestations of the global networked society. In answering this question, I would start from the observation that the global networked society – or at least several of its manifestations – is full of temptations, not in the least because of its connection with global capitalism, and thus has a tendency to draw people in. To this comes the fact that the global networked society is indeed to a large extent everywhere, which means that it is quite difficult not to be subjected to its lures.

But to be subjected is precisely the opposite of what subjectification – becoming-subject – is about. Here the old saying that if you stand for nothing you will fall for anything, is educationally very relevant, because to resist the temptations of the global networked society – or at least to make engagement with aspects of the global networked society the outcome of a deliberate decision rather than just an automatic reflex – requires indeed what we might refer to as a certain 'strengthening' of the subject. This is of course tricky terrain – and I will in a moment show that this is only half of the task of education in response to the global networked society – but it can be connected to what I see as one of the most fundamental educational issues or challenges, which is the transformation of what is desired into what is desirable (see Biesta, 2010a). That is to see education as assisting the process where we rise 'above' our desires by always exploring whether what I do desire is also what I should desire, i.e., whether what is *de facto* desired is also desirable. If, for a moment, we use the words 'weak' and 'strong' in a rather simplistic way, we could say that following one's desires weakens subjectivity whereas engaging with the question which of one's desires is actually desirable strengthens subjectivity.

The idea that education has something to do with strengthening the subject – and in this sense with resisting adaptation to what is – does, however, come with a risk, namely that of disengaging the subject from the world. If the subject becomes too strong, one could say, there is a risk that it becomes self-enclosed, shielded off from others, and thus shielded off from the world. Strengthening the subject, resisting the tendency to simply adapt to what is, should therefore not result in a withdrawal from the world. The challenge for education, therefore, is both to strengthen subjectivity *and* support engagement with the world. Education is about the double task of engaging with and emancipating from, in the words of Meirieu (2008, p. 91). One could of course say that this is an impossible task, as it pulls education into two very different directions. I don't think that this is necessarily so because resistance and engagement actually have a different 'object' – there is a need to resist adaptation to what is, whereas there is a need to engage with a world that is not yet, a world of possibilities, a world of alternatives, a world that can be different from what is.

If these suggestions make sense, if they begin to articulate what I would see as a more responsible response to the so-called realities of the global networked society, it puts the school in a very interesting position. Perhaps the briefest way to summarise what I have in mind is to say that we need a school that is *closed towards society but open towards the world*. It is a school that is shielded off from direct demands from society so that an engagement with the world as a world of possibilities, a world of alternatives, becomes possible. It is the school as a space of suspension, a moratorium. This image of the school fits quite well with one of the original meanings of the Greek word *schole*, which means leisure or free time, which we should not so much see as time where you can do what you want, but time that is not determined by particular demands, particularly not the demands of society (see also Masschelein & Simons, 2010). To say that this puts the school in a very interesting position, is also to say that I do not think that in the global networked society we can do without the school. It doesn't mean that the school becomes obsolete; on the contrary, we need this space free from the immediate demands of society perhaps even more than ever.

This brings me to the third and final step of my chapter, which is the question of democracy, about which I will make two brief observations in order to bring the themes of my chapter – networks, education and democracy – together.

Democratic Education for the Global Networked Society?

I have started my chapter by hinting at the democratic potential of the kind of networks that seem to be characteristic of the global networked society, that is 'flat' networks or, as I have called them in my more detailed exploration, *decentred* networks. That such networks have a democratic potential is obvious, but we should be mindful that it is a potentiality, not an actuality. The point is that while it could be argued that democracy is necessarily decentred, this does not mean that every decentred network is automatically democratic. The difference between the twitter revolutions and the Facebook riots is a helpful demonstration of this point. While I have characterised both events as popular events, that is events of the people, one could say that they were informed by a different set of values. Whereas the twitter revolutions were orientated towards the democratic values of equality and freedom, the Facebook riots to a large extent lacked this orientation, particularly where these riots turned destructive (see also Biesta, 2011a).[13]

The first point to make, therefore, is that decentred networks are only *potentially* democratic, and that it depends on the values that inform the actions of individuals within such networks whether this democratic potential can become actual. Rather than simply celebrating the democratic potential of the global networked society, there is a need for hard work and constant vigilance if, that is, we are interested in making this democratic potential in some way real. For this it is also important to be aware of the potential threat of what I have referred to as pseudo-decentred networks, that is, networks that while, lacking an obvious centre of control, are nonetheless contributing to the production of asymmetries and inequalities. Again, this proves the point that there is no such thing as 'the' global networked society – there are a number of different manifestations of it, and we need to look very carefully at the differences that manifest themselves.

If we are interested in making the democratic potential of the global networked society real, it is not only important to acknowledge that this requires that our actions are informed by an orientation towards the democratic values of equality and freedom – even if they can only exist in a paradoxical tension (see Mouffe, 2000). It is also important to see that a democratic orientation towards freedom is not simply about maximising one's own freedom but is about maximising the freedom of everyone – which means that in a sense the democratic orientation is first and foremost an orientation towards the freedom of others. What this means in practice is that we should not understand democracy in arithmetical terms, that is as a process of expressing and counting preferences, but as a transformative process in which there is always the question whether the preferences that are expressed can be legitimately 'carried' by the collective. It is at precisely this point that we can see a similarity between education and democracy in that both education and democracy come with a requirement for not simply accepting what is desired or preferred, but for transforming such desires and preferences into what legitimately can be seen as desirable (a theme I explore in more detail in Biesta, 2011b).

This is then where the educative and the democratic intersect, precisely because in a sense they come with the same 'demand' or the same challenge of *not* to live one's life by one's desires, but always to ask whether one's desires are truly desirable. One might argue that what is different in the case of democracy is that a judgement about what is desirable always brings in the perspective of

others, so that the judgement as to whether certain preferences can indeed be
seen as desirable always need to engage with the question how my preferences
interfere with the preferences of others. This is what I meant with the question
whether certain preference can legitimately be 'carrier' by the collective.

I wish to suggest, however, that this is actually not different in the case
of education. If I am correct that the challenge for education is the double
challenge of strengthening subjectivity *and* supporting engagement with the
world, then any judgement about the question whether what one desires is
also desirable necessarily needs to bring this worldly 'dimension,' which is
the dimension of the other, into consideration. From this angle – but with a
rather different set of assumptions and ideas – I do think that John Dewey
was right about the intrinsic connection between democracy and education,
in that education is necessarily democratic just as democracy is automatically
educative. Or to be a bit more precise: that 'good' education as outlined here is
necessarily democratic, just as 'good' democracy as outlined here is automatically educative.

For the discussion in this chapter this means then, that the responsible
response to the phenomenon of the global networked society that I have tried
to outline, points in the direction of a connection between school and world
that is necessarily of a democratic nature.

Conclusion

In this chapter I have tried to formulate an answer to the question what kind
of education we might need for the global networked society. On the one hand
I have offered some conceptual tools for formulating more precise questions
about the relationship between education and the global networked society.
For that I have made a distinction between different qualities of global networks – the distinction between *centred, decentred* and *pseudo-decentred* networks – and between different functions of education and different domains of
educational purpose – the distinction between *qualification, socialisation* and
subjectification. In my chapter I have taken what could be characterised as a
political approach. Although I would see that as a fair characterisation – I have,
after all raised questions about power, interest, asymmetry, and inequality – I
would also, and perhaps first and foremost, characterise my response as an
educational response, perhaps with the explanation that for me education cannot be done or understood outside of the domain of the political.

The reason for this is that for me education is itself never a value-neutral
'technical' enterprise, but rather what I would call an *interested* endeavour.

And I have tried to make clear that for me the main, and perhaps even the ultimate educational interest is an interest in the human being as a subject of action and responsibility. That is why I have warned against a too optimistic embrace of the global networked society and why I have questioned educational responses that are just *responsive* in that they simply accept the global networked society and see the only task of education as that of making children and young people ready for this reality.

While my argument does not amount to a wholesale rejection of the global networked society, it points at a need to resist at least aspects of the global networked society. In order for this to be possible we need spaces where the 'demands' of the global networked society can at least be suspended. I have suggested that the school could and should be such a space. While this means that, as I have put it, the school should in this respect be closed towards (the demands of) society I have argued that at the same time it should be open towards (the possibilities of) the world. It should be closed towards what presents itself as given and inevitable and should be open towards a world of possibilities, a world in which there are always alternatives. It is here, in the school's openness towards the world, that I see the educative and the democratic interest come together (see also Winter, 2011). That is why, in conclusion, I wish to argue that a responsible educative response to the global networked society has to be a democratic one.

Notes

1   An earlier version of this text was presented as an invited keynote address at the 14th Biennial Conference of the European Association for Research on Learning and Instruction (EARLI). This earlier version also appeared as Biesta, G. J. J. (2013). Responsive or responsible? Education for the global networked society. *Policy Futures in Education*, *11*(6), 734–745.

2   See http://www.bbc.co.uk/news/10569081 [accessed 4 September 2012].

3   See https://www.wirelessintelligence.com/analysis/2011/07/china-to-surpass-1-billion-mobile-connections-in-may-2012/ [accessed 4 September 2012].

4   See http://www.them.pro/One-billion-mobile-phone-subscribers-China [accessed 4 September 2012].

5   This is not only well known in China where there are ongoing issues about access to the world wide web, but also in the UK where the government, in response to the street riots of 2011, suggested that it should have the power to black out social networking sites during civil unrest. The Chinese government could indeed not resist pointing out the irony of this suggestion.

6   Bruno Latour's Science in Action (1987) is an interesting example of the analysis of the operation of modern science according to these principles.

7   Complexity theory with its notions of emergence and self-organisation is particularly suited for understanding the dynamics of such decentred networks (see, for example, Cilliers, 1998; Osberg & Biesta 2010).

8   See, for example, IPhone 3, IPhone 4, IPhone 5, but we can also think how a company such as H&M operates with cycles of about 3 weeks for bringing new clothing designs into their shops.

9   See http://www.p21.org [accessed 4 September 2012].

10 See http://www.p21.org [accessed 4 September 2012].

11 These ideas are discussed and developed in more detail in Biesta (2009a, 2010a).

12 The reason to prefer the word 'subject' is partly a technical/philosophical one (see Biesta, 2010a, for more detail). I could also have used the word 'person' there (although the technical argument here is that person is a more individualistic notion that subject). The word I would not prefer to use in this context is that of identity. Identity for me has to do with question of 'identification with' and therefore belong more to the domain of socialisation. Also, identity for me is more a psychological and sociological than an educational notion.

13 I am aware that more complex readings of the difference are possible and probably also necessary as the Facebook riots can at least partly be understood as an expression of a certain desire for equality. That is why I am highlighting the fact that they turned against the values of equality and freedom when they became destructive, thus blocking the freedom of others. While – again to a certain extent – I can understand such a response in the light of the banking crisis and the destructive effects this has had, it does not justify the riots, nor, of course, is there any justification for the amoral and destructive behaviour of bankers, and perhaps we can add: of the global financial network itself.

CHAPTER 2

How General Can *Bildung* Be? Reflections on the Future of a Modern Educational Ideal

Introduction[1]

In the beginning of the nineteenth century the journey from London to Plymouth, one of the longest east–west journeys between major towns in England, took about 22 hours by mail coach. At Plymouth the traveller would find that the local time was 20 minutes later than it was in London, but this was a trifling difference, easily adjusted. As the national railway system developed, however, time differentials soon became an impediment. The two lines that ran almost directly from east to west therefore adopted Greenwich time for all purposes from their opening in 1838 and 1841 respectively. Greenwich time was also used by the companies that in 1841 formed the line from Leeds to Rugby, where it joined the London & Birmingham Railway, which, however, still observed local time. Henry Booth, secretary of the Liverpool & Manchester Railway, advocated the adoption of Greenwich time by all railway companies. His own company petitioned Parliament to impose it in 1845. That attempt failed, but his arguments soon came to be accepted as inevitable. They were indisputable when the electric telegraph enabled time signals to be transmitted instantaneously. By 1852 Greenwich time was established everywhere along the railways in Britain.

The change made itself felt elsewhere too. In 1847 the Manchester Corporation ordered all clocks in the town to be set to Greenwich time. The number of public clocks now began to multiply. The railways themselves provided many of them, placed conspicuously above their stations. Clock towers came to be widely adopted as public monuments, standing in the streets of towns all over the country. Time, and more specifically Greenwich time, thus came to be quietly forced into the minds of people living in Britain. Greenwich time came to be referred to in ordinary speech as railway time and, when the railways' victory was complete, as London time – a silent reminder of the increasing power of the capital (see Simmons & Biddle, 1997, pp. 512–513).

© KONINKLIJKE BRILL NV, LEIDEN, 2019 | DOI: 10.1163/9789004401105_003

A Brief History of *Bildung*[2]

If today we raise the question as to whether *Bildung* has a future and if so, what this future might look like, we must begin with an exploration of the history of *Bildung*. Only on the basis of an understanding of this history can we decide whether the future of *Bildung* can in any sense be a continuation of that history or whether a break with the past is required – if such a break is possible in the first place.

The history of *Bildung* has a double face: one face is educational and the other is political. On the one hand *Bildung* stands for an educational ideal that emerged in Greek society and that, through its adoption in Roman culture, humanism, neo-humanism and the Enlightenment, became one of the central notions of the modern Western educational tradition (Klafki, 1986, p. 455; Tenorth, 1986, p. 10). Central in this tradition is the question of what constitutes an educated or cultivated human being. The answer to this question is not given in terms of discipline, socialisation or moral training, that is, as an adaptation to an existing external order. *Bildung* refers, rather, to the cultivation of the inner life, that is, of the human soul, the human mind and the human person; or, to be more precise, the person's humanity.

Initially the question of *Bildung* was approached in terms of the contents of *Bildung*. An educated person was one who had acquired a clearly defined set of knowledge, ideas and values. A decisive step was taken when the activity of the acquisition of the contents of *Bildung* became itself recognised as a constitutive aspect of the process of *Bildung* (for example, by Herder, Pestalozzi, von Humboldt; see Groothoff, 1978, p. 36). Since then *Bildung* has always also been self-*Bildung*.[3]

The Enlightenment brought about a further development of the idea of *Bildung* in that the process of self-*Bildung* now became defined in terms of rational autonomy. Kant provided the classical definition of Enlightenment as "man's [sic] release from his self-incurred tutelage [Unmündigkeit] through the exercise of his own understanding" (Kant, 1992, p. 90). Kant also argued that the human being's "propensity and vocation to free thinking" – which he considered to be the human being's "ultimate destination" and the "aim of his existence" (Kant, 1982, p. 701) – could only be brought about by means of education. It was for this reason that he argued in his treatise on education (*Über Pädagogik*) that the human being is not only the sole creature that has to be educated, but also the sole creature that can become human only through education.[4] Kant argued, in other words, that in order to reach the state of rational autonomy education was a necessity.

By conceiving of rational autonomy as man's 'ultimate destination' and the 'aim of his existence' Kant gave *Bildung* a strong anthropological orientation

(Groothoff, 1978, p. 39). Any attempt to block the process of Enlightenment, Kant argued, would be nothing less than a crime against human nature (see Kant, 1992, p. 66). Yet for Kant – but not only for him – *Bildung* was more than only an educational ideal. It was also, and perhaps even primarily, an answer to the question about the role of the subject in the emerging civil society, viz., as a subject who can think for himself (not yet herself; see Rang, 1987, pp. 53–54) and who is capable of making his own judgements (Klafki, 1986, pp. 457–458; see also Bauman, 1992, p. 3). In this respect the modern conception of *Bildung* has a political history as well (see Sünker, 1994).

Bildung Lost, *Bildung* Regained

In the 1960s the concept of *Bildung* largely disappeared from the Continental educational scene.[5] In many European countries the discourse of education (that is, educational theory, educational research) underwent an 'empirical turn' (Roth, 1963) and in its wake the notion of *Bildung* was exchanged for psychological and sociological notions like qualification, socialisation, integration and learning (Koring, 1990, p. 70).

In the 1980s, however, a renewed interest in the idea of *Bildung* emerged. The context of this interest was the debate about general education ('allgemeine *Bildung*'), that is, about the kind of non-vocational education that every person should engage in (Tenorth, 1986). Although some authors explored a broad, culture-oriented approach,[6] the question of general *Bildung* or general education was quite often approached in a rather simplistic and instrumentalist manner. In the United States E. D. Hirsch compiled lists of what every American needed to know in order to count as culturally literate (Hirsch, 1987, 1989). In many other countries the question of general education came down to the institution of national curricula, which often revealed a narrow-minded instrumental and centralist conception of education.

The fact that the notion of *Bildung* returned in the context of discussions about general education is, as such, understandable. The globalisation of the economy and of information and the increase in migration and mobility have brought about a heightened awareness of plurality and difference. In those cases where plurality is considered to be a problem (and I will not go into the reasons for this but simply note that this is the case), there is a strong tendency to look for a uniting force or a common ground. Quite often, this task is approached in terms of knowledge and values that are supposed to be generally shared or even universal. The idea, in other words, is to overcome plurality through the institution of a 'generality' or 'universality' that binds us all or should bind us all.

The relationship between *Bildung* and what is general or universal is not new. Although in the modern conception of *Bildung* the focus is on notions like self-determination, freedom, emancipation, autonomy, rationality and independence (Klafki, 1986, p. 458), it is acknowledged that individuals can only achieve rational autonomy by relating to subject matter that is not of their own making but that, to use Klafki's formulation, consists of objectivisations of the cultural history of mankind (see ibid., pp. 459–460). The idea here is that the individual should not be seized by (and hence adapt to) reality as it is, nor be led only by his or her own particular interests in relation to that reality. The idea is that relationships that bring about *Bildung* should be relationships that, through the concrete and the particular, bring the individual in touch with what is general or universal and enduring (Vanderstraeten, 1995, p. 108).

How General Can *Bildung* Be?

The foregoing history of *Bildung* reveals that the modern conception of *Bildung* articulates an educational ideal that, through the Enlightenment, has gained a political significance in that it has become intimately connected with an emerging civil society and with a specific conception of the ideal citizen in such a society. This citizen should have the capacity to make use of his own understanding (rational autonomy), and *Bildung* should provide the modern citizen with the opportunity to acquire this capacity.[7] The process of *Bildung* is itself understood in terms of a relationship that goes 'beyond the present and the particular' (Bailey, 1984). It is a relationship, in other words, with something that is general.[8]

If this is the path that leads to the rational autonomy needed in modern society, then it immediately raises the question how we should understand the idea of 'the general' in *Bildung*. What, to put it differently, makes certain subject matter general, that is, non-particular subject matter, subject matter that is equally valid for everyone everywhere? What makes knowledge into general knowledge, knowledge that is equally valid for everyone everywhere? What makes values into general values? And how should we conceive of 'the general' and 'generality' as such? These are the questions that I want to address in the following pages.

I will first present two answers that have been given to these questions in the context of the modern tradition of *Bildung*. The first is the epistemological answer in which the general is understood as the universal. The second is the answer from the sociology of knowledge in which the general is understood as a social construction. I will discuss the strengths and weaknesses of both positions. Against this background I will present a third approach, taken from the anthropology of science. I will argue that this approach can solve some of the problems of the other two approaches. In the final section I will return to the question about the future of *Bildung* in a postmodern world, a world in which the idea of a general or universal perspective has become a problem.

The Epistemological Interpretation: The General as the Universal

Traditionally – and this tradition lasts up to the present day – the general has been conceived as an epistemological category. In this tradition the general is thought of as an intrinsic quality of knowledge. Knowledge is considered to be general if it is valid and can be applied everywhere and at any time. In the epistemological interpretation the universal validity and applicability of knowledge is taken as proof of the fact that this knowledge represents reality 'as it is.' The epistemological interpretation is based on two assumptions: the idea that reality itself is univocal and universal (which means that ultimately there exists only one reality), and the idea that knowledge represents (this) reality. Taken together, these two assumptions guarantee that general knowledge is objective knowledge. Or, to put it the other way around, that objective knowledge is general and universal knowledge.

Philosophically the epistemological interpretation goes back to the Greek distinction between doxa (opinion) and episteme (true and certain knowledge). Historically the epistemological identification of the general with the universal and the objective is mainly the result of the succession of three revolutions: the scientific revolution, the industrial revolution and what I would like to refer to as the technoscientific revolution.

The scientific revolution brought about the idea that through science – that is to say experimental natural science –we can penetrate the most fundamental layers of reality. The scientific revolution, to put it differently, gave us the idea that through science we can read the book of nature. With the help of the telescope and the microscope the scientist can reveal what really lies behind the world of everyday perception.

In the industrial revolution this reality appeared as the object of manipulation and control. What was new about the industrial revolution was not the fact that human beings started to intervene in nature. This was already the case in pre-industrial societies, for example, in pre-industrial agriculture. What was new was the scale and manner of the intervention. The pre-industrial relationship with nature was primarily a relationship of cultivation and the optimisation of existing processes. In this relationship human beings basically remained dependent on the unpredictable forces of nature. The main characteristic of the industrial revolution was that the forces of nature themselves became the object of manipulation and control. This was made possible, according to Cipolla (1976), because societies came into possession of endless amounts of sheer mineral energy (Bauman, 1998, pp. 48–53).

In the technoscientific revolution, and presumably not much earlier, the core processes of both revolutions (the acquisition of knowledge and technology respectively) became intertwined. In some cases, this happened according to a pattern in which scientific research in the form of pure research preceded the technological application of its findings. More and more, however, technology – itself pushed forward by commercial interests – came to define and direct the course of scientific research (Boehme et al., 1978). An early example of the intertwinement of science, technology and business is the work of Edison in Menlo Park (see Hughes, 1979). The most recent example is, without doubt, biotechnology.

The close relationship between science and technology that was central to the technoscientific revolution promoted the idea that modern technology was made possible by the knowledge that was provided by natural science. This, in turn, led to the assumption that the success of modern technology – which, among other things, appeared to be evident from the universal applicability of the artefacts and techniques of modern technology – proved that the knowledge upon which technology was based was true.[9] I will refer to the idea that the omnipresent success of technology proves the truth of the knowledge upon which it is based as the technology-argument.

The Interpretation from the Sociology of Knowledge: The General as a Social Construction

While in the epistemological interpretation the general is conceived as an *intrinsic* quality of knowledge, the interpretation from the sociology of knowledge claims that the general is *extrinsic* to knowledge. Sociologists of knowledge argue that all knowledge is historically and socially determined (see, for example, Zijderveld, 1974, p. 219). Unlike the epistemological interpretation in which knowledge is assumed to reveal reality as it really is, undisturbed by human intervention, the sociology of knowledge acknowledges the role that human beings play in the process of the acquisition of knowledge. It does so by relating knowledge to socio-economic, sociocultural and political circumstances (ibid., p. 12). Karl Marx, one of the earliest sociologists of knowledge, maintained that "man's social being determines his thought and

consciousness" (Woolgar, 1988, p. 22). This provided a basis for the explanation of false consciousness, which can be seen as a sociological explanation
of error. Karl Mannheim not only introduced a broader conception of the
social than class position alone. He also went beyond Marx in his claim that
both true and false knowledge can be explained sociologically. For Mannheim
this meant that all knowledge is ideological; or, to put it more positively, that
'truth can only be said to exist within the specific world-view of its adherents'
(ibid., p. 23).

An example of the approach of the sociology of knowledge can be found
in recent discussions about the curriculum. Traditionally, curriculum questions have been approached and understood in epistemological terms. After
all, Herbert Spencer's famous question 'Which knowledge is of most worth?'
suggests that the criterion for decisions about what to include in the curriculum is the quality of knowledge. Recent historical and sociological research,
however, has put forward the claim that the actual content of the curriculum
is not the result of a rational deliberation about the quality of this content,
but always rather the provisional outcome of a complex struggle between a
wide variety of interest groups (Kliebard, 1986; Apple, 1993). We should not
only think of this process as one in which a group or a coalition of groups raises
its knowledge or worldview to the status of 'official knowledge' by managing
to make it part of the official curriculum. Being part of the curriculum has
itself 'legitimising effects,' which in turn reinforces the status and power of the
group or groups concerned (Apple, 1993, p. 10). What the sociological analysis
of the development of the curriculum shows, in other words, is that behind
Spencer's question lies another question: 'Whose knowledge is of most worth?'
(ibid., p. 46).

The sociology of knowledge suggests, in sum, that the general is a social
construction. It suggests, in other words, that what is general (or what is taken
to be general) is an expression and a product of social relationships, and hence
an expression and a reinforcement of a certain way in which power in a society
is distributed.

A Critical Theory of *Bildung* and Critical Pedagogy

If the sociology of knowledge is correct in claiming that truth is historically
and socially determined, then this raises serious problems for the idea and
even the possibility of *Bildung*. Its claim is that the general is nothing but a
social construction—nothing, that is, but an expression of the way in which
power is distributed at a certain moment in time (and hence, that the general

is in fact a specific manifestation of the particular). If *Bildung* follows from a relationship with what is general and enduring, a relationship, in other words, with what lies beyond the present and the particular, then the sociology of knowledge implies that *Bildung* is no longer possible. *Bildung*, in other words, itself becomes an ideology.

There is, however, a solution to this problem – a solution that can be found already in the very intentions of the sociology of knowledge. This solution, which is also central to the critical theory of *Bildung* and to some forms of critical pedagogy, comes down to a redefinition of the 'task' of *Bildung* in the very terms of the sociology of knowledge. The aim of critical education is precisely specified as the acquisition of the capacity to decipher the operations of power behind the status quo, behind what presents itself as necessary, natural, general and universal. The aim of a critical approach to *Bildung* becomes specified in terms of demystification (see, for example, Mollenhauer, 1982; McLaren, 1997). In this way the possibility of going beyond the present and the particular is rescued.

An example of this approach is the idea of 'critical literacy' (see Apple, 1993, p. 44; Lankshear & Lawler, 1988). Critical literacy is a form of literacy that does not simply provide an introduction into the existing culture, into the existing state of affairs, but that consists in the ability to look through what presents itself as necessary, natural and general in order to reveal the power relations that lie behind this. Critical literacy, according to Apple, "enables the growth of genuine understanding and control of all the spheres of social life in which we participate" (Apple, 1993, p. 44).

It may seem as if the critical approach is able to rescue the modern project of *Bildung*. In a certain sense – at least this is what proponents of the critical approach would argue – the sociology of knowledge makes it possible to free ourselves from the naivety of the epistemological approach. It makes it possible to free ourselves from the idea that knowledge simply 'is,' that truth simply 'is.' Although I agree that we should not be satisfied with what is simply 'given,' however, I do not think that the sociology of knowledge and the critical theory of education built upon it solve all our problems. There are at least two problems left.

The first problem is a theoretical, but also a practical, a political and a pedagogical problem. It concerns the status of the sociology of knowledge itself and is known as the problem of reflexivity (Woolgar, 1988; for the sociology of scientific knowledge, see Bloor, 1976). We have seen that the central claim of the sociology of knowledge is that all knowledge is an expression of social relations, which are understood as power relations. The problem is, however, that if the sociology of knowledge wants to offer an insight into these power relations, it can only do so, first, if its own knowledge about power relations stands outside of the realm determined by these relationships, and, second, if it can assume that the knowledge that the sociology of knowledge itself provides offers a correct representation of the social and historical situation upon which our knowledge is said to depend.

As Zijderveld (1974) argues, there is indeed a tendency among the 'traditional' sociologists of knowledge to look for an Archimedean point from which they can perform their critical analyses – a point that itself stands outside of the social and historical determination and that for that very reason makes critique possible. This means, however, that the sociology of knowledge eventually falls back upon the same epistemological structures of thought for which it sought to provide a (critical) alternative. The critical impetus of the sociology of knowledge can only exist, in other words, if it is possible to provide knowledge about or to speak the truth about social reality.

A second problem that should be mentioned is that it is difficult for the sociology of knowledge to provide an adequate explanation for the success of modern technology. If knowledge is 'only' a social construction, if knowledge is essentially an expression of social relations of power, how then can we explain the fact that knowledge is instrumentally effective? And how can the sociology of knowledge explain that some knowledge seems to work and seems to be true everywhere, irrespective of particular social, cultural or political configurations? The problem here is, in other words, that the sociology of knowledge is not able to provide an adequate answer to the technology-argument.

Does this mean that the epistemological interpretation of the general – that is, the idea of the general as the objective and universal – is the only feasible interpretation? Does it mean that the omnipresence of successful technology indeed forces us to accept the truth of the knowledge upon which it is based? Before we accept this conclusion, I want to present one more interpretation of the idea of the general – an interpretation that takes as its point of departure precisely the apparent success of modern technology, and one that starts precisely from the question whether the epistemological interpretation of the successful omnipresence of technology is the most adequate interpretation. This approach has been developed by the French philosopher and 'anthropologist of science,' Bruno Latour.

The Network Approach: The General as the Asymmetrical Expansion of the Local

In the epistemological interpretation of the success of 'techno-science,' in Latour's phrase, it is assumed that techno-scientists construct facts and machines that are then distributed to the world outside of the laboratory in which they were constructed. The successful distribution of facts and machines—or, to be more precise: the fact that facts and machines appear to be able to survive outside the laboratory—is taken as a sign of the special (intrinsic) quality of these facts and of the knowledge that lies at the basis of these machines.

Latour sees no reason for doubting that techno-scientists are indeed able to create facts and machines in their laboratories.[10] He also sees no reason to doubt the fact that at a certain moment in time facts and machines show up at other places than where they were originally produced. But what Latour does challenge is the claim that what has happened in the meantime is a displacement of these facts and machines from the 'safe' environment of the laboratory to the 'real' world outside. Latour argues that what in fact has happened is a displacement of the laboratory, that is, a displacement of the only conditions under which the facts and machines can exist and operate successfully. It is not the facts and machines that have moved into a world outside of the laboratory. The outside world has been transformed into laboratory: "No one has ever seen a laboratory fact move outside unless the lab is first brought to bear on an 'outside' situation and that situation is transformed so that it fits laboratory prescriptions" (Latour, 1983, p. 166).

Latour's work provides many fascinating examples of this process. In his book on the work of Louis Pasteur, Latour shows that the success of Pasteur's approach was not the result of the distribution of a robust technique from Pasteur's laboratory to the farms in the French countryside. It could only happen because significant dimensions of French farms were transformed into Pasteur's laboratory. It is, as Latour argues, "only on the conditions that you respect a limited set of laboratory practices [that] you can extend to every French farm a laboratory practice made at Pasteur's lab" (Latour, 1983, p. 152). What took place, therefore, was a pasteurisation of France (Latour, 1988).

Latour refers to "this gigantic enterprise to make of the outside a world inside of which facts and machines can survive" as *metrology* (Latour, 1987, p. 251). Metrology can be conceived as a process of creating 'landing strips' for facts and machines (ibid., p. 253). Metrology is a transformation of society, an incorporation of society into the network of techno-science, so that, as a result, facts and machines can spread out comfortably and apparently as a result of some inner, intrinsic force. There is, as Latour puts it, "no outside of science but there are long, narrow networks that make possible the circulation of scientific facts" (Latour, 1983, p. 167).

The idea of metrology provides an answer to the question how technology and knowledge can become general or universal that is both different from the epistemological approach and from the sociology of knowledge. In contrast to the latter, metrology does not need to question that we have technology and that we have knowledge. It only questions the idea that technology and knowledge contain an intrinsic force or quality that makes their easy movement through space and time possible.

Latour does not doubt the fact that we can make mobile phones. He only points to the fact that these phones only work everywhere – only become general – after a network of transmitters and receivers that provides 100 per cent coverage has been set up. Similarly, Latour sees no reason to doubt the fact that medical techno-science has developed effective therapies and treatments (which is not say that all of them are good or desirable and that there are no alternatives). The only point that he wants to make is that the apparent universal applicability of products of medical techno-science is the result of a transformation of society so that it fits the conditions under which the products of medical technoscience can work.[11] One 'landing strip' for medical techno-science to which it can retreat if it turns out that it cannot prove its truth and effectiveness 'out on the street' is, of course, the modern hospital.

Latour's contribution to my exploration of the idea of the general first of all shows that the apparent universality of modern techno-science should not be accounted for in terms of some inner quality of facts and machines. It is important to see, however, that Latour does not so much provide a different explanation for the universal presence of techno-science. He rather argues that we are dealing with a different phenomenon: not the displacement of facts and machines to a world outside of the laboratory, but an incorporation of the outside world into the order of the laboratory.

Latour thus criticises the main idea of the epistemological interpretation, which is that it is the special quality of the knowledge invested in facts and machines that makes their universal movement possible. But – and this is crucial as well – Latour does not simply reverse the argument. He does not say that the spreading of facts and machines causes the knowledge invested in them to become general. (This is what the sociology of knowledge would argue, claiming that interest groups try to gain power by spreading 'their' facts and machines as widely as possible.) The crux of Latour's analysis is that there is no movement of facts and machines at all. They just stay where they are. It is only because more and more 'points' (places, locations, people) become incorporated into a network that the illusion of movement and the illusion of universality arises. But in fact, it is not that facts and machines move from the centre to the periphery. It is rather that the margins are moved towards the centre. By connecting all railways and stations in Great Britain with the centre, they became part of the centre. London time remained as local as it had ever

been. What happened was, that all corners of the country became incorporated into the local time of London.

This, then, provides a different way to understand the relationship between
the local and the universal, between the particular and the general. With
Latour we can see the world as a plurality of local practices. Some of these
practices have been more successful in incorporating and transforming the
world 'outside' than others. Latour refers to this situation as asymmetry. It is
important to see that this asymmetry is not to the expression of qualitative,
intrinsic or epistemological differences.

There is no doubt that there are qualitative differences between these practices, depending, among other things, upon the criteria we use to evaluate
them. But these differences in quality do not cause asymmetry. Asymmetry
denotes only that some networks are bigger, longer and stronger than others.

What appears to be general or universal is, from this point of view, nothing
more (and nothing less) than an extension of a particular local practice. This
does not say anything about the quality or value of such a practice, although,
as Latour argues, scientists (and others) often try to define asymmetry in qualitative terms (for example, in terms of the rational versus the irrational). But
apart from the rhetorical gain, there is no real point in doing this. Local time in
Plymouth is not better than local time in London. Problems only arose when,
through the railways, the two places became part of one network.

Concluding Remarks

In this essay I have presented three different ways to understand the idea of
the general in relation to the general character of the content of *Bildung*. My
aim has not only been to show that the general can be understood in different ways. My aim has also been to suggest that different conceptions of the
general imply different conceptions of *Bildung*. In conclusion I want to offer
three observations that may help us in finding an answer to the question as to
whether there can be a future for *Bildung* in our times.

I have argued that a central component of the modern understanding of
Bildung is the idea that rational autonomy can only be achieved by means
of a movement that goes beyond the present and the particular towards the
general and the enduring. The argument makes sense in that a rational and
autonomous subject indeed should not be seized by reality as it is, and should
not be subjected to its own inclinations and propensities. Yet this movement
of liberation or emancipation only seems to be possible if we can make 'hard'
distinctions between the particular and local, on the one hand, and the general

and universal, on the other. This is, as I have argued, what the epistemological interpretation of the general tries to do.

One of the most compelling arguments in favour of the epistemological interpretation is the technology-argument. The omnipresence of technology in our everyday lives and the apparent ease with which technology spreads all over our globe, makes it very difficult not to think of the knowledge that lies behind this technology as general and universal. I believe, however, that Latour's work provides an adequate critique of the technology-argument. On the one hand Latour, unlike the sociology of knowledge, is able to acknowledge that technology is possible, that is, that we can put a man on the moon, that we can cure more than fifty per cent of all cases of cancer, and everything else that is impressive in modern techno-science. Yet Latour can also make clear that the apparent 'generality' of techno-science says nothing at all about the quality of the knowledge upon which techno-science seems to be based.

The importance of this achievement can hardly be overestimated since what it makes possible is an 'escape' from positivism, that is, from the situation in which science not only claims cognitive authority (that is, where it claims to provide the ultimate truth about reality), but where, on the basis of this cognitive authority, it is also claims normative authority over our lives.

There is, of course, a price to be paid for this 'escape,' in that we have to give up the idea of a hard distinction between the particular or local on the one hand and the general or universal on the other. What appears as universal is rather the effect of the successful extension of a specific local practice. The implication of this line of thought for the concept and even for the very possibility of *Bildung* as it has been conceived in the modern educational tradition, is that we will have to concede that beyond the present and the particular we will only find another present and another particular, and never the general and universal.

In a sense, as this is my second point, this conclusion comes remarkably close to what the sociology of knowledge can offer us. After all the sociology of knowledge also claims that all knowledge is an expression of a specific social and historical state of affairs. We have seen how in certain versions of the critical theory of *Bildung* and critical pedagogy this was not taken as the end of the possibility of *Bildung*. It provided rather the starting point for a more general and more critical conception of *Bildung* as the ability to 'read' power behind knowledge. I have argued that this is problematic since the only way in which such a project is possible is by relying upon a deeper or more encompassing form of understanding—which, eventually, brought the sociology of knowledge quite close to the very epistemological approach for which it wanted to provide an alternative.

The issue here has everything to do with the (modern) tradition in which it is assumed that there is an original division between knowledge and power on the basis of which knowledge can not only be used to illuminate how power works but, in doing so, can also be put to work to combat the workings of power—which, I believe, can stand as a very brief encapsulation of Enlightenment thought. Latour's work gives reason to question the assumption that knowledge and power are ontologically separate entities. Latour's analysis does suggest that there exist asymmetries between networks. But he claims neither that these asymmetries are caused by operations of power, nor that it is possible to stand outside the field of competing networks to give an objective description of the state of affairs that can then be used to erase existing asymmetries.

This does not imply the end of critique. What it does suggest – and at this point the implications from Latour's work come remarkably close to some insights offered by Foucault (Biesta, 1998a, 1998b) – is the end of the critical style of the modern tradition where knowledge operates against power. Foucault's insight is that we are not operating in a field where we can use knowledge to combat power. Instead, we are always operating in a field of power/knowledge constellations, in a field, to put it in Latour's terms, of (weaker and stronger) networks. This suggests a style of critique that is no longer theoretical but thoroughly practical. It is a style of critique where the point is not one of theoretically revealing the power behind strong networks, but rather one of building different networks – we can perhaps call them counter-networks or counter-practices (see also Biesta, 1998a) – in order to show that what appeared to be universal and necessary was only one possible way in which things can be, without, however, claiming that this counter-practice relies upon a deeper understanding or a more truthful knowledge of the situation. The crucial point, in other words, is to show that things can be different (which is not to claim that the alternatives are automatically better). This is less certain and presumably more dangerous than the Enlightenment style of critique as demystification. But it seems to me that this is at least one viable way in which we can retain the critical impetus of the sociology of knowledge for *Bildung* without having to fall back upon the epistemological model.

This may not be a popular message in an educational climate in which there is a strong tendency to eradicate any form of plurality (for example, through national curricula or international standardised testing). Under the pretence of equality of opportunity, schools and educational systems more generally are veering more and more towards uniformity. The epistemological defence of this development, as we may now be able to see, is that each child should have the right to go beyond his or her own particular situation in order to engage with knowledge, beliefs and values that are general and enduring. With Latour we can understand such developments as national curricula as extensions of a specific network and hence as processes in which schools contribute to the creation and reproduction of specific asymmetries. This suggests that real equality of opportunity has nothing to do with uniformity, but should be concerned with cutting through the very networks that keep impeding asymmetries in place.

What, to conclude, does this signify for the future of *Bildung* and for a future *Bildung*? Is there still a place for *Bildung* in a world where we are trying to come to terms with the fact that there is no 'outside,' no safe haven from which we can oversee and judge reality, a world without generality, a world where we have only a multiplicity of practices and no neutral yardstick – which does not mean that we can no longer measure, evaluate, judge, but where it becomes visible that we are ourselves responsible for the yardsticks we use? And to what extent can a future ideal of *Bildung*, a *Bildung* of the future still be related to or take inspiration from its modern articulation?

These are complex questions to which there is no simple answer. One thing that we should keep in mind, however, is that *Bildung* has never been an abstract educational idea; the tradition of *Bildung* with which we are connected – the modern conception of *Bildung* that was coined in the Enlightenment – was first and foremost an answer to the question of how to respond to, and deal with, the new political situation that emerged at the end of the eighteenth century. This suggests that any answer to the question whether there is a future for *Bildung* in a postmodern world, a world in which the idea of a general or universal perspective has itself become a problem – and in this chapter I have presented some dimensions of this problem – will have to be an answer to the question of how to respond to, how to deal with, how to understand this very world.[12]

Notes

1   An earlier version of this chapter appeared as Biesta, G. J. J. (2002). How general can *Bildung* be? Reflections on the future of a modern educational ideal. *British Journal of Philosophy of Education*, 36(3), 377–390.

2   This is a chapter about *Bildung*, one of the key ideas in the Continental educational tradition. It is, however, an extremely difficult concept to translate into English (see Cleary & Hogan, 2001 for some helpful insights). I have chosen not to attempt to translate '*Bildung*.' Instead, I provide a brief history of the idea of *Bildung*, which hopefully will help the reader not only to understand what *Bildung* is about, but also to see that the meaning of '*Bildung*' has itself changed over time.

3 For a contemporary defence of this idea see Gadamer (2001). For a fascinating account of the paradoxical relationship between *Bildung* and self-*Bildung*, see Wimmer (2001).

4 The original text reads: "Der Mensch ist das einzige Geschöpf, das erzogen werden muss ... Der Mensch kann nur Mensch werden durch Erziehung" (Kant, 1982, pp. 697, 699).

5 In Germany one of the few exceptions was Heydorn (see Rang, 1987, p. 51; Sünker, 1989). It could be argued that in other countries there were educational theorists working in a language and framework that was akin to the Continental tradition of *Bildung*. In the UK one can think of the writings of Michael Oakeshott and R. S. Peters. This can be taken as an indication that the ideas of the tradition of *Bildung* did not completely disappear; indeed, one could well argue that the intuitions of the tradition of *Bildung* have always been part of modern educational discourse more generally (see, for example, Arcilla, 1995; and regarding *Bildung* in John Dewey's work, see Biesta, 1995a). But my point here is to highlight a rupture in the tradition of *Bildung* insofar as this understood itself as a tradition. I am talking, in other words, about the demise of the idea of *Bildung* in Continental educational thought.

6 In Germany one can think of the work of Klaus Mollenhauer (1983). In the USA perhaps Allan Bloom (1987).

7 Kant stressed that this citizen should also have the courage to make use of his own understanding (see Kant, 1988, p. 59), although he did not make clear how this courage could be acquired.

8 I deliberately use the word 'general' and the not the word 'universal.' I am aware that the word 'general' is less precise than the word 'universal,' and that this may even lead to some initial confusion with English readers (readers familiar with German can read 'general' as a translation of 'allgemein'). However, I prefer to use the less precise word in order to be able to show that to think of what is general as what is universal, or even universally valid, is only one way in which what is general can be understood (see below). I ask the reader to bear with me in my exploration of different ways to articulate what is general.

9 This is, for example, the argument Ernest Gellner uses to 'prove' the superiority of the Western worldview (see Gellner, 1992).

10 For the way in which Latour understands the process of the construction of facts and machines, see Latour and Woolgar (1986).

11 One crucial factor in this transformation is undoubtedly health education which, among other things, teaches us to define our own health in terms of medical techno-science.

12 I wish to thank Pádraig Hogan for helpful comments and suggestions on an earlier version of this chapter.

CHAPTER 3

Becoming World-Wise: An Educational Perspective on the Rhetorical Curriculum

Introduction[1]

From one angle, the educational interest in rhetoric is hardly remarkable, as one could argue that one of the main ambitions of educational processes and practices is that they convince – or, in the stronger language of the tradition of rhetoric: that they persuade. The educational curriculum is, after all, never just an option that students can either take or leave but represents a particular selection of all that can possibly be learned and, more specifically, an intended and powerful selection. Wherein the power of the curriculum actually resides, has been an ongoing issue in curriculum scholarship, ranging from Spencer's contention in 1854 that the 'question of all questions' for the development of a 'rational curriculum' had to be 'What knowledge is of most worth?' (see Spencer, 1909) – to which his answer was 'science' – and up to Apple's rephrasing of Spencer's question in the 1980s as that of 'Whose knowledge is of most worth?' (see Apple, 1979, 1986), thus shifting the curricular question from the realm of epistemology to the realm of sociology. The rhetorical account of the curriculum is closer to the sociological than to the epistemological understanding of the power of the curriculum, because its interest is not so much in why a particular curriculum might convince or persuade, but first and foremost in the question how the curriculum convinces or persuades, irrespective, so we might say, of its 'intrinsic' epistemological quality.

The sociological thrust is particularly prominent in the shift from 'traditional' rhetoric to 'new rhetoric' (see Burke, 1951; Perelman & Olbrechts-Tyteca, 1958, 1969). This is particularly so because of the emphasis of authors like Burke on rhetoric as a tool for identification that is of 'inducing cooperation in beings that by nature respond to symbols' (Burke, 1996, p. 41). In the hands of Burke, new rhetoric thus focuses on how language can overcome division and bring people together or, as Rutten and Soetaert (2012) put it, on 'the role of rhetoric in our socialization into communities and in the creation of cultural and social rules.' Scholarship in the context of new rhetoric not only focuses on the analysis of such practices of identification but also on the community building 'effects' that follow from it – a line that is prominent in the contributions from Enoch and Mortensen to this special issue. There is also a more

© KONINKLIJKE BRILL NV, LEIDEN, 2019 | DOI: 10.1163/9789004401105_004

programmatic line that focuses on the question how the rhetorical curriculum might be put to 'work,' so to speak, for example, through the idea that education should contribute to making people 'symbol-wise' (Burke, 1955, p. 260; see also Enoch, 2004). These questions are more prominent in the contributions from Zappen (2012) and from Rutten and Soetaert (2012).

In what follows, I aim to look at the (renewed) interest in rhetoric and the curriculum from an educational angle – an angle which, as I will argue, should be distinguished carefully from a sociological perspective on education (see also Biesta, 2007a). I will do this in relation to three themes that, in my view, are of central concern for the discussion in this special issue. I first focus on the different conceptions of education that figure in the discussion, highlighting the distinction between the Greek tradition of paideia and the (neo-)humanist tradition of *Bildung*. I then discuss in more detail some of the educational implications of a rhetorical approach to education and the curriculum, focusing specifically on the way in which language is conceived in the discussion. In the third and final step, I ask to what extent the 'rhetorical turn' in curriculum scholarship is connected to the idea of education-as-empowerment or education-as-emancipation. While I do think that a rhetorical perspective has something new to offer to the field of curriculum studies – something that is significantly different from a sociological analysis of curriculum – I have some doubts about the ways in which the 'rhetorical turn' is utilised programmatically, that is, in order to outline a different approach to education. I introduce the distinction between education aimed at becoming 'symbol-wise' and education aimed at becoming 'world-wise' as a brief summary of a wider set of challenges that in my view need to be taken up in order to utilise the educational potential of the rhetorical turn in a more consistent and more radical way.

Education, Paideia and *Bildung*

As Rutten and Soetaert point out in their contribution (Rutten & Soetaert, 2012), the educational dimensions of rhetoric first came to the fore in the idea of paideia which, in classical Athens, stood for a broad process of cultivation of the person towards virtue (ἀρετή) and, more specifically, towards civic virtue. Among the subjects that were supposed to lead to such cultivation we do indeed find rhetoric, and also grammar, mathematics, music, philosophy, geography, natural history and gymnastics – a set of subjects which in medieval times re-emerged in the trivium (grammar, rhetoric and logic) and quadrivium (arithmetic, geometry, music and astronomy) which, together, constituted the seven liberal arts that were seen as the core of 'higher learning.' Paideia was conceived as the kind of education that would bring human beings to their true form – that is, achieving 'excellence' in what was considered to be distinctively human which, for Plato and Aristotle, was the ability for reason (man as a 'rational animal' in Aristotle's formulation). Paideia was, however, confined to free men in order to further their freedom as citizens and stood therefore in opposition to the education that was meant for manual labourers and artisans, the 'banausoi' (βάναυσοι), Paideia was an education which required free time or schole (σχολή), rather than that it was connected to the domain of work and production (see, e.g., Jaeger, 1945).

There is a clear although not direct or uninterrupted line from paideia to *Bildung*, in that both paideia and *Bildung* articulate an interest in the formation of the person and, thus, in an understanding of education that is not just about training and adaptation. In the neo-humanist approach of Wilhelm von Humboldt *Bildung* became understood as a process of self-formation ('Selbstgestaltung') through the dialectical interaction of the individual with culture and society. This not only raised the question about which aspects of culture and society were deemed worthy enough for 'real' or 'true' *Bildung* to occur – and here Von Humboldt looked favourably at Greek and Roman antiquity (see Ballauff & Schaller, 1970). It also raised the question about the role of the individual in the process of *Bildung*, thus highlighting that *Bildung* is not a 'blind' process in which individuals simply adopt existing cultural and social ways of doing and being, but has to be understood as a reflexive process, that is a process in which the individual establishes a relationship with existing culture and society and, more importantly, develops a stance towards existing culture and society (see Kron, 1989, p. 66). In this regard, *Bildung* emerges as a process that always involves the evaluation ('Bewertung') of existing culture and society. Both aspects return in the work of 20th-century authors such as Heydorn and Klafki. Klafki not only highlights more explicitly that *Bildung* has to be understood as a process of 'double disclosure' – that is the disclosure of both 'self' and 'world' (see Klafki, 1969). He also orients *Bildung* more explicitly towards the idea of emancipation, thus adding an explicit political dimension to it (see Klafki, 1964; see also Klafki, 1986; Heydorn, 1972).

While paideia and *Bildung* both exemplify an interest in the formation of the person, the important difference between the two – and here lies a clear discontinuity between paideia and *Bildung* – lies in the fact that the orientation of paideia is that of cultivation – that is, the formation of the person in light of existing traditions and standards – whereas the orientation of *Bildung* is that of self-formation ('Selbstgestaltung') and thus ultimately of emancipation.[2] In modern terms, we might say that paideia is orientated towards identity – that is, identification with existing ways and forms of doing and being – while *Bildung* is more explicitly orientated towards the achievement of subjectivity or 'subject-ness.' While Miller (2007, p. 186), for example, might be right, therefore, in suggesting that there is 'close correspondence' between the idea of paideia and the idea of *Bildung* in that both focus on the formation of the person, what he seems to overlook is the crucial difference in the 'form' of personhood that paideia and *Bildung* are after. The distinction between paideia and *Bildung* is important because it exposes a difference that remains largely invisible in the English language, particularly when the discussion only makes use of the word 'education,' because when using that word it remains unclear whether the interest is in socialisation – the insertion of 'newcomers' into existing ways of being and doing – or in subjectification (for this term see Biesta, 2009a) – that is, the process of becoming a subject of action and responsibility.

The distinction I am highlighting here is relevant for the discussion about the rhetoric and the curriculum in a number of ways. On the one hand, it shows – and this is consistent with the interpretation of paideia I am offering – that 'old' rhetoric, understood as the art of persuasion, can, from an educational perspective, indeed be understood in terms of socialisation, since an education in rhetoric makes the individual ready for effective operation within a given socio-political 'order.' The shift from 'old' to 'new' rhetoric broadens the outlook from an emphasis on persuasion to an interest in how language functions more generally, and, more specifically, how language functions in the establishment of social relationships. Yet, the shift from 'old' to 'new' rhetoric does not simply coincide with the difference between paideia and *Bildung*, that is, with the difference between socialisation and subjectification. There are two reasons why the situation is more complex. One has to do with the fact that, as I have mentioned, the rhetorical approach to education is being deployed in two different ways: analytically and programmatically. With regard to this distinction, I wish to argue that the analytical use of ideas from the new rhetoric predominantly looks at education through the lens of socialisation. When Burke claims that every given terminology is not only a reflection of reality, but also at the very same time a selection of reality and, therefore, also a deflection of reality (see Burke, 1966, p. 45), he opens the way for an analysis of the curriculum – both the official curriculum of schools, colleges and universities and the everyday curriculum of popular culture – as a 'terministic screen' (see also Rutten & Soetaert, 2012), that is, as a 'mechanism' of reflection, selection and deflection. Hence, this approach calls for the study of curriculum as rhetoric in order to make visible how particular curricula manage to convince – particularly in light of the fundamental contingency of meaning (for the latter see Rutten & Soetaert, 2012) – and thus how particular curricula have socialising effects, effects that provide individuals with particular social positions and identities.

The contribution by Mortensen (2012) is a good example of how this works in terms of literacy and illiteracy, both at the level of making visible how literacy and illiteracy are rhetorically produced, and in terms of how stories about the production of literacy and illiteracy themselves have socialising effects, that is effects on our beliefs about what it means to be literate or illiterate. The importance of such analytical work – and here I do think that the rhetorical approach offers an innovation for curriculum scholarship – lies in the fact that it provides a clear alternative for more 'traditional' sociological approaches, particularly approaches from the sociology of knowledge. The difference has to do with the fact that rhetorical analysis is first and foremost interested in revealing how curricula manage to convince and is less interested in trying to identify those individuals or groups who aim to make the curriculum convincing in particular ways, for particular purposes, and in relation to particular audiences. In this regard, the rhetorical approach appears to be more 'neutral' – or perhaps we should say more 'agnostic' – than the sociology of knowledge with regard to the question of underlying interests. This, in turn, explains, as Rutten and Soetaert (2012) also mention, why new rhetoric runs the risk of being characterised as relativistic in its intentions and consequences.

The second reason why the shift from 'old' to 'new' rhetoric does not simply coincide with the difference I have highlighted between paideia and *Bildung* – that is with an orientation towards socialisation or an orientation towards subjectification – brings us to the programmatic use of insights from the new rhetoric in education.

Becoming 'Symbol-Wise' or Becoming 'World-Wise'?

As mentioned, the new rhetoric does not only provide a particular framework for the analysis of curricula and educational processes and practices more generally, but can also be used in a more programmatic way, that is, as a framework for the development of particular educational approaches. This is one way in which we might understand the idea of the rhetorical curriculum, although it is perhaps better to speak of educational approaches informed by insights from the new rhetoric. Rutten and Soetaert (2012) provide some insights into what this might look like, particularly in relation to Burke's own ideas about the educational potential of his work. This goes back to Burke's (1955) essay 'Linguistic Approaches to the Problem of Education,' a detailed discussion and analysis of which can be found in Enoch (2004). While it is important to distinguish the analytical and programmatic use of new rhetoric in education, this does not mean that the two are disconnected. On the contrary, one of the key ideas that can be found in Burke's work is that of becoming 'symbol-wise' (see Enoch, 2004), and one could say that becoming symbol-wise is precisely about developing the ability to look at reality – and specifically social reality – through the eyes of the framework of the new rhetoric, a framework that helps to see how our interaction is 'structured,' so we might say, by language, symbols and meaning. In one of his letters, Burke formulates his educational ambition as that of "[sharpening] awareness of the ways in which terms are related to one another and of the momentous role that terminology plays in human thought and conduct" (Burke, quoted in Enoch, 2004, p. 276). Enoch (2004) characterises this as a 'pedagogy of critical reflection' and shows how there are both similarities with and differences from the ideas of Paulo Freire. (I return to this below in relation to the role of empowerment and emancipation in education.)

It is important to see that for Burke, the idea of becoming symbol-wise was about more than the formal capacity to become aware of the role of language in understanding and interaction. Burke contrasted being symbol-wise with approaching the world in a 'symbol-foolish' way (Burke, 1955, p. 260) and believed that being symbol-wise embodied an orientation towards cooperation rather than combat and competition. As Enoch shows, teaching students to become symbol-wise was for Burke explicitly aimed at countering competitive tendencies by prompting students "to disengage from moments of aggressive argumentation and, instead reflect upon the ways language contributes to such conflicts" (Enoch, 2004, p. 273). The technique of "preparatory withdrawal" Burke proposed for this was explicitly meant to make "methodical the attitude of patience" (Burke, quoted in Enoch, 2004, p. 273). Enoch also shows that for Burke all this was closely connected to the threat of the Cold War and, in this regard, his educational proposals can be read as an explicit response to this threat (see Enoch, 2004).

Zappen (2012) explicitly follows this line in his exploration of the educational potential of Burke's ideas in connection with Bakhtin's views about dialogue, polyphony and heteroglossia, pointing out their relevance for contemporary inter-, multi- and trans-cultural education. A key idea in this regard is the notion of 'frame of reference,' which expresses that the world can be viewed, understood and approached in many different ways and that, as Zappen (2012) puts it, "different perspectives are not necessarily right or wrong but simply different, not antithetical but potentially complementary." Burke thus envisages an educational trajectory that proceeds from indoctrination, to knowing something about other points of view in order to combat them, to learning to appreciate other groups in all their varied habits, strengths and shortcomings, to situating multiple voices in relation to each other in search of ways whereby the various voices, in mutually correcting one another, will lead towards a position "better than any one single" (Burke, quoted in Zappen, 2012) – a process where we ultimately are in a position, where we not only understand other people's perspectives but can also actually learn from them, thus contributing to what Zappen describes as "mutual respect and reciprocal learning." In this context, Zappen highlights an important difference between multiculturalism and transculturalism, where multiculturalism operates on the assumption "that each culture is complete and perfect by itself" (Zappen, 2012) and transculturalism, on the other hand, operates on the assumption that "each culture is partial and incomplete without the others" (Zappen, 2012). Bakhtin's ideas on dialogue, as Zappen argues, provide theoretical support for the latter understanding of culture.

The 'pedagogy of critical reflection' (Enoch, 2004) that emerges from the ideas of the new rhetoric sounds, in a sense, quite familiar, particularly given the fact that the idea that students should become reflective and critical has become an influential idea in contemporary education. What the rhetorical perspective adds to this is a particular focus on the critical analysis of the ways in which language frames our understanding, doing and being and how such an understanding can help to engage in what is often referred to in the educational literature as 'dialogue across difference.' Enoch (2004) particularly highlights the similarities between Burke's idea of becoming symbol-wise and ideas from North American pragmatism and critical pedagogy which, indeed, also focus on equipping students with the skills to critically analyse the operation of language, particularly in order to expose how the functioning of language contributes to the creation of inequalities and injustice. But the 'metarhetorical shift' (Rutten & Soetaert, 2012) which characterises the rhetorical pedagogy of critical reflection is not without problems. These problems are partly of a philosophical, ethical and political nature, but also have repercussions for education. Let me briefly indicate these problems.

A major philosophical problem has to do with the reliance of the new rhetoric on what, since Davidson's landmark paper 'On the very idea of a conceptual scheme' (Davidson, 1974), is known as 'scheme-content dualism,' which is the assumption that it is possible to make a distinction between the empirical content of our experiences and the conceptual schemes with which we 'make sense' of such experiences. Davidson argues, in my view convincingly, that such a distinction is untenable, which, among other things, means that there is never some 'pure' empirical content that we observe through different conceptual schemes or frames of reference, but that content and scheme always appear 'together,' so we might say – although it is even more precise to say that the distinction itself simply cannot be made. This raises serious questions for the idea that it is possible to become 'symbol-wise' or that inter/multi/ transcultural education should focus on gaining knowledge about each other's frames of reference. While this does not mean that we cannot learn from each other, this can, in my view, no longer be understood as a process in which we become acquainted with each other's perspectives on the world. Instead, it has to be seen as a process through which we become acquainted with each other's worlds (on this distinction see also Biesta, 2010d). This then suggests an educational orientation towards becoming 'world-wise' rather than becoming 'symbol-wise' – which, in turn, raises the question whether this can still be 'contained' within a rhetorical perspective or begins to articulate a position that moves beyond that of the new rhetoric.

The problem is, however, not only philosophical, but also has ethical and political dimensions. The main issue I wish to highlight in relation to this is the fact that the emphasis of the new rhetoric on languages and symbols runs the risk of interpreting all difference as 'merely cultural,' that is, as the 'effect' of different cultural and conceptual schemes. There are two problems here. The first is that many important differences between people are precisely not conceived as just cultural differences, that is, as having to do with different cultural perspectives or frames of references. The 'culturalist' tendency in the educational application of the new rhetoric thus runs the risk of putting all differences under the same rubric and thus of doing injustice to other ways in which difference can be understood, articulated and experienced. To this comes the fact that to suggest that all differences can be understood (and in a sense ought to be understood) as 'linguistically produced,' so to speak, is ultimately a totalising gesture that in the very moment in which it makes difference visible also eradicates all differences. This point has, in my view, most forcefully been made by Bhabha in his book *The Location of Culture* (Bhabha, 1994), where he argues that culture is never a kind of neutral 'layer' that is added to a world that, in itself, is objective and shared. Culture is rather 'located' in a 'third space' of enunciation that is the product of interaction but that, in itself, is unrepresentable (see Bhabha, 1994, p. 55). Culture, in other words, is always 'in translation,' always emerging, so that any attempt to 'pin it down,' that is, to suggest that the workings of culture – and of wider systems of language and meaning – can be made transparent, is in that sense an attempt to make a particular local position into something that is universal. From the perspective of post-colonial theory, this can be characterised as a typical colonial gesture (see, e.g., Andreotti, 2011; also Biesta, 2010d).

It is interesting to see that Zappen (2012) in discussing Burke's ideas in conjunction with those of Bakhtin actually comes quite close to this insight, particularly when he connects the difference between the two authors to the difference between multiculturalism and transculturalism. Yet, in discussing the educational implication of the rhetorical turn he stays, in my view, (too) close to Burke, thus missing the more radical implications that a truly dialogical approach brings with it, implications that would move education – and particularly education under the aegis of 'culture' – significantly beyond an agenda of 'mutual learning towards broader cultural understanding' and 'mutual respect.' The issue here not only has to do with the question whether such understanding is indeed what inter/multi/ transcultural education should aim for – and again Zappen (2012) goes some way in showing that such forms of education should actually operate under a double imperative of cultural understanding and social justice. But by focusing on mutual learning for cultural understanding, he seems to be less aware of the limits of cultural understanding in relation to a wider social justice agenda. One of the key questions here is whether better understanding of the other is the best way towards achieving more just relationships with the other – a predicament perhaps expressed most poignantly in Homer Simpson's infamous statement 'Just because I don't care, doesn't mean I don't understand.' (A more academic discussion of this predicament in relation to democratic education is given in Biesta, 2010c.)

Empowerment or Emancipation?

This, then, brings me to the final point I wish to make in response to the contributions in this special issue – a point that brings me back to the question whether the rhetorical turn and, more specifically, the adoption of ideas from the new rhetoric can contribute to forms of education that are not just about socialisation – that is the insertion of 'newcomers' into existing cultural and socio-political 'orders' – but can contribute to what I have termed subjectification, that is, the process of becoming a subject of action and responsibility. Several of the authors in this issue, either implicitly or more explicitly, highlight the potential of the rhetorical approach for empowering students. The key 'mechanism' here is that the adoption of a rhetorical approach can provide students with the skills that allow them to critically analyse the workings of language – a point also emphasised by Enoch (2004). Rutten and Soetaert characterise this as a 'meta-rhetorical shift' in that it provides us with 'a method for analysing our interpretations of reality (and in this way, it offers a

meta-perspective about language and culture' (Rutten & Soetaert, 2012). While
the notion of 'meta' seems to suggest that the rhetorical approach can provide
some kind of 'escape' – at least by locating the position from which rhetorical
analysis is performed as being one level 'up' from where rhetoric 'takes place' –
I wish to argue that the 'escape' that is suggested here, to stay with the metaphor
for a moment, is only an escape to a different floor in the edifice of language,
but does not provide an escape from this edifice itself. The educational potential of the new rhetoric, in other words, can contribute to empowerment within
a world that is viewed through language and symbols – and I wish to emphasise that such empowerment is not insignificant – but it remains confined to
such a linguistic worldview, and in the previous section I have tried to indicate
what I see as some of the limits and limitations of such a worldview.

This is why the use of the word 'empowerment' is actually quite appropriate if, that is, it is granted that there is an important distinction to be made
between the idea of 'empowerment' and the idea of 'emancipation' (on this
see also Biesta, 2010b, 2012). I wish to suggest that empowerment has to do
with processes that provide individuals with power to operate within a particular 'order' (which can be a linguistic order, a social order, a cultural order
or a political order). Empowerment thus operates within the confines of what
Jacques Rancière has helpfully characterised as a 'distribution of the sensible'
(2004, p. 85). Emancipation, on the other hand, is to be understood as a process
that challenges the particular orders that grant individuals the power to speak
and act, so that new ways of speaking and acting, and ultimately new ways of
being become possible. Emancipation is, therefore, not a process of identification – of obtaining an identity within a given distribution of the sensible –
but always has to be understood as a moment of dis-identification (see Biesta,
2010b, 2011b), that is, of instituting ways of speaking, acting and being that are
'out of order,' so to speak. This is another way of understanding the distinction
between what, above, I have referred to as socialisation and subjectification –
a distinction I have used to suggest a possible critical difference between the
tradition of paideia and the tradition of *Bildung*, although it has to be said that
not everything that is written about or done in the name of *Bildung* operates
on this distinction (which means that there are also understandings and practices of *Bildung* that go no further than forms of socialisation).

While some would say that language awareness and critical reflection precisely allow us to emancipate ourselves from existing ways of doing and being –
and this idea has been central in modern education from Kant's work on
Enlightenment up to 20th-century critical pedagogy – I have tried to indicate
above (and also in much more detail in other writings; see, with regard to the
limits of critical pedagogy, particularly Biesta, 2005), that language awareness

and critical reflection may contribute to empowerment but do not allow for the kind of 'escape' and perhaps a better phrase here is a redistribution of the sensible which, for Rancière, is the moment at which democratic politics 'occurs' (see Biesta, 2011b) – that would characterise 'moments' of emancipation. Looking at the educational adoption of insights from the new rhetoric, I am therefore inclined to say that it constitutes a programme of empowerment but not a programme of emancipation and that, for this reason, it remains more closely connected to a sociological approach to education – that is education-as-socialisation – than one that I, in the clumsy formulation that is possible in the English language, could be characterised as an educational approach to education, that is, one focused on education-as-subjectification (see Biesta, 2009a).

The distinctions I am working with here may be perceived a subtle – and perhaps as too subtle – but they are nonetheless important, not only to appreciate the educational implications of the rhetorical turn but also, so I wish to suggest, the political implications of what is at stake. This has to do with a point raised by Rutten and Soetaert (2012) – a point not really taken up by the other contributors in this issue – where they try to connect the new rhetoric explicitly with a post-foundational perspective on knowledge (their formulation). In response to this, I am inclined to say that the new rhetoric does exemplify a 'linguistic turn' in our understanding of education and the curriculum, but not a post-foundational one. The new rhetoric operates with what we might characterise as a linguistic worldview – and perhaps we should even say that it is a form of 'linguistic foundationalism,' in that it operates on a certain 'belief' about language. The fact that Rutten and Soetaert connect this to anthropology – with the idea of rhetoric as 'an anthropological fact' – is perhaps the strongest indication of a kind of linguistic foundationalism that underlies the new rhetoric.

The Challenge

It is precisely at this point that I think that there lies an important challenge for rhetorical scholarship in education and curriculum studies. In educational terms, the challenge is whether it is possible to deploy rhetoric in such a way that it goes beyond empowerment and towards emancipation. Or, in the vocabulary which I have introduced in relation to the discussion of paideia and *Bildung*, that it goes beyond socialisation and towards subjectification. In philosophical terms, the challenge is whether it is possible to develop an approach to rhetoric – or a rhetorical approach – that is consistently post-foundational.

This, so I wish to suggest, does not require that one gives up the linguistic perspective altogether – as that would mean the end of what is specific about a rhetorical approach – but it does require an abandonment of the idea of language as something transparent, as a 'scheme' that operates on 'content' and a move towards approaches that situate language more radically within interaction and dialogue. In political terms, then, the challenge is to move the rhetorical approach away from what I see as a rather outdated view of culture towards an approach that is able to see that culture is only one of the ways in which difference can be understood, and not necessarily the one that allows for the most just ways of relating to the other. The educational, philosophical and political challenges are, of course, closely connected. What I have tried to do in this contribution is not only highlighting where they are at play in current discussions about rhetoric and the curriculum, but also where there are potential problems arising from this, thus indicating areas where there is still work to be done. The rhetorical turn definitely has the potential to bring something new to curriculum scholarship. The challenge is to explore this potential more consistently and, so I wish to suggest, in a more radical manner.

Notes

1 An earlier version of this chapter was published as a discussion piece in a special issue of the *Journal of Curriculum Studies* on the rhetorical curriculum (see *Journal of Curriculum Studies*, 44(6), 2012). The articles I refer to in this chapter can be found in the special issue.
2 The distinction between cultivation and emancipation is the central point in this chapter. In hindsight I am less sure whether this can be mapped that easily onto the traditions of paideia and *Bildung*.

CHAPTER 4

Critical Thinking and the Question of Critique: Some Lessons from Deconstruction

Deconstruction, if such a thing exists, should open up.
JACQUES DERRIDA (1987, p. 261)

∴

Philosophy, Critique, and Modern Education[1]

Ever since philosophy has lodged itself into Western thought, or to put it more self-consciously: ever since philosophy has inaugurated Western thought, it has understood itself as a critical enterprise. Socrates is undoubtedly the main icon of the critical style of philosophy. By a constant questioning of received opinions he tried to reveal that these could not be sustained as easily as was assumed. In his later dialogues Plato translated the Socratic approach into a distinction between knowledge (*episteme*) and belief (*doxa*). This was not only a formalisation of the Socratic style. It also entailed a division of tasks – and thereby a distinction – between the common man, who could only achieve *doxa*, and the philosopher, who could have *episteme*, who could have knowledge of an ultimate reality beyond mere convention and decision.

Apart from a justification of the superior position of the philosopher in the *polis*, Plato's distinction also articulated a specific understanding of the *resources* for critique. For Plato it was the very knowledge of ultimate reality, i.e., of the world of Ideas, which provided the philosopher with a *criterion* so that *krinein* – distinction, separation, decision, disputation, judgement – became possible. In a similar vein Aristotle stressed the indispensability of a criterion. "There must be certain canons," he wrote, "by reference to which a hearer shall be able to criticize" (Aristotle, *De Partibus Animalium*, I.1, 639a, 12).

While Western philosophy has travelled many different routes since Socrates, Plato and Aristotle, the critical temper has certainly not been lost. It seems more accurate to say that the critical motive has become a, if not *the* central concern for modern philosophy, especially since it had to renounce its claim to a higher form of knowledge about the natural world (meta-physics) as a result of the emergence of the natural sciences (see Rorty, 1980).

© KONINKLIJKE BRILL NV, LEIDEN, 2019 | DOI: 10.1163/9789004401105_005

A crucial step in the development of the critical face of modern philosophy was the *generalisation* of the idea of critique. Pierre Bayle – the other philosopher from Rotterdam – was among the first modern scholars who went beyond the idea that only texts could be the object of critique (see his *Dictionaire Historique et Critique* from 1715). From then on institutions like church and state, and society more generally, became possible targets for critical examination (see Röttgers, 1990). This culminated, a few decennia later, in Kant's rather bold claim that our age is the true age of critique, a critique to which everything must be subjected (see Röttgers, 1990, p. 892).

Kant's three *Critiques* still stand out as a major attempt to articulate what it could mean for philosophy to be critical. But Kant has not said the last word. His idea of critique as a tribunal of reason was challenged by Hegel and Marx from a perspective in which a much more historical orientation came to the fore (see Röttgers, 1990). Both orientations – reason and history – have continued to play a central role in the two main critical traditions of 20th century philosophy, namely Popper's critical rationalism and the critical theory of the Frankfurt School.

From the Enlightenment onwards, the question of critique has become intimately connected with the question of education. As Usher and Edwards (1994, p. 24) have argued, the very rationale of the modern understanding of education is founded "on the humanist idea of a certain kind of subject who has the inherent potential to become self-motivated and self-directing." Consequently, the main task of education became that of bringing out this potential so that subjects could become "fully autonomous and capable of exercising their individual and intentional agency" (ibid., pp. 34–35; see also Mollenhauer, 1982, pp. 9–16).

It was, again, Kant who provided an explicit argument for linking critique and education. Kant not only defined Enlightenment as "man's release from his self-incurred tutelage through the exercise of his own understanding" (Kant, 1992, p. 90). He also argued that man's "propensity and vocation to free thinking" – which he considered to be man's "ultimate destination" and the "aim of his existence" (Kant, 1982, p. 701) – could only be brought about by means of education. Kant not only considered man to be the only creature that *has to be* educated. He even argued that man could *only* become human *through education*. Man is therefore everything he is because of what education has made him to be.[2]

Critical Thinking and the Question of Critique

Over the past decades one of the most explicit manifestations of the critical vocation of education has been developed under the name of *critical thinking*.

Robert Ennis's 1962-article "A concept of critical thinking" (Ennis, 1962) is often credited as the starting point for the present interest in critical thinking in the English speaking world (see, e.g., Siegel, 1988, p. 5; Thayer-Bacon, 1993, p. 236; Snik & Zevenbergen, 1995, p. 103). In his article Ennis defined critical thinking as "the correct assessing of statements" (Ennis, 1962, p. 83) and identified several aspects and dimensions of critical thinking. In later publications Ennis revised his definition to "reasonable reflective thinking that is focused on deciding what to believe or do" (Ennis, 1987, p. 10), arguing that one must both have the skills necessary to be a critical thinker *and* the inclination to use these skills.

Ennis's work has not only been an important factor in the resurgence of interest in critical thinking as an educational ideal. It has also provided an important point of reference for subsequent debates concerning critical thinking and education. Besides Ennis, key participants in these discussions include McPeck (e.g. 1981, 1990), Paul (e.g. 1992) and Siegel (e.g. 1988, 1997) (for more recent contributions to the debate see Norris, 1992; Portelli & Bailin, 1993; Walters, 1994; Thayer-Bacon, 2000; see also Haroutunian-Gordon, 1998).

Although more traditional questions about the nature and scope of critical thinking continue to surface, one issue that has become increasingly central in recent years is the question whether the idea(l) of critical thinking is a neutral, objective, universal and self-evident idea(l), or whether it is in some way *biased* (e.g., by culture, class or gender). Although the bias-question is part of the more general question concerning the *justification* and *justifiability* of the idea(l) of critical thinking,[3] it is special in that it has not so much emerged from the internal development of the debate about critical thinking but mainly from the ways in which the idea(l) of critical thinking has been challenged from the 'outside.' Postmodernist, feminists and (neo-)pragmatists are among those who have questioned the neutral, self-evident character of the idea(l) of critical thinking (see, e.g., Orr, 1989; Garrison & Phelan, 1990; Thayer-Bacon, 1992, 1993; Alston, 1995; Garrison, 1999). They have not done this, so it must be stressed, in order to reject the idea(l), but rather to come to a more encompassing articulation – a "redescription" (Thayer-Bacon, 1998) – of it.

Any answer to the question whether or not the idea(l) of critical thinking is biased, is intimately connected with the way in which we conceive of the idea of critique itself. It is intimately connected, in other words, with our conception of "criticality" (see for this term Burbules, 1999). In this chapter I wish to contribute to the ongoing discussion about critical thinking by focusing on the more general and in a sense also more fundamental issue of the status of critique. I will discuss three different conceptions of 'criticality' to which I will refer as *critical dogmatism, transcendental critique,* and *deconstruction.* These conceptions not only differ in their understanding of what it is to be critical – which means that they entail different definitions of the critical 'operation.' They also rest upon different justifications for 'being critical.' They provide, in other words, different answers to the question as to what gives each of them the *right* to be critical.

The argument that I will pursue in the following pages consists of the following steps. The first conception of criticality that I discuss (critical dogmatism) conceives of critique as the application of a criterion. The main problem with this position concerns the justification of the criterion. While some argue that the uncritical acceptance of the critical criterion is inevitable, others have argued that it is possible to justify the critical criterion in a non-dogmatic manner. In doing so, the second approach (transcendental critique) not only provides a different answer to the question of the justification of the critical criterion. It also entails a different 'style' of critique. While this conception of criticality provides a less uncritical and hence more consistent approach to the question of critique, it is still problematic in that it entails a totalising style of critique. The third conception of criticality (deconstruction) can be seen as an attempt to articulate a non-totalising conception of critique.

The main aim of this chapter is to provide some philosophical groundwork for the discussion about the idea(l) of critical thinking, more specifically with respect to the question as to whether this ideal is biased. I will show that "critique" is not a univocal and monolithic notion, but that different conceptions of criticality can be distinguished. My main assumption is that if we want to take the critical vocation of philosophy seriously, we must continuously be vigilant for uncritical 'remainders' in any conception of criticality. My main claim is that in precisely this respect deconstruction provides the most consistent approach available.

Critical Dogmatism[4]

The first way in which we can conceive of what it is to be critical, is to think of critique as the application of a criterion in order to evaluate a specific state of affairs. I propose to refer to this style of critique as *critical dogmatism*. The operation can be called *critical* in that it gives an evaluation of a specific state of affairs. Yet the operation is *dogmatic* in that the criterion itself is kept out of reach of the critical operation. Critical dogmatism, so we could say, derives its right to be critical from the *truth* of the criterion (see also Masschelein & Wimmer, 1996, chapter 1).

In education we can find many examples of this style of critique. Critical work is, for example, carried out by means of a definition of what counts as education (see, e.g., Peters, 1966). Such a definition can then be used to evaluate educative practices and theories which can then turn out be, e.g., non-educative or indoctrinary. A further example can be found in the work of those educators who take 'emancipation' as the general criterion for the evaluation of educational theory and practice, as is the case in critical pedagogy (see, e.g., Mollenhauer, 1973; McLaren, 1995).

Although I refer to this style of critique as dogmatic, there is as such nothing objectionable about this approach. That is to say, there is nothing objectionable *as long as one recognises and accepts its dogmatic character*. In his *Treatise on Critical Reason* (Albert, 1985) Hans Albert has even suggested that critical dogmatism is inevitable. He argues, in what has become known as the *Münchhausen trilemma*, that any attempt to articulate foundations – and in critical dogmatism the criterion is the foundation of the critical operation – inevitably leads to a trilemma, i.e., "a situation with three alternatives, all of which appear unacceptable" (Albert, 1985, p. 18). According to Albert we are forced to choose between (1) an *infinite regress*, because the propositions that serve as a fundament need to be founded themselves; (2) a *logical circle* that results from the fact that in the process of giving reasons one has to resort to statements that have already shown themselves to be in need of justification; or (3) breaking off the attempt at a particular point by *dogmatically* installing a foundation. Since neither the first nor the second option appear to lead to any satisfactory results in finding and founding a criterion, the conclusion has to be that the only possible foundation for critique *is* a dogmatic foundation, so that the only possible form of critique *is* critical dogmatism.

While there are reasons to conceive of critique as criterion-based evaluation, it is not difficult to see that there is at least a tension, presumably a paradox, and possibly even a contradiction at stake in this conception of criticality. All depends, of course, on whether one accepts Albert's conclusion and, not unimportantly, on whether one recognises that a specific criterion for critique indeed only has a conventional basis. With respect to the latter point, it has been argued most strongly by postmodern thinkers that the foundations that play a central role in modern philosophy – such as: the subject, consciousness, reality or truth – are not as solid and self-evident as has for a long time been assumed (see, e.g., Biesta, 1995b).

Although I do not want to suggest that the application of certain criteria has never had any positive effects or that all critical work in education along this line has been in vain, I do wish to argue that the justification critical dogmatism provides for being critical is unsatisfactory. Is it possible to circumvent the paradox of critical dogmatism? According to the 'style' of critique that I will discuss next, this is indeed possible.

Transcendental Critique

Like critical dogmatism, transcendental critique conceives of the critical operation as the application of a criterion. The main difference between the two critical styles lies in the way in which this criterion is justified, namely by means of a transcendental form of argumentation.

The transcendental style of critique must be understood against the background of the way in which philosophy had to reconsider its position as a result of the emergence of the scientific worldview. From then onwards philosophy could no longer claim to provide knowledge of the natural world, nor could it claim to provide knowledge of a more fundamental reality (meta-physics). As a result, philosophy lost its role as a foundational discipline. It was Kant who put philosophy on a new track – the *transcendental* track – where it became the proper task of philosophy to articulate the *conditions of possibility* of true (scientific) knowledge (and, within the Kantian project, also of true metaphysical knowledge, i.e., knowledge of the synthetic judgements a priori; see Kant, 1956).

Although transcendental philosophy opened up a whole new field for modern philosophy, Kant's program was almost immediately criticised for the reflexive paradox it contained. It was Hegel who exposed the problematic character of the attempt to acquire knowledge of something of which the existence had already to be presupposed (namely the capacity to acquire knowledge) in order to be able to acquire any knowledge at all.[5] The main reasons why Kant did not perceive this paradox had to do with the framework in which he operated, which was the so-called philosophy of consciousness. For Kant, the "Ich denke" (I think), the "transcendental apperception," was "that highest point to which we must ascribe all employment of the understanding, even the whole of logic, and conformally therewith, transcendental philosophy" (Kant, 1929, B134).

Karl-Otto Apel's Transformation of Philosophy
The work of Karl-Otto Apel can be seen as a re-articulation (or transformation; see Apel, 1980, p. 973) of transcendental philosophy which tries to circumvent the dogmatic element in Kant's position by making a shift from the framework of the philosophy of consciousness to the philosophy of language. The main difference between Kant and Apel lies in the latter's recognition of the fact that all knowledge is linguistically mediated. While Kant assumed that the

acquisition of knowledge is an individualistic enterprise, Apel argues that our individual experiences must be lifted to the level of a language game in order to become knowledge. The link between experience and language is, however, not automatically established. The question of the validity of our individual experiences has to be answered by means of *argumentation*. Because argumentation only makes sense within a language game, within a specific "community of communication," Apel concludes that this community is the condition of possibility of all knowledge.

Apel's 'linguistic turn' thus results in the recognition of the *a priori* of the community of communication. For Apel this community is "das Letzte, Nichthintergehbare," i.e., that what cannot be surpassed (Apel quoted in Van Woudenberg, 1991, p. 92). Because we can never get 'behind' or 'before' the actual use of language in a specific community of communication, any reflection on language in formal terms can only take place in and hence is only made possible by a specific language game, that is, within a specific community of communication. The pragmatic dimension of language is therefore the most basic dimension, which is the reason why Apel refers to his position as *transcendental pragmatics*.

Although Apel establishes a strong link between transcendental pragmatics and really existing communities of communication – a manoeuvre, which seems to give his project a strongly conventionalistic basis – he introduces a critical element which is meant to enable him to go beyond mere convention. This is the idea of the *ideal community of communication* or the *transcendental language game*. Apel claims that a participant in a genuine argument is at the same time a member of an actual community of communication *and* of a counterfactual *ideal* community of communication, a community that is in principle open to all speakers and that excludes all force except the force of the better argument. Apel argues that any claim to intersubjectively valid knowledge implicitly acknowledges this ideal community of communication, as a meta-institution of rational argumentation, to be its ultimate source of justification (see Apel, 1980, p. 119).

Reflexive Grounding

For Apel, then, the idea of the ideal community of communication provides a criterion that makes critique possible. What distinguishes Apel's position from critical dogmatism is, that this criterion is *not* installed dogmatically but by means of a process to which Apel refers as *reflexive grounding* ("Letztbegründung durch Reflexion"). With respect to this process Apel claims that he can circumvent the dogmatic implications of the Münchhausen trilemma. How does this work?

The first thing to acknowledge is that the first and third option of the Mün-
chausen trilemma – infinite regress and dogmatism – hang together. Both follow from the fact that Albert thinks of the process of foundation in terms of
deduction. It is evident that if we talk about foundations in a deductive way,
i.e., if we raise the question of the "foundation of the foundation," we immediately enter an infinite regress, which can only be stopped arbitrarily. Apel
admits that if we understand founding in this deductive sense, we will never
find foundations. But, so he argues, this does not mean that we should give
up the idea of foundation as such, but only that we need another way to bring
foundations into view.[6]

Apel's approach starts from the recognition that the conditions of possibility of argumentation have to be presupposed in all argumentation (otherwise
they would not be conditions of possibility). From this it follows that one cannot argue against these conditions without immediately falling into a *performative contradiction*. This is the situation where the performative dimensions of
the argument, i.e., the act of arguing, contradicts the propositional content,
i.e., what is being argued (like in sentences as "I claim that I do not exist," or
"I contend – thereby claiming truth – that I make no truth claim"). This implies
*that all contentions that cannot be disclaimed without falling into a performa-
tive contradiction, express a condition of possibility of the argumentative use of
language.* The principle of the avoidance of the performative contradiction,
in short the principle of *performative consistency*, thus is the criterion which
can reveal the ultimate foundations of the argumentative use of language, i.e.,
those propositions that do not need further grounding because they cannot be
understood without knowing that they are true.[7]

Although Apel articulates the method and the criterion by which the ultimate foundations of the argumentative use of language can be revealed, he
doesn't say much about what these foundations actually are (on this point see
Van Woudenberg, 1991, pp. 134–135). Yet what the application of the principle
of performative consistency can bring into view are precisely the foundations,
or, as Apel calls them, the 'meta-rules' of all argumentative use of language.
These meta-rules, which include such things as that all communication aims
at consensus, that all communication rest upon the validity of claims to truth,
rightness and truthfulness, and that these claims can in principle be redeemed,
outline the *ideal* community of communication (see Van Woudenberg, 1991,
pp. 134–135).

Transcendental Grounding

Apel's transcendental pragmatics provides an attempt to articulate the criteria for critique in a non-dogmatic way. The importance of Apel's position lies

in the fact that it goes beyond the individualism of Kantian transcendental philosophy. Apel brings the transcendental approach into the realm of argumentation and communication.[8] More than simply another conception of critique, Apel's position suggests that critical dogmatism – at least in so far as it concerns the dogmatic, or what Popper calls the irrational choice for a rational form of life – is an untenable position, because "any choice that could be understood as meaningful already presupposes the transcendental language game as its condition of possibility" (Apel, 1987a, p. 281). Only, therefore, "under the rational presupposition of intersubjective rules can deciding in the presence of alternatives be understood as meaningful behavior" (ibid.).

From this, so Apel concludes, is does not follow that every decision is rational, but only, that *a decision in favor of the principle of rational legitimation of criticism* is "rational a priori" (ibid., p. 282). Reason, so Apel argues, in no way needs to replace its rational justification, for "it can always confirm its own legitimation through reflection on the fact that it presupposes its own self-understanding of the very rules it opts for" (ibid.).

These remarks reveal that for Apel the criticality of transcendental critique is motivated by the principle of *rationality*. After all, so we could say, the 'sin' of the performative contradiction is a sin against rationality. In this respect rationality gives transcendental critique its 'right' to be critical. Transcendental critique suggests a style of critical thinking that is primarily aimed at spotting performative contradictions. It can therefore be understood as a specific form of internal critique, where the main critical work consists of the confrontation of a position or argument with its often implicit conditions of possibility, in order to reveal whether such a position or argument is rational or not.[9]

The main advantage of the transcendental style of critique lies in the fact that it brings a critical programme into view that doesn't rest upon an arbitrary, dogmatic choice for criteria. In doing so transcendental critique outlines a stronger and more consistent critical program than critical dogmatism. It will be clear, however, that the strength of transcendental critique rests upon the validity of the transcendental style of argumentation. It is at this point that the third conception of criticality that I wish to discuss raises some important issues.

Deconstruction

The writings of Jacques Derrida, to which I will refer as the philosophy of *deconstruction*, can be understood as yet another reaction to the Munchausen trilemma. Like Apel, deconstruction rejects the possibility of grounding by deduction. Like Apel, deconstruction seeks a solution along the lines of the second option of the trilemma, i.e., the option of the reflexive paradox. But unlike Apel, deconstruction doesn't try to escape the paradox by means of a transcendental movement. It rather chooses to stay within this paradoxical terrain in order to explore its critical potential. In doing so it not only offers yet another way to think about critique and criticality. It also provides a profound critique of the transcendental approach in that it questions the very possibility of articulating conditions of possibility in an unambiguous way. In this respect deconstruction moves the discussion about conceptions of criticality one step 'forwards.'

The Metaphysics of Presence

Derrida sees the history of Western philosophy as a continuous attempt to locate a fundamental ground, an Archimedean point which serves both as an absolute beginning and as a centre from which everything originating from it can be mastered and controlled (see Derrida, 1978). Since Plato, this origin has always been defined in terms of *presence*. The origin is thought of as fully present to itself and as totally self-sufficient. The "determination of Being as *presence*," Derrida holds, is the matrix of the history of metaphysics. This "metaphysics of presence" (Derrida, 1978, p. 281) includes a *hierarchical axiology* in which the origin is designated as pure, simple, normal, standard, self-sufficient and self-identical, in order *then* to think in terms of derivation, complication, deterioration, accident etcetera. This, so Derrida argues, is "*the* metaphysical exigency," that which has been "the most constant, most profound and most potent" (Derrida, 1988, p. 93).

Derrida wants to put the metaphysical gesture into question. He acknowledges that he is not the first to do so. But unlike Nietzsche, Freud, Heidegger and all the other "destructive discourses," Derrida argues that we can never make a total break, that we can never step outside of the tradition that has made us. "There is no sense," he argues, "in doing without the concepts of metaphysics in order to shake metaphysics. We (...) can pronounce not a single destructive proposition which has not already had to slip into the form, the logic, and the implicit postulations of precisely what it seeks to contest" (Derrida, 1978, p. 280). While Derrida definitely wants to shake metaphysics, he acknowledges that this cannot be done from some neutral and innocent place outside of metaphysics.[10] What is more to the point, to put it simply, is to say that Derrida wants to shake metaphysics by showing that it is itself always already 'shaking,' by showing, in other words, the impossibility of any of its attempts to fix or immobilise being through the presentation of a self-sufficient presence.

Deconstruction is therefore not something that is applied to the (texts of the) metaphysical tradition from the outside, which is why he stresses that deconstruction is not a method "and cannot be transformed into one" (Derrida, 1991, p. 273). Deconstruction rather is "one of the possible names to designate (...) what occurs [ce qui arrive], or cannot manage to occur [ce qui n'arrive pas à arriver], namely a certain dislocation which in effect reiterates itself regularly – and everywhere where there is something rather than nothing" (Derrida & Ewald, 1995, pp. 287–288).

Différance and Deconstruction

One way in which Derrida articulates the occurrence of deconstruction is through the "notion" of différance. Derrida develops his ideas about différance in the context of a discussion of the structuralism of Ferdinand de Saussure (see Derrida, 1982, pp. 1–28). Saussure had argued that language should not be understood as a naming process, a process of attaching words to things, but that it should rather be seen as a structure where any individual element is meaningless outside the confines of that structure. Language, so we could say, only consists of differences. These differences, however, are not differences between positive terms, that is, between terms that in and by themselves refer to objects outside of the system. In language there are only differences without positive terms. From this insight – which I can here describe only briefly – two conclusions follow.

First of all, the idea of differences without positive terms entails, that the "movement of signification" is only possible if each element "appearing on the scene of presence, is related to something other than itself" (Derrida, 1982, p. 13). What is called "the present" is therefore constituted "by means of this very relation to what it is not" (ibid.) This contamination is a necessary contamination: for the present to be itself, it already has to be other than itself. This puts the non-present in a double position, because it is the non present which makes the presence of the present possible, and yet, it can only make this presence possible by means of its own exclusion. What is excluded thereby, in a sense, returns "to sign the act of its own exclusion, " and it is this apparent complicity, which "outplays the legality of the decision to exclude" in the first place (Bennington, 1993, pp. 217–218; see also Derrida, 1981, pp. 41–42).

If this is what deconstruction can bring into view, we can already get an idea of its critical potential, because at the heart of deconstruction we find a concern for the 'constitutive outside' of what presents itself as self-sufficient. This reveals that deconstruction is more than just a destruction of the metaphysics of presence. Deconstruction is first and foremost an affirmation of what is excluded and forgotten. An affirmation, in short, of what is other (see Gasché, 1994).[11]

Deconstruction Is Justice

There is, however, a complication, which concerns the question *how* deconstruction can bring that what is excluded into view. For if it is the case that in language there are only differences without positive terms, then we have to concede that we can no longer articulate the differential character of language itself by means of a positive term (like, for example, 'differentiation'). Difference without positive terms implies that this dimension must itself always remain unperceived, for strictly speaking, it is unconceptualisable. Derrida thus concludes that the "play of difference," which is "the condition for the possibility and functioning of every sign, is in itself a silent play" (Derrida, 1982, p. 5).

If we would want to articulate that which does not let itself be articulated and yet is the condition for the possibility of all articulation – which we may want to do in order to prevent metaphysics from re-entering – we must acknowledge that there can never be a word or a concept to represent this silent play. We must acknowledge that this play cannot simply be exposed, for "one can expose only that which at a certain moment can become *present*" (ibid.). And we must acknowledge that there is nowhere to begin, "for what is put into question is precisely the quest for a rightful beginning, an absolute point of departure" (ibid., p. 6). All this is expressed in the new word or concept – "which is neither a word nor a concept" (ibid., p. 7) but a "neographism" (ibid., p. 13) – of *différance*.

The reason why Derrida introduces that "what is written as *différance*" (ibid., p. 11) is not difficult to grasp. For although the play of difference is identified as the condition for the possibility of all conceptuality, we should not make the mistake to think that we have finally identified the real origin of conceptuality.[12] The predicament can be put as follows: because we are talking about the condition of possibility of all conceptuality, this condition cannot belong to that what it makes possible, i.e., the 'order' of conceptuality. Yet the only way in which we can *articulate* this condition of possibility is from within this order. Because the condition of possibility is always articulated in terms of the system that is made possible by it, it is, in a sense, always already too late to be its condition of possibility (which implies that the condition of possibility is at the very same time a condition of impossibility; see Gasché, 1986, pp. 316–317).

At this point the critical potential of deconstruction returns in an even more radical way. The idea here is that because conditions of possibility are always already contaminated by the 'system' that is made possible by them, this 'system' is never totally delimited by these conditions. *Différance* is therefore a quasi-transcendental or quasi-condition of possibility. As Caputo (1997, p. 102) puts it, *différance* "does not describe fixed boundaries that delimit what can happen and what not, but points a mute, Buddhist finger at the moon of uncontainable effects."

Deconstruction thus tries to open up the system in the name of that which cannot be thought of in terms of the system and yet makes the system possible. This reveals that the deconstructive affirmation is not simply an affirmation of what is known to be excluded by the system. Deconstruction is an affirmation of what is wholly other (*tout autre*), of what is unforeseeable from the present. It is an affirmation of an otherness that is always to come, as an event which "as event, exceeds calculation, rules, programs, anticipations" (Derrida, 1992, p. 27). Deconstruction is an openness towards the unforeseeable in-coming (*l'invention*; invention) of the other (see Caputo, 1992, p. 47). It is from this concern for what is totally other, a concern to which Derrida sometimes refers as *justice*, that deconstruction derives its 'right' to be critical, its right to deconstruct – or, to be more precise, its right to reveal deconstruction.[13]

From Critique to Deconstruction

It is not too difficult to see the profound difference between deconstruction and critical dogmatism. Derrida points out that "the instance of *krinein* or of *krisis* (decision, choice, judgement, discernment) is ... one of the essential 'themes' or 'objects' of deconstruction" (Derrida, 1991, p. 273), for which reason he even concludes that "deconstruction is deconstruction of critical dogmatism" (Derrida, 1995a, p. 54). Derrida tries to show in many different ways that there is no safe ground upon which we can base our decisions, that there are no pure, uncontaminated, original criteria on which we can simply and straightforwardly base our judgements. At the basis of our decisions, as he puts it, lies a radical *undecidability* which cannot be closed off by our decisions, but which "continues to inhabit the decision" (Derrida, 1996, p. 87).

The distance between deconstruction and transcendental critique is perhaps more difficult to grasp. Yet I wish to argue that deconstruction, while in a sense staying remarkably close to the main intuitions of transcendental pragmatics, also puts a serious challenge to this program. Apel and Derrida agree on the fact that we are always on the inside of language and history, so that the language game that made us who we are, that gives us to possibility to speak in the first place, is, in Apel's words, "nichthintergehbar" (unsurpassable). This is why Derrida stresses that there cannot be a total rupture from the language game of metaphysics (which comes close to Apel's claim that a total critique of reason is impossible). Difficulties arise, however, as soon as we want to say something about that which makes our speaking – and more specifically in the case of Apel: argumentation – possible.

Although Apel hesitates to give a positive description of the conditions of possibility of the argumentative use of language, he at least believes that these conditions can be identified in a positive way by means of the principle of performative consistency. This, as I have argued, leads him eventually to the meta-rules that constitute the ideal community of communication.

Derrida is much more radical in his rejection of the possibility to identify and articulate the conditions of possibility of our speaking in any positive and unambiguous way. This is the whole point of *différance*, which is nothing less than an attempt to express the inexpressible, to point out the predicament that a condition of possibility has to be 'outside' of the system that is made possible by it in order to be a condition of possibility, and yet at the very same time can only be articulated from the 'inside' of the system that it has made possible. *Différance* is, therefore, at the very same time inside and outside, it is both origin and effect, for which reason it can only be understood as a "quasi-condition of possibility" which, as I have shown, does not describe fixed boundaries that delimit what can happen and what not.

The crucial difference between transcendental critique and deconstruction lies precisely here. If I see it correctly, Apel has to assume that the conditions of possibility control the system that is made possible by them. It is only on the basis of this assumption that a performative contradiction can arise, because such a contradiction can only occur when all possible performances in the system are controlled by these conditions. What Derrida brings to the fore, is that conditions of possibility can never be articulated independent of the system, that they can never be articulated from some safe metaphysical position outside of the system. And it is precisely because of this that they cannot have total control over the system. What is possible, so we could say, is always more than what any condition of possibility allows for. Deconstruction wants to do justice to this unforeseeable excess.

In this respect deconstruction can be seen as offering yet another conception of criticality (although it should by now be clear that after deconstruction both the idea of a conception and the idea of criticality have to be understood differently, just as the 'after' of after deconstruction is not simply an after) in that it envisages another way to go beyond the present and the given, another way, in short, for judgement to become possible. Unlike critical dogmatism, this judgement doesn't come from some allegedly safe place 'outside.' Unlike transcendental critique, it doesn't come from the inside either – as a form of internal critique through a test of performative consistency. Deconstruction suggests that *both* resources of critique are not as pure and self-sufficient as is assumed. The critical work of deconstruction, so we could say, consists in revealing the impurity of the critical criteria, it consists in revealing that they are not self-sufficient but need something other than themselves to be(come) possible. *Not*, as is so often claimed about deconstruction in particular and postmodern and poststructural thought more generally (see for an example Hill et al., 1999), to subvert the very possibility of critique, but rather to open up critique for its own uncritical assumptions – albeit *not* from some higher position or higher form of insight or knowledge (see also Biesta, 1998a). Not, in other words, to destroy but rather to *affirm* what is excluded and forgotten; to open up the possibility for the unforeseeable.

Conclusion

In the foregoing pages I have shown that 'critique' is not a monolithic concept, but that there are several ways to understand and articulate what 'being critical' is. I have also shown that different conceptions of criticality rest upon different justifications of the critical operation. These, in turn, relate to different answers to the question as to what gives each position the 'right' to be critical, to which I have referred as truth, rationality, and justice respectively. I have argued that critical dogmatism is problematic because it rests upon a *dogmatic* instalment of the critical criterion, although I have shown that it is possible to argue that such dogmatism is inevitable. I want to stress once more that critical dogmatism is more prevalent than is often assumed – although here everything depends on whether one is willing to concede that there is a dogmatic element involved in one's critical stance (see on this also Biesta, 1998a). The transcendental style of critique provides in a sense a more consistent conception of criticality. I have suggested, however, that it remains problematic in that it assumes that it can bring the foundations of critique into vision (albeit by a more sophisticated line of argumentation, namely the transcendental line). In this respect, so I wish to argue, transcendental critique displays a totalising tendency. Deconstruction – "if such a thing exists" – tries to go beyond this tendency in that it tries to open up, neither in order to install a new totality, nor by means of another, new totality.

While the foregoing pages may provide some new insights for the ongoing discussions about critical thinking, it will be clear that this is only a first step and that many issues still need to be addressed. This, however, lies well beyond the scope of the current contribution in which I have mainly tried to open up our understanding of critique and criticality. If, against this background, we return briefly to the question as to whether the idea(l) of critical thinking is biased, we can first of all conclude that critical dogmatism is without doubt a biased position. It may, however, be more appropriate to think of it as an *interested* position. After all, the bias-question has primarily to do with the assumption that the idea(l) of critical thinking is a self-justifying idea(l) – which is a central claim in the work of those who apply a transcendental approach to critical thinking. With respect to this question, however, it appears that transcendental critique and deconstruction take diametrically opposed positions. One way to frame the issue at stake is to ask whether rationality should have priority over justice, or whether justice should have priority over rationality. Siegel, an astute defender of the transcendental approach, is not only acutely aware of this issue but is also very explicit in outlining his position when he writes that "the philosophical enterprise does not have as its goal the bringing about of social justice" (Siegel, 1995, p. 22). I would want to argue, however, that if rationality is to have any value at all – and I do not wish to contest that it might be valuable – this value should eventually stem from its contribution in furthering the case of justice (see also Biesta, 1999b). This, in sum, is the direction in which I think that a redescription of critical thinking that takes the lessons from deconstruction into consideration, should go.

Notes

1　An earlier version of this chapter was co-authored with Geert-Jan Stams and published as Biesta, G. J. J. & Stams, G. J. J. M. (2001). Critical thinking and the question of critique. Some lessons from deconstruction. *Studies in Philosophy and Education,* 20(1), 57–74.

2　"Der Mensch ist das einzige Geschöpf, das erzogen werden muss. (…) Der Mensch kann nur Mensch werden durch Erziehung. Er is nichts, als was die Erziehung aus ihm macht" (Kant, 1982, pp. 697, 699).

3　Siegel is one of the few participants in the discussion who has dealt with this issue extensively (see e.g., Siegel, 1987, 1988, 1990; see also Snik & Zevenbergen, 1995, p. 112).

4　In the next three sections of this chapter I make use of an argument that was developed in a slightly different context in Biesta, 1999a.

5　"Die Forderung ist also diese: man soll das Erkenntnisvermögen erkennen, ehe man erkennt; es ist dasselbe wie mit dem Schwimmenwollen, ehe man ins Wasser geht. Die Untersuchung des Erkenntnisvermögens ist selbts erkennend, kann nicht zu dem kommen, zu was es kommen will, weil es selbst dies ist …" (Hegel, quoted in Sas, 1995, p. 508) Nietzsche would later express this concern quite poignantly in the following way: "(E)ine Kritiek des Erkenntnisvermögens ist unsinnig; wie sollte das Werkzeug sich selbst kritisieren können, wenn es eben nur *sich* zur Kritik gebrauchen kann? Es kann nicht einmal sich selbst definieren" (Nietzsche, 1964, section 486).

6 In a sense we could say that Apel uses the middle option of the trilemma, the logical circle, to find his way out (cf. Sas, 1995, pp. 506–511).

7 In Apel's own words: "(dieses) Kriterium ... ist in der Lage, unbestreitbare Präsuppositionen der Argumentation als reflexiv-letztbegründete Sätze aufzuzeichnen: d.h., Sätze, die keiner *Begründung aus etwas anderem* bedürfen, weil *man sie nicht verstehen kann, ohne zu wissen dass sie wahr sind*" (Apel, 1987b, p. 185; emphasis in original).

8 Although the transcendental approach plays a central role in the debates about the justification of rationality as the central principle of critical thinking (see, most notably, the work of Harvey Siegel), Apel's approach, which to my understanding provides the most sophisticated version of transcendental philosophy available today, has hardly been explored in the context of these discussions. One of the few exceptions is Zevenbergen (1997).

9 This line of thought is quite often used to argue that claims by so-called minority groups to have the right to educate their children in group-specific ways cannot be sustained since such claims rest upon non-group-specific principles.

10 In so far as critique operates through the application of an external criterion, this means that deconstruction is *not* a critique (see Derrida, 1991, p. 273; see also Norris, 1987, p. 56).

11 Although I present these ideas in the context of a discussion about language, they have a larger significance than the field of language alone. See for a brilliant application of these ideas on issues concerning politics and political theory Honig (1993).

12 Strictly speaking, there is only one way to avoid this mistake, which is by acknowledging that the differences that constitute the play of difference "are themselves *effects*" (Derrida 1982, p. 11). This means, then, that in the "most classical fashion," that is in the language of metaphysics, we would have to speak of them as effects "without a cause" (ibid., p. 12).

13 Over the past years a whole body of literature on Derrida's rather idiosyncratic use of the idea of justice has been published. Besides Derrida (1992), see also Derrida (1999) and Critchley (1999).

CHAPTER 5

Philosophy, Exposure, and Children: How to Resist the Instrumentalisation of Philosophy in Education

What Might Philosophy Achieve?[1]

I fear that this chapter boils down to two questions: "What is philosophy?" and "What might it achieve?" The reason for using the word 'fear' is that both questions are in a sense impossible to answer – and perhaps, therefore, even impossible to ask. The question as to what philosophy *is* has been one of the perennial questions in the writings of those who call themselves philosophers. The answers that have been generated are extremely diverse, ranging from claims for some kind of essence of philosophy to views which emphasise the arbitrariness of what counts as philosophy, such as in Richard Rorty's idea of philosophy as 'a kind of writing' (Rorty, 1978) or Peter Sloterdijk's characterisation of the philosophical tradition as a community of letter-writing friends (Sloterdijk, 2009). Discussions about the definition of philosophy are often also attempts at policing the borders of the field – a 'good' example being the opposition from a number of philosophers to the proposal to award Jacques Derrida an honorary doctorate at the University of Cambridge (see Derrida, 1995b). The question as to what counts as philosophy is virtually impossible to answer, therefore, because it belongs to the very nature of the genre to reflect upon its identity and its borders, and to do so without the hope for a final settlement. The question as to what philosophy might achieve is similarly difficult to answer, because philosophy in its many forms and guises may achieve many things – both things that lie within and things that lie beyond our control and imagination. Nonetheless, questions of definition and effect are important when philosophy is being mobilised to do something, and they are perhaps even more important when philosophy is being mobilised to do something *educational,* such as in the case of philosophy for children. In this regard, then, the two questions are at the very same time impossible and inevitable.

The use of philosophy in educational programmes and practices under such names as philosophy for children, philosophy with children, or the community of philosophical enquiry, has become well established in many countries around the world. This is first of all due to the efforts of Matthew Lipman and colleagues, but is also the result of the work of numerous others who have followed in their footsteps or have taken inspiration from the work. The main attraction of the educational use of philosophy – which I will use as the phrase to cover a range of approaches – seems to lie in the claim that it can help children and young people to develop skills for thinking critically, reflectively and reasonably. By locating the acquisition of such skills within communities of enquiry, the further claim is that engagement with philosophy can foster the development of moral reflection and sensitivity and of social and democratic skills more generally. Claims like these provide a set of arguments for the inclusion of philosophy in the school curriculum that goes well beyond philosophy as just another curricular subject or body of knowledge. Here is, for example, how the website of SAPERE, the UK Society for Advancing Philosophical Enquiry and Reflection in Education, lists the wider benefits of philosophy for children ('P4C').

> Independent research during 2003–2004 in 100 English schools showed that P4C raises achievement, IQ and test scores, and improves self-esteem and motivation across the ability range. Controlled tests in America in the 1980's showed that not only could children's reasoning powers be enhanced through philosophical enquiry, but so could their reading and mathematical skills. Reading and comprehension improvements were also shown by UK studies in Derby and South Wales in the 1990's. Teachers have found that the Community of Enquiry approach suits a holistic concern for their students: self-esteem rises with children's ability to communicate in a personally meaningful way with their peers. There was support for this in the late 1990's, in very positive OFSTED [the English School Inspection Organisation; GB] reports on two schools with philosophical enquiry in their curriculum. (http://www.sapere.org.uk/content/index.aspx?id=46; last accessed 22 July 2010)

Although I do not wish to doubt that engagement with certain forms of philosophy can have these kinds of effects – albeit that there is the question what the exact 'cause,' the exact 'effect,' and the exact relationship between the two is (see also Biesta, 2007b, 2010e) – and although I can see the attraction of this particular way of making a case for the inclusion of philosophy in the curriculum, the case for philosophy that is presented along these lines is not without problems. The ambition of this chapter is to raise some questions about the conception of education that appears to inform the discussion about the educational use of philosophy. My aim is to suggest an *additional* rather than an alternative view about the educational use of philosophy. This means that I do not have the ambition to suggest a new programme for philosophy in education but rather wish to suggest a perspective that can act as a reminder of a different way in which one can engage with philosophy – which in a sense can also be read as a reminder about how philosophy might engage with us. The philosophical distinction in terms of which my argument is phrased is that between humanism and post-humanism[2] – and I wish to make clear from the outset that 'post-humanism' does not stand for an approach which tries to do away with the humanity of the human being, but rather articulates an approach which, in the words of Emmanuel Levinas, denounces human*ism* "because it is not sufficiently human" (Levinas, 1981, p. 128). The guiding concept in this additional view is that of 'exposure' (and the 'absent-present' in my argument – already in brackets – is the child).

Philosophical Enquiry or Scientific Enquiry?

Given the sheer diversity of schools, views and positions within the field of philosophy, one of the important questions in relation to the educational use of philosophy concerns the particular selection(s) made from the field. One thing that is remarkable in relation to this is the strong orientation towards knowledge and truth. Hannam and Echeverria (2009), for example, argue that in the community of philosophical enquiry "the purpose is to construct knowledge together" and the aim is "to promote cooperation in illuminating a path to come closer to the truth of things" (Hannam & Echeverria, 2009, p. 8). Although this is not the whole of what happens or may happen in the community of philosophical enquiry, and although there is also a strong emphasis on the provisional character of all claims to truth (see ibid.), this, and the wider pedagogy of the community of philosophical enquiry, gives the impression that at least to a certain extent the approach is less about a community of *philosophical* enquiry and more about a community of *scientific* enquiry, one based, moreover, on a particular rational-epistemological view of what scientific knowledge is and how it is brought about. Here is, for example, how the website of SAPERE summarises the pedagogy of 'P4C.'

Key Principles of P4C
– The key practice that starts and drives the whole thinking process is enquiry (interpreted as going beyond information to seek understanding).
– The key practice that results in significant changes of thought and action is reflection.
These aims and processes can be made more explicit if the teacher asks appropriate questions. These can range from a general invitation (such as: Can anyone respond to that?) to more specific calls that require a considered response.

There are ten key elements the teacher can introduce to elicit a considered response.

1. *Questions* (What don't we understand here? What questions do we have about this?)
2. *Hypotheses* (Does anyone have any alternative suggestions or explanations?)
3. *Reasons* (What reasons are there for doing that? What evidence is there for believing this?)
4. *Examples* (Can anyone think of an example of this? Can someone think of a counter-example?)
5. *Distinctions* (Can we make a distinction here? Can anyone give a definition?)
6. *Connections* (Is anyone able to build on that idea? or Can someone link that with another idea?)
7. *Implications* (What assumptions lie behind this? What consequences does it lead to?)
8. *Intentions* (Is that what was really meant? Is that what we're really saying?)
9. *Criteria* (What makes that an example of X? What are the things that really count here?)
10. *Consistency* (Does that conclusion follow? Are these principles/beliefs consistent?)
    (see http://www.sapere.org.uk/content/index.aspx?id=45; accessed 22 July 2010; emphases in original)

That the educational engagement with philosophy tends to model itself on a rational-epistemological interpretation of the community of scientific enquiry is also visible in its focus on the development of thinking skills, and particularly higher order thinking skills (see ibid.). Hannam and Echeverria argue, for example, that the development of thinking skills takes place through the interaction between four "key elements" which are listed as critical thinking, creative thinking, collaborative thinking and caring thinking (Hannam & Echeverria, 2009, p. 13) and four "categories of skill," namely good reasoning skills, investigatory skills, conceptual skills, and translation skills (see ibid., pp. 91, 159). Particularly the first three of the latter set give the strong impression that the community of philosophical enquiry is more like a community of scientific enquiry which proceeds towards truth though the employment of reasoning, investigation and conceptual development, while the skills listed under the category of 'translation' are not that far away from the four norms of scientific practice as articulated by Robert K. Merton (1942): communalism, universalism, disinterestedness and organised scepticism. This again shows that at least part of what occurs within the community of philosophical enquiry is modelled upon a particular conception of scientific enquiry.

While this does raise the question about the *justification* for this particular selection from the philosophical tradition – to which I turn below – the other thing to bear in mind at this point is that the conception of scientific enquiry informing the practice of the community of philosophical enquiry is in itself a very specific reconstruction of the way in which science is thought to pro-ceed. It represents the practice of science predominantly in epistemological and procedural terms and, in this regard, can be characterised as *ideological,* not in the least because there are radically different accounts of how we should understand the practice and culture (Pickering, 1992) of science, including ones that say that epistemology and rational procedure are the least helpful in making sense of science (see, for example, Latour, 1987; Bloor, 1991).

Lipman (2003) tries to address this point by arguing that the idea of the community of enquiry should not be understood as "an attempt to substitute reasoning for science" but rather as an effort "to *complement* scientific inquiry" (Lipman, 2003, p. 111; emphasis added). Nonetheless his focus for what the community of enquiry is about, is based on an acceptance of the epistemologi-cal understanding of science – and perhaps we could even say that it is based on an uncritical acceptance of this view – and sees reasoning exclusively as having to do with knowledge. As he explains:

> The information derived from science – its theories, data and procedures – are not in dispute. What reasoning helps do is (a) *extend* knowledge through logical inference; (b) *defend* knowledge through reasons and arguments; and (c) *coordinate* knowledge through critical analysis. (Lipman, 2003, p. 111; emphasis in original)

A Performative Contradiction

Yet even where the community of philosophical enquiry is focused less on knowledge and truth and more on meaning and understanding, it still artic-ulates a particular selection from the philosophical tradition. This, in itself, should not be seen as a problem as the philosophical tradition – including all the work that occurs 'on' and, according to some, even 'beyond' its borders – is too vast and too diverse to be represented in full. At the same time, however, there is something uncomfortable about a too self-assured presentation of a particular selection of the tradition as representing all of philosophy. While there is a strong emphasis in the literature on the provisional and always revisable character of *knowledge*, this is less so with regard to philosophy itself. This, of course, brings us back to the impossible question I started this chapter with. Rather than to get into this discussion, I simply wish to log the question about the representation of philosophy *within* philosophy for and with children and *within* the community of philosophical enquiry as an issue for further scrutiny.

There is, however, another level at which the question of the particular conception of philosophy can be asked. This is not about how philosophy is explicitly *represented* – which is the question of selection – but about the way in which philosophy is *deployed* in and through the educational use of philosophy. This, in a sense, brings us to the question as to what philosophy might *achieve*, rather than about what philosophy *is*.

What is noticeable in the educational use of philosophy within philosophy for/with children and the community of philosophical enquiry is an *instrumental* use – and also an instrumental positioning – of philosophy (see also, for example, Long, 2005; Murris, 2008). Philosophy is deployed as an instrument that is supposed to work *upon* individuals so that they can develop and/or acquire certain qualities, capacities and skills. While this tendency might be characterised as a psychologisation of philosophy, I prefer to use the more general term of instrumentalisation – philosophy as an instrument for 'producing' something – albeit that within the literature there is indeed a strong emphasis on the ways in which individuals, through engagement with philosophy in the community of philosophical enquiry, are supposed to *develop* a range of skills, including cognitive and thinking skills, moral and social skills, and democratic skills.

Hannam and Echeverria (2009), who focus their discussion on philosophy with teenagers, add an extensive discussion on identity development during adolescence to the mix of possible outcomes of the engagement with philosophy In addition they emphasise the potential impact of the community of philosophical enquiry on emotional development and emotional well-being and "healthy perceptions of others" (see ibid., p. 43), on the "growth in cognitive competencies which in turn facilitate the development of understanding and tolerance of different points of view" (ibid., p. 44), on the development of the "personal qualities of self-governance [and] self-control" (ibid., p. 65), and on the development of literacy skills (see ibid., p. 84). SAPERE, as I have shown above, lists such potential effects as an increase in achievement, IQ and test scores, the improvement of self-esteem and motivation, and the enhancement of reasoning powers and reading and mathematical skills.

These claims may all be true, and they may all be considered important. My aim here is not to contest these potential effects in themselves – although I do wish to repeat my concern about the extent to which it is possible to identify causes, effects and their interrelationships. I rather wish to highlight the underlying conception of the human being as a kind of 'developing organism' or, in the words of Usher and Edwards (1994, p. 24), as "a certain kind of subject who has the inherent potential to become self-motivated and self-directing" – a conception which seems to inform the pedagogy of the community of philosophical enquiry conceived as a process aiming at facilitating the development of a range of qualities, competencies and skills. When we look at the educational use of philosophy from this angle it becomes clear that the whole project – in its intentions, its effects, and its pedagogy – is not only based on a particular *conception* of the human being but also and, from a philosophical point perhaps more problematically, on a particular *truth* about the human being.

My concern here is not with the particular conception of the human being that seems to inform the work, but with the implications of the fact that the educational use of philosophy appears to be based on a particular truth about the human being. It is the latter which situates the educational use of philosophy more explicitly within what philosophers such as Heidegger, Levinas and Sloterdijk have characterised as 'humanism,' understood as the idea that it is possible to know and articulate the essence or nature of the human being – an idea which is often accompanied by the assumption that it is possible to use this knowledge as the foundation for subsequent action in such domains as education, politics or ethics. Levinas characterises such a form of humanism as entailing "the recognition of an invariable essence named 'Man,' the affirmation of his central place in the economy of the Real and of his value which [engenders] all values" (Levinas, 1990, p. 277).

One way to identify a potential problem – or at least raise a topic for discussion – in relation to this, is to point at the possible contradiction between an ethos of reflection and questioning at the level of the *practice* of the community of philosophical enquiry and an unreflective foundation of this practice enacted through a particular pedagogy and a wider justification of this practice which sees (engagement with) philosophy as an instrument to 'produce' a particular kind of human subjectivity. The contradiction here is a performative one, as it is not that questions about the human being and about being human are not or cannot be on the agenda of the community of philosophical enquiry. The contradiction rather arises from the tension between what the community of philosophical enquiry is committed to and the assumptions that appear to inform its justification and pedagogy.

This is also the point made by Vansieleghem (2005) in her critique of instrumentalist tendencies within philosophy for children, particularly with regard to the ambition to contribute to the formation of the democratic person. The question Vansieleghem raises in this context is whether we should think of education as the production of a pre-defined identity or whether education, if it has an interest in the human subject and its freedom, should always remain open to something else, something new. Vansieleghem argues that philosophy for children, "with its emphasis on critical thinking and autonomy," is actually "nothing more than the reproduction of an existing discourse," which is why "the autonomy the child gains through Philosophy for Children by critical thinking and dialogue is nothing more than the freedom to occupy a pre-constituted place in that discourse" (Vansieleghem, 2005, p. 25).

The issues for discussion, then, are (1) how and why this contradiction is a problem, and (2) how we might be able to overcome it. A partial and quick answer to the first question is that it *does* matter to find dogmatic elements within any philosophical endeavour – which is not to say that it is always easy to overcome such elements (on this see also the previous chapter; and Biesta, 2009b). But in order to explore the wider implications and articulate the outlines of a different pedagogy, some more detail is needed.

The Trouble with Humanism, Particularly in Education

In 20th century philosophy humanism has basically been challenged for two reasons. On the one hand questions have been raised about the *possibility* of humanism, that is, about the possibility for human beings to define their own essence and origin. Foucault and Derrida have both shown the impossibility of trying to capture our own essence and origin – an impossibility which has become known as the 'end of man' or the 'death of the subject' (see Foucault, 1970; Derrida, 1982). On the other hand, questions have been raised about the *desirability* of humanism. This line has particularly been developed by Heidegger and Levinas (see Biesta, 2006a for more detail; see also Derrida, 1982, pp. 109–136). For Levinas the "crisis of humanism in our society" began with the "inhuman events of recent history" (Levinas, 1990, p. 279). Yet for Levinas the crisis of humanism is not simply located in these inhumanities as such, but first and foremost in humanism's inability to effectively counter such inhumanities and also in the fact that many of the inhumanities of the 20th century – Levinas mentions "the 1914 War, the Russian Revolution refuting itself in Stalinism, fascism, Hitlerism, the 1939–1945 War, atomic bombings, genocide and uninterrupted war" (ibid.) – were actually based upon and motivated by particular definitions of what it means to be human. This is why Levinas concludes – with a phrase reminiscent of Heidegger – that "humanism has to be denounced (...) because it is not *sufficiently* human" (Levinas, 1981, p. 128; emphasis added).

The problem with humanism is that it posits a *norm* of what it means to be human and in doing so excludes those who do not live up to or are unable to live up to this norm. This point is not simply a general and philosophical one; it also has important educational ramifications. From an educational point of view the problem with humanism is that it specifies a norm of what it means to be human *before* the actual manifestation of 'instances' of humanity. It specifies what the child, student or newcomer must become before giving them an opportunity to show who they are and who they will be (see also Vansieleghem, 2005). This form of humanism thus seems to be unable to be open to the possibility that newcomers might radically alter our understandings of what it means to be human. The upshot of this, to put it briefly, is that education becomes focused on the 'production' of a particular kind of subjectivity.

A Post-Humanist Theory of Education: Action, Uniqueness and Exposure

The challenge to overcome humanism is, therefore, a double challenge, as there is not only the question how this might be done *philosophically*, but also the question how it might be achieved *educationally* – and the two questions are partly separate as I do not wish to see educational theory as simply the application of philosophy. In my own work I have responded to this challenge through a combination of two sets of ideas – captured in the notions of 'coming into the world' and 'uniqueness' – which, together, constitute what might be characterised as a post-humanist theory of education (see particularly Biesta, 2006a, 2010a). On the one hand I have suggested that instead of understanding education as having to do with the production or promotion of a particular kind of subjectivity, we should think of education as being interested in how new beginnings and new beginners can come into the world. The idea of 'coming into world' thus aims to articulate an educational interest into human subjectivity but does so without a template, that is, without a pre-defined idea about what it means to be and exist as a human being. It thus tries to overcome a humanistic determination of human subjectivity.

A focus on how individuals come into the world bears resemblance to forms of child-centred and student-centred education. But whereas extreme forms of child- and student-centred education would simply accept anything and anyone that announces itself (on this see Oelkers, 1996), I have emphasised the there is always a need for *judgment* about what and who comes into the world. My only point is that such judgment should occur *after* the event of coming into the world, not before. Moreover, 'coming into the world' should not be understood as a 'one-off' event but has to do with the ongoing stream of initiatives, which means that the question of judgement is one that poses itself continuously (see below). There is, of course, a risk entailed in this,[3] but the question here is not whether we should try to do away with this risk. The question is whether in order to prevent a new Hitler or a new Pol Pot from coming into the world we should forfeit the possibility of a new Mother Theresa, a new Martin Luther King or a new Nelson Mandela from coming into the world as well. It is as simple – and of course also as complicated – as that. The other notion I have used in order to respond to the challenge outlined above is the idea of *uniqueness*, where uniqueness is precisely about the way in which each individual is not a specimen of a more general definition of what it means to be human.

Coming into the World

The idea of 'coming into the world' draws inspiration from the writings of Hannah Arendt, particularly her ideas on *action*. For Arendt to act first of all means to take initiative, that is, to begin something new. Arendt characterises the human being as an *initium*: a "begin*ning* and a begin*ner*" (Arendt, 1977, p. 170; emphasis added). Arendt compares action to the fact of birth, since with each birth something 'uniquely new' comes into the world (see Arendt, 1958, p. 178). But it is not only at the moment of birth that something new comes into the world. We *continuously* bring new beginnings into the world through our words and deeds. Arendt connects action to freedom but emphasises that freedom should not be understood as a phenomenon of the will, that is, as the freedom to do whatever we choose to do, but that we should instead conceive of it as the freedom "to call something into being which did not exist before" (Arendt, 1977, p. 151). The subtle difference between freedom as sovereignty and freedom as beginning has far-reaching consequences. The main implication is that freedom is not an 'inner feeling' or a private experience but by necessity a public and hence a political phenomenon. "The raison d'être of politics is freedom," Arendt writes, "and its field of experience is action" (ibid., p. 146). Arendt stresses again and again that freedom needs a "public realm" to make its appearance (ibid., p. 149) Moreover, freedom only exists in action, which means that human beings are free – as distinguished from their "possessing the gift of freedom" – as long as they act, "neither before nor after" (ibid., p. 153). The question this raises is how freedom can appear.

To answer this question, it is crucial to see that 'beginning' is only half of what action is about. Although it is true that we reveal our 'distinct uniqueness' through what we say and do, everything depends on how others will take up our initiatives. This is why Arendt writes that the agent is not an author or a producer, but a subject in the twofold sense of the word, namely one who began an action and the one who suffers from and is subjected to its consequences (see Arendt, 1958, p. 184). The upshot of this is that our 'capacity' for action – and hence our freedom – crucially depends on the ways in which others take up our beginnings, which immediately means that the 'capacity' for action is not a capacity that can ever be in our possession or under our control (and in this way the 'capacity' for action is not a skill or disposition). The 'problem,' after all – and again Arendt argues that this actually is far from a problem – is that others respond to our initiatives in ways that are unpredictable and beyond our control.

Although this frustrates our beginnings, Arendt emphasises again and again that the "impossibility to remain unique masters of what [we] do" is at the very same time the condition – and the *only* condition – under which our beginnings can come into the world (ibid., p. 244). We can of course try to control the ways in which others respond to our beginnings. But if we were to do so, we would deprive others of their opportunities to begin. We would deprive them of their opportunities to act, and hence we would deprive them of their freedom. Action is therefore never possible in isolation. Arendt even goes as far as to argue that "to be isolated is to be deprived of the capacity to act" (ibid., p. 188). This also implies that action in the Arendtian sense of the word is never possible without plurality – or to be more precise: action in the Arendtian sense is never possible without the exposure to otherness and difference. As soon as we erase plurality – as soon as we erase the otherness of others by attempting to control how they respond to our initiatives – we deprive others of their actions and their freedom, and as a result deprive *ourselves* of the possibility to act, and hence of our freedom. All this is captured in Arendt's concise but profound statement that "plurality is the condition of human action" (ibid., p. 8). This statement should, however, not be read as an empirical statement but rather as the normative core of Arendt's philosophy, a philosophy committed to a world in which everyone has the opportunity to act, appear and 'achieve' freedom.

Uniqueness

The notion of 'uniqueness' plays an important role in the ideas I have taken from Arendt, particularly her claim that we disclose our 'distinct uniqueness' through action – which, as I have shown, implies that we can only disclose this uniqueness if we are willing to run the risk that our beginnings are taken up in ways that are different from what we intended. What is important about Arendt's views is that they can help to approach the question of uniqueness in relational, political and existential terms, as she links the idea of 'uniqueness'

to the particular ways in which we *exist* with others (on the political significance of such a existential view see Biesta, 2010c). But the idea of disclosing
one's distinct uniqueness through action runs the risk of conceiving of uniqueness in terms of characteristics or qualities of the subject – and would thus
conceive of uniqueness in terms of what we *have* or *possess*. It would, to put it
differently, turn the question of uniqueness into a question of identity.

There are several problems with this way of understanding uniqueness. One
is that if we think of uniqueness in terms of the characteristics we have, we
must assume that there is some underlying 'substratum' that is the carrier of
such characteristics. This brings us close, again, to the idea of an underlying
human essence, and thus would bring humanism in through the backdoor.
There is, however, a second problem which in my view is the more important
one. This has to do with the fact that if we would only relate to others in order
to make clear how *we* are different from *them*, there would, in a sense, be nothing at stake in our relationships with others. Or, to put it differently, we would
only need others in order to find out and make clear how we are different
from them – how my identity is unique – but once this has become clear we
wouldn't need others any more. Our relationship with others would therefore
remain instrumental.

The philosopher who has helped me most to think through these issues and
articulate an alternative way of approaching the idea of uniqueness is Emmanuel Levinas. What is most significant about Levinas's work is *not* that he has
generated a new theory about the uniqueness of the human being – and I
would argue that he actually has not develop any theory at all – but that he
has introduced a different *question* about uniqueness. Instead of asking what
makes each of us unique – which is the question of identity – Levinas has
approached the question of uniqueness by asking when it *matters* that I am
unique, that I am I and no one else. Levinas's answer to this question, to put
it briefly, is that my uniqueness matters in those situations in which I cannot
be replaced by someone else, that is, in those situations where it matters that *I*
am there and not just anyone. I have referred to this idea as 'uniqueness as irre-
placeability' in order to distinguish it from 'uniqueness as difference,' which is
the question of identity (see Biesta, 2010a, chapter 4).

Exposure

The situations Levinas has in mind are those in which I find myself in a position of responsibility for a concrete other; that is, in a situation in which someone calls me, singles me out so to speak, and where it is up to me to respond.
It is, therefore, in situations where I am *exposed* to the other – or to be more
precise: where I am exposed to an 'imperative' (see Lingis, 1994, p. 111, for this

term) – that my uniqueness matters, as it is in those situations that it is for *me* to respond and not just for anyone. It is important to mention that for Levinas this responsibility is not issued from our will or our decision to become responsible, nor from a judgement that we should take up our responsibility. For Levinas responsibility comes *before* subjectivity, which is why he has argued that responsibility is "the essential, primary and fundamental structure of subjectivity" (Levinas, 1985, p. 95). Uniqueness, then, ceases to be an ontological notion – it is not about what we possess or are in terms of identity – but becomes an *existential* notion that has to do with the ways in which we are exposed to others, are singled out by them.

One important implication of these ideas is, that they do not lead to some kind of educational programme through which action and uniqueness can be produced. Action and uniqueness are phenomena that are structurally *beyond* our control – which means that as soon as we try to control then, as soon as we try to bring them into our grasp, they actually disappear. Although action and uniqueness cannot be produced – and in this sense are beyond the reach of any educational programme – it is of course possible to create situations in which it becomes very unlikely that action and uniqueness will appear. This is the case when we block any exposure to otherness and difference. It is the situation in which we are made 'immune' for any interruption from the outside, for any intervention of the other (on immunisation see Masschelein, 1996; Masschelein & Simons, 2004). The choice, therefore, is between education that contributes to immunisation and education that keeps the possibility for interruption and intervention open – with no guarantee, of course, that anything may emerge from this. (For a thoughtful discussion of some of the tensions in the ideas of exposure and interruption in education see Bonnett, 2009.)

Conclusion: A Different Philosophy for Different Children

In this chapter I have focused on the assumptions underlying the pedagogy of the educational use of philosophy. I have characterised this pedagogy as an *instrumental* pedagogy in that it focuses on the way in which engagement with philosophy can produce an individual with certain qualities and skills. I have brought the wider set of assumptions informing this pedagogy in relation with humanistic thinking in education. I have suggested that the educational use of philosophy appears to be based on a particular idea – and perhaps we can say a particular truth – about what the human subject is and how the human subject can become 'better,' for example as a more critical, reflective and reasonable thinker. This at least partly seems to be connected with a tendency to see the community of philosophical enquiry first and foremost as a community of *scientific* enquiry. This, as I have argued, is not only problematic because it enacts a rather narrow representation of what philosophy can be about, but also raises problems because the particular depiction of science as a disinterested search for truth is itself ideological.

In order to overcome the instrumentalist tendencies in the educational use of philosophy I have suggested that we not just need a different pedagogy, but actually need to shift the assumptions informing our pedagogy. This led me to the wider discussion about the humanist foundations of modern education and to some suggestions for a post-humanist understanding of education, one that is not based on a particular truth about the nature and destiny of the human subject but rather wants to see education as a concern for the ways in which individuals-in-their-uniqueness might come into the world. The central educational concept emerging from these ideas is that of *exposure*. Exposure is not an educational technique to produce unique individuals. Exposure rather denotes a 'quality' of human interaction and engagement that may make the event of the 'arrival' of uniqueness possible. Exposure is the moment when I am singled out, so to speak; it is the moment where I am exposed in my singularity. Exposure is therefore not about the revelation of a unique, pre-existing identity; it rather is about the *constitution* of me as being irreplaceable in the face of an appeal, in the face of a call. In this sense exposure does not produce – it only interrupts.

A pedagogy focusing on exposure and interruption is therefore no longer a pedagogy that aims to produce a particular kind of subject or particular qualities of the subject or that aims to equip the subject with a range of useful skills. A pedagogy focusing on exposure and interruption is a pedagogy that may bring about hesitation (see Chapter 6), an experience of not knowing, an experience that makes us stop rather than that it rushes us into the pseudo-security of questions, hypothesis, reasons, examples, distinctions, connections, implications, intentions, criteria, and consistency. There are parts of the philosophical tradition that have the potential to make us hesitate, to put us on the spot, to put our normal ways of being and doing into question. This, however, has to do with a quality of philosophy that is rather far away from the model of scientific enquiry, as it is not focused on knowing and the improvement of knowledge, but has an orientation towards *not*-knowing. One could even say that when engagement with philosophy leads to interruption and hesitation, it puts us, in a sense, in the position of the child as the one whose seeing, thinking and doing is not yet filled with the knowledge, categories and ways of speaking of others. I am not referring here to a kind of romantic unmediated wholeness-with-the-world, but to a situation in which we cannot rely on existing knowledge, patterns, structures and traditions so that it is up to us to invent a unique response and thus to invent ourselves uniquely in and through this response. This child-like position of not-knowing that can follow from exposure may well suggest an entirely different set of possibilities for the educational engagement with philosophy and may well give the phrase 'philosophy for children' an entirely new meaning.

Notes

1 This chapter is based on Biesta, G. J. J. (2011). Philosophy, exposure and children: How to resist the instrumentalisation of philosophy in education. *Journal of Philosophy of Education*, 45(2), 305–319.

2 Since writing this chapter, and since doing the work that cumulated in my book *Beyond Learning* (Biesta, 2006a) in which I explicitly criticise philosophical humanism and its role in modern education, a whole area of scholarship has emerged around issues of post-humanism. Perhaps my work has been a forerunner in what is currently going on – a judgement that will have to be made by others and in the future. Although it could also be that the angle I took, and am also presenting in this chapter, is (slightly) different. In this chapter I present my case in the best possible way; I leave it to readers to make up their mind about the significance, or not, for more recent discussions.

3 This is precisely the beautiful risk that is the central topic of Biesta (2014a).

CHAPTER 6

No Education without Hesitation: Exploring the Limits of Educational Relations

Introduction[1]

In a publication from 1894, the German philosopher Wilhelm Dilthey (1833–1911) wrote that "die Wissenschaft der Pädagogik kann nur beginnen mit der Deskription des Erziehers in seinem Verhältnis zum Zögling" – which roughly translates as "the science of education can only begin with a description of the educator in his or her relation to the one being educated" (Dilthey, 1961, p. 190). In the 1930s, Dilthey's student Hermann Nohl (1879–1960), by then professor of education at the university of Göttingen, would put the educational relation at the centre of his conception of education (see Nohl, 1963), thus making it into one of the key concepts of 20th century German educational theory (see Kron, 1989, pp. 190–210).

The idea that relations matter in education – and that they matter in a crucial and fundamental way – is difficult to contest. It is difficult to envisage education *without* relation, and in this regard, it may well be true, to quote the title from the book edited by Charles Bingham and Alexander Sidorkin (2004), that there is indeed no education without relation. Yet to say that there is and can be no education without relation, is not entirely without risk. At a practical level the risk is that we may try to relate *too much*, that is, that we may try to get too close to our students – for example on the assumption that we need to know as much as possible about our students, about their history, their background, their identity, their feelings, their sense of self, in order to be able to teach them successfully – and therefore leave no space for something educational to happen, for the 'event' of education to occur (see also Caputo, 2012). Here we can take inspiration from Anton Makarenko who, precisely for this reason, refused to have any knowledge about the history of the juvenile delinquents he worked with at the Gorky Colony (see Meirieu, 2007, pp. 109–110). At a theoretical level the risk is that, by focusing too much on the relational dimensions of education, we lose sight of the gaps, the fissures, and the disjunctions, the disconnections and the strangeness that are part of educational processes and practices as well – and, more importantly, we run the risk that we lose sight of the educational significance of these dimensions.

© KONINKLIJKE BRILL NV, LEIDEN, 2019 | DOI: 10.1163/9789004401105_007

While I do not wish to contest, therefore, that there is no education without *relation*, I wish to *add* to this that there is also no education without *hesitation*. This involves what we might call 'practical hesitation' – the subtle moments where we hold back, where we do not want to know, where we leave space for something to happen that is fundamentally beyond our intentions and control – and 'theoretical hesitation' – an awareness of the importance of those aspects of educational processes and practices that are 'beyond' or 'outside' of a common (or perhaps we should say: an all too superficial) understanding of education-as-relation. It is to the latter task that I aim to make a modest contribution by exploring what, in the title of this chapter, I refer to as the limits of educational relations.

In what follows I explore some dimensions of educational processes and practices that highlight the 'unrelated' and the 'non-relational' dimensions that emphasise separation and distance rather than connection and closeness. I will focus on three themes: that of communication, that of speech, and that of teaching. My approach will be broad more than that it will be deep, in that I aim to identify a number of arenas in which questions about the non-relational dimensions of education can be raised. My ambition, therefore, is to offer a number of starting points for further discussion, rather than that I will be able to pursue all aspects of these discussions in full detail. Before I start, however, I need to say a few things about what I am increasingly seeing as one of the most unhelpful and most imprecise words in our field – which is the word 'education.'

The Multiple Meanings of 'Education'

While other languages and traditions of theorising have a whole range of different words to talk 'in' and 'about' education – in no particular order: *Pädagogik, Didaktik, Bildung, Erziehung, Ausbildung, Unterricht, Lehren, danning, utdanning, dannelse, bildning, utbildning, opvoeden, onderwijzen, vormen* – the English language is seriously lacking in its ability to make meaningful distinctions. While I have no magical solution for bridging the gap between forms of educational thinking and doing that have emerged in the English language and those that have developed in other contexts and languages (for a first exploration see Biesta, 2011d), and while I would also argue that the ambition should less be one of bridging the gap than acknowledging the strangeness of each other's vocabularies, I have found it useful to make a distinction between three domains of educational function and purpose (see Biesta, 2010a). The distinction I have suggested is between *qualification* (the domain of the transmission and acquisition of knowledge and skills); *socialisation* (the domain of the reproduction and adoption of traditions and practices, of ways of doing, thinking and being); and *subjectification* (the domain that is concerned with the formation of the human person, in whatever way we may wish to understand this task). These domains are of course not separate, at least not in their function – the research on the hidden curriculum shows, for example, that transmission of knowledge always also confirms existing social structures and stratifications – and probably also not in their intention, something we know at least since Johann Friedrich Herbart promoted the idea of 'erziehenden Unterricht' (see Geissler, 1970), that is – in inadequate translation – that of 'teaching-which-also-aims-to-educate.' With these distinctions in mind, I now turn to three areas – or arenas, as I have called them – in which I wish to explore non-relational dimensions of education.

'Mind the Gap!'

It is perhaps not without significance that the chapter I contributed to the book *No Education without Relation* was titled 'Mind the gap' (Biesta, 2004). The particular focus of my contribution there was on education as a process of communication and, more specifically, the communication of meaning – which puts the discussion mainly in the domain of qualification and, to a lesser extent, that of socialisation. The argument in the chapter is based on a discussion of different theories of communication, and the main opposition is between the co-called sender-receiver model of communication in which communication is mainly seen in logistical terms – as the transportation of bits of information from a sender to a receiver – and the understanding of communication developed by the pragmatists, most specifically John Dewey and George Herbert Mead. In the view of Dewey and Mead communication is seen as a process of practical creation and transformation, that is, in Dewey's words, as a process in which things are "literally made in common" (Dewey, 1958, p. 178). While the idea of 'making something in common' may suggest the kind of closeness and fusion that would perhaps begin to highlight the relational character of educational communication – one could, after all, say that we need to relate or, in the terms of pragmatism, need to co-ordinate our actions, in order to make something in common – Dewey defines communication as a process in which something is made in common "in at least two different centers of behavior" (ibid.), thus suggesting that the process of making something in common is not a process of producing something that is identical for both partners in communication (for more detail see Biesta, 2006b).

While the sender-receiver model is based on a logic of identity, the pragmatist understanding of communication is based on a logic of difference, based on the idea that while we can co-ordinate our actions, this neither requires identity (of action, meaning and self) nor does it result in identity (of action, meaning and self). The pragmatists therefore provide us with an effective argument against the idea that communication is only possible on the basis of a common understanding – a common ground – that needs to be established before communication can start. They rather depict communication as the ongoing task of producing or living a common world (note that the word 'in' is not missing here).

The difference between these two conceptions of educational communication can also be articulated with the words 'mechanism' and 'event,' in that the sender-receiver model depicts educational communication ultimately as a mechanistic process, whereas the pragmatist approach sees it as an event, that is, as a happening with always unpredictable outcomes. Yet this also shows – and we have to be honest here and not fall into the trap of accusing only one position of (crypto-)normativity – that both conceptions of communication articulate a norm of good, desirable or ideal communication. While the sender-receiver model sees communication ideally as a process where the intentions of the sender arrive safely with the receiver, the pragmatist model sees communication ideally as a process of creation, production and transformation. This also leads to a different position for the self. Whereas in the sender-receiver model we might say the self is subjected to communication, in the pragmatist model the self is a subject of communication.

What is interesting about the pragmatist model is that it highlights a fundamental gap between the partners in communication, and what is also interesting is that there is no ambition or desire to bridge or close this gap. The theorist who perhaps has pushed the idea of a gap between the partners in communication to its logical conclusion is Homi Bhabha who, in his book *The Location of Culture* (Bhabha, 1994), makes the case that the 'third space of enunciation' that emerges in the encounter between interlocutors (be they individuals, be they cultures), is "unrepresentable in itself" (Bhabha, 1994, p. 37). The reason why this is so, has to do with the fact that any attempt at representing this third space – the in-between space in which meanings emerge – can only be undertaken from the position of one of the interlocutors and not from some kind of neutral position outside of this. This means that any attempt to represent a third space of enunciation will only ever produce a further third space that will forever escape our attempts to grasp it. To acknowledge that what emerges in communication can never be owned or totalised by any of the partners in communication is, therefore, not only an epistemological point but also, and first and foremost, an insight with ethico-political bearings (see also Biesta, 2009[a]).

The theme of educational communication thus gives us a first case of an educational situation where gaps and disconnections seem to matter. If we tend to think about relations in terms of connection and the bridging of gaps – which is, of course, a point for further discussion – then we may have an example of an aspect of education that reveals some of the limits of educational relations. There is, however, an important educational point to make, which has to do with the fact that much educational activity is actually orientated towards reproduction and faithful transmission. After all, irrespective of how much some constructivists would want to convince us that learning is a process in which students construct their own meanings and insights, at the end of the day two and two still equals four. And while we may wish to praise the creativity and ingenuity of the student who can argue that 2 and 2 should also equal 5, education, particularly when it operates in the qualification mode, has little scope for tolerance (in the technical sense of the word).

This is not only the case in the domain of meaning, knowledge and understanding, but even more so in the domain of practical learning where identity between what is taught and what is learned tends to be the predominant orientation. There is, after all, only so much divergence and creativity that can go into learning to drive a car, learning to drill for oil, or learning to fly an Embraer ERJ 145. While perhaps from the perspective of subjectification, education has and should have an orientation towards keeping the gap open and using it generatively, from the perspective of qualification (and probably also that of socialisation) the normative educational ambition is strongly orientated towards reduction, reproduction and closure – and these are real aspects of education as well.

The main 'mechanism' for closing the gap between teaching and learning is that of assessment, as assessment can be seen as the process through which selections are made from the divergent productions of students so that some of these productions are sanctioned as being 'right' and others as being 'wrong' (elsewhere – Biesta, 2010g – I have referred to this as a process of 'retrospective complexity reduction'). Given that assessment, rather than teaching or pedagogy, is the key process in closing the educational gap, it is perhaps not without significance that teaching and pedagogy are increasingly being replaced by and being redefined as assessment (see, for example, Black et al., 2003), thus running the risk of driving the event out of education (see also Biesta, 2014a).

'Being Addressed'

The second arena in which I wish to explore some of the limits of educational relations continues the theme of communication, but now in relation to the question of speech. The familiar way to engage with the question of speech in education, is by asking how children learn to speak and, more generally, how they learn to communicate. This puts speech at the end of a developmental trajectory in which some kind of learning is supposed to lead to the ability to speak. There is a lot of developmental information that might be relevant here and, looking at it from an empirical angle, it is quite difficult to deny that learning to speak is a kind of developmental process where, at one point in time a child is unable to produce words and sentences whereas at a later moment in time the child has acquired this ability. But what might happen if we approach the question of speech from a different angle, that is, not as the question how children *learn* to speak but as the question *how it is possible* for the child to speak – how it is possible, in other words, for the child to be a speaking subject and a subject of speech.

The first thing we need to establish for this, is that it is not possible to speak in isolation. One can produce sounds in isolation, but one cannot speak in isolation, that is, one cannot utter sounds that mean or have meaning. If we follow this line of thinking, then we might say that in order to transform sounds into speech, one needs to learn what one's sounds mean, which seems to imply that *others* need to tell you what *your* sounds mean. This suggests a trajectory of learning in which the speaking that is made possible is the speech of the other, that is, the speech that already exists. On this account to learn to speak becomes a process of socialisation into an existing order of speech, and the speech that is made possible in this way is speech as repetition. It is speech, in other words, where the subject has dropped out and identity – as identification with an existing order of speech – has taken over. Also note that on this trajectory the guiding assumption on the side of the educator is that the child cannot *yet* speak. It thus starts from an assumption of *in*capacity.

This is, however, not the only way in which we can think about the way in which the child can come to speech and can become a subject of speech. The alternative view I wish to explore, is one that does not start from the assumption of incapacity but from the assumption of capacity. It starts, in other words, from the assumption that the child is able to speak or, to keep the discussion away from questions of ability and inability: it starts from the assumption *that the child is already speaking* (see also Biesta, 2010f). This is indeed nothing more than an assumption. It is an assumption from which we can start; an assumption that can inform our educational actions. Rancière (1991) would call it an assumption that 'asks' for verification, but not in the theoretical sense of establishing its truth, but in the practical sense of *making it true*, that is, enacting its truth. How might this assumption be enacted? I can see three different options, and it is by working through them that I will reach another point of disconnection and non-relatedness in education.[2]

The first option, which has become very prominent in recent scholarship (see, for example, Haroutunian-Gordon, 2004; Waks, 2010; Thompson, 2011), is to say that to enact the assumption that the child is speaking means to *listen* to the child. There is something I like about this suggestion, as it is indeed true that to listen enacts the assumption that the person one is listening to is speaking and has something to say. But there is also something I am concerned about, perhaps first and foremost the fact that listening seems to keep the sovereignty of the listener mostly in place – the listener remains in control of what he or she wants to hear. And maybe I am also concerned that listening may get us too much into questions of interpretation, understanding and translation, and thus runs the risk of bringing the question of speech back to that of repetition, that is, of trying to decipher meaning rather than to acknowledge a speaking being.

A second option, also prominent in recent discussions, is that of *recognition* (see, for example, Bingham, 2001; Stojanov, 2006). Here the enactment of the assumption that the child is speaking, would take the form of me recognising that the other is speaking and me recognising the other as a speaking being. One concern I have about the idea and the logic of recognition, is that it tends to operate from a position of power, that is, where I claim the power to recognise you as a speaking being or not, and where I therefore make your existence dependent upon my decision either to recognise you or not to recognise you. (I am aware of the further complexities of work in this area, particularly the issue concerning mutual recognition and the subsequent struggle for recognition.)

Rather than in terms of listening or recognition, I wish to approach the enactment of the assumption that the child is speaking in terms of the event of *being addressed*.[3] While listening and recognition can be configured as acts of benevolence, 'being addressed' works in the opposite direction. Here it is not for me to recognise the other, but rather to recognise that the other is addressing me – that I am being addressed by another human being – and for me to act upon this recognition. This suggests that if any recognition is involved, it is recognition that is directed towards the *self*, not towards the *other*. To say, therefore, that the child is speaking and to act on this assumption, is not to make an empirical claim, but to make a choice, a choice that is at the very same time educational and political. But we must be careful with the word 'choice' in order not to fall back on the idea that it lies within my powers to choose whether I want to be addressed or not. Zygmunt Bauman's reading of Levinas in his *Postmodern Ethics* (Bauman, 1993) is helpful here, in that he clarifies that the responsibility that is at stake is not our responsibility for the other – this responsibility is simply 'there' – but the responsibility we take for this responsibility.

What is interesting about this third way in which the assumption that the child is speaking can be enacted, is that, unlike listening and recognition, it does not rely on a 'relating gesture' – if that is a proper way of putting it – but rather on the creation of a certain distance. The recognition, after all, is directed towards the self, not towards the other. The teacher does not reach out to the student – neither as listener nor as recogniser – but rather turns towards the self. In a paper with the intriguing title 'Alone in the presence of others,' Glenn Hudak (2011) provides an important exploration of these ideas by focusing on educators working with "youth labelled as autistic" (Hudak, 2011, p. 58). What makes his exploration relevant for my discussion, is the fact that he focuses on a 'category' – and I immediately apologise for the word 'category' here – where the general assumption appears to be one of individuals who are unable to speak, communicate or even relate.

One could of course accept this definition – this knowledge about the other – and use it as the assumption to guide one's actions. In that case any educational activity would simply repeat what is already assumed to be there. It would be tied to what allegedly *is* (on this problem see also Biesta & Säfström, 2011). Hudak, however, argues for the opposite case, suggesting that the possibility for education is precisely opened up when the educator acts on basis of three presumptions: the presumption of *competence*, the presumption of *imagination* and the presumption of *intimacy*. And in each case Hudak makes the point that the onus is not on the young person to communicate and relate in an 'accepted' manner, so to speak, but on the educator "to figure out how we can help those with physical impairments better communicate their experience, and hence be included into discussions rather than remaining on the side-line, spoken for by others" (ibid., p. 61).

The task for the educator, therefore, "is not to interpret the world for those labelled autistic [but rather] to *presume* that the person labelled autistic is a thinking, feeling [and, so I wish to add: speaking] person" (ibid., p. 61; emphasis added). Hudak makes similar points in relation to the other two presumptions – those of imagination and intimacy – and with regard to all three he argues that they pose "at once a philosophical and political challenge" (ibid., p. 66), in that they not only require us to fundamentally rethink what it means to speak, communicate and relate, but, by acting upon these assumptions, also challenge "dominant structures of power" (ibid.) and dominant definitions "of what it means to be human" (ibid., p. 62; see also Biesta, 2006a, p. 1).

And this, as Hudak concludes, is not only relevant "for those labelled 'disabled'" but actually for "all of us" (Hudak, 2011, p. 69). And I agree.

What I find interesting about the idea of 'being addressed,' as mentioned, is that it denotes a significantly different gesture than the gesture of listening and the gesture of recognition. What Hudak's discussion highlights is that, through the idea of 'being addressed,' questions of speech, coming to speech and being a subject of speech become disconnected from question about individual skills and capacities, and particularly from skills and capacities that are often seen as essential for any relationship to be possible. Speech, so we might say, is no longer a matter of the *acquisition* of a competence by the speaker. It is not even a matter of me making an effort to speak and be understood. My 'ability' to speak, so we might say, is there when someone is addressed by my speech, even if this speech has no recognizable form – like the babble of a baby or the silence of a person labelled as autistic. This also means that the question of speech and coming to speech viewed in this way is no longer a question of qualification and socialisation but ultimately a question of subjectification.

'You Must Change Your Life'

The final arena in which I wish to explore the limits of educational relations has to do with what we might perhaps characterise as the most general and most fundamental educational 'gesture' of all, which is the fact that education always in some way implies a call, an evocation, and perhaps even a demand for *change*. When educators speak and act, they hardly ever do so in order to confirm what is already there – and perhaps they never do so – but always with the suggestion that something ought to change. This call for change occurs across the three domains of educational function and purpose – qualification, socialisation, and subjectification – albeit that what it means concretely is different in each domain. The call for change does not necessarily come with a clear specification of *what* this change should be, nor does it necessarily come with a clear specification of *how* this change should occur. But when the teacher teaches or the educator educates, the overriding orientation is that of change.

Why do I bring this up in the discussion about relations and 'non-related-ness' in education? The main reason for this lies in the fact that the *educational* call for change is a call that comes from the *outside* and, so I wish to suggest, should *necessarily* be understood as a call that comes from the outside. This is one of the main reasons why the discourse of learning and the discourse of education are fundamentally different discourses. One can, of course, always decide for oneself that one wishes to change, and one can, of course, always decide to engage in learning in order to effect change. But the educational logic works differently, not least because it works in a different direction, that is, from the outside-in rather than from the inside-out. Yet this brings us to a question with a long pedigree in the philosophy of education, which is the question whether it is possible for education – and more specifically for teaching – to bring anything radically new into a situation, to bring anything that really comes from the outside. This question goes straight back to Plato's *Meno*, to Socrates and to what is known as the 'learning paradox.' I am aware that the issue of the interpretation of Socrates as an educator is a tricky one and, moreover, one about which almost every philosopher of education appears to have an opinion. Let me proceed, therefore, with one possible reading in order to make the point I would like to make, not claiming that this is the one and only or ultimate interpretation (or even claiming that what is at stake in my argument is the question of the correct interpretation of Socrates).

Socrates' way out of the learning paradox is to argue that all learning is a matter of recollection. This is why he can deny that he actually has anything to teach at all and why he can represent his educational efforts as entirely *maieutic*: bringing out what is already there. But whereas Socrates says that he is not involved in any teaching and, by doing so even seems to want to deny the very possibility of teaching, this is not consistent with what he may actually be doing. Sharon Todd, in her book *Learning from the Other*, argues that Socrates "cannot simply be taken at his word" (Todd, 2003, p. 23) and shows, through a subtle reading of the Meno, that there is actually quite a lot of teaching going on in the way in which Socrates tries to convince Meno's slave boy that he already possesses the knowledge he did not realise he possessed.

Todd particularly highlights the teaching performed by Socrates that has an impact on the slave boy's subjectivity, a process through which the slave boy is being taught that he is indeed a slave boy, and also the process through which the slave boy is being taught that he is a learner, that is, a "subject of pedagogy" (ibid., p. 24). Todd thus presents Socrates as "the teacher, who, like the perfect murderer, makes it appear that teaching has not taken place, who leaves the scene without a trace, and who, moreover, is convinced of his own innocence" (ibid.). Yet, so she argues, by proclaiming his questions to be innocent, Socrates actually "obscures the fundamental structures of alteration and asymmetry that are present between teacher and student" (ibid., p. 25).

Søren Kierkegaard, under the pseudonym of Johannes Climacus, provides a similar critique of the Meno, by asking whether it is possible to think of teaching outside of, and different from, the idea of maieutics. Whereas the maieutic conception of teaching sees teaching as accidental to learning, Climacus raises the question as to "what would have to be true *if* there were to be an alternative to Socrates' account of knowledge as recollection, *if* the teacher were really to teach so that the relation to the teacher would be essential rather than accidental" (Westphal, 2008, p. 25; emphasis in original). The answer Kierkegaard gives, is that the teacher not only needs to give the learner the truth but also needs to give the learner the condition of recognising it as truth, because "if the learner were himself the condition for understanding the truth, then he merely needs to recollect" (Kierkegaard, 1985, p. 14). This 'double truth giving' is what Climacus characterises as revelation. Revelation therefore means not merely "that the teacher presents the learner with some knowledge not already possessed, but more importantly, also [with] the condition for recognizing it as truth" as it is only in the latter case that "the relation to the teacher becomes essential" (Westphal, 2008, p. 25; emphasis added).

Climacus helps us see that a notion of teaching that is essential rather than accidental to learning, is not simply about presenting students with something they do not yet know. It rather is about presenting students with something that "is neither derivable from nor validated by what [they] already know" (ibid., p. 26), but that truly transcends what they already know. This is why Levinas writes that Socratic teaching is characterised by the "primacy of the same," that is, "to receive nothing of the Other but what is in me, as though from all eternity I was in possession of what comes to me from the outside" (Levinas, 1969, p. 43). In contrast to this, Levinas is after a relationship in which I receive from the Other "beyond the capacity of the I" – which not only means "to have an idea of infinity" but also means "to be taught" (ibid., p. 51). And it is this teaching which can be called revelation (see ibid., p. 67).

Merold Westphal, in his discussion of these ideas in the work of Levinas and Kierkegaard (Westphal, 2008), highlights that both Levinas and Kierkegaard link the notion of revelation to that of authority. After all, if teaching is about presenting students with something that is 'neither derivable from nor validated by' what they already know, then they have to take it on the authority of the teacher. The wider significance of this insight lies in the fact that, as Westphal (2008, p. 26) puts it, "for both Levinas and Kierkegaard the basis of the ethical and religious life lies in an authoritative revelation that in its immediacy comes to us from beyond our own powers of recollection." In the 1965 essay "Phenomenon and Enigma" Levinas refers to this revelation as 'enigma' in order to highlight that what is revealed is not a phenomenon, not something that is comprehensible and comprehended by me, but rather something that is 'beyond' my cognition and comprehension – and therefore even "beyond being" (Levinas, 1987, p. 62) and "beyond reason" (ibid., p. 61). Enigma is about a way of 'manifesting oneself without manifesting oneself.' It stands for that which "signifies itself without revealing itself" (ibid., p. 73). It is about God who literally "comes to mind," as Levinas would put it, rather than a mind trying to comprehend God (see Levinas, 1998).

Elsewhere (Biesta, 2011c) I have summarised this line of thought by suggesting that teaching, if it is to have any meaning that goes beyond the now so popular idea of the facilitation of learning, needs to carry with it a notion of transcendence, a notion of a radical exteriority that comes to me rather than that it is produced by me. This is also why I think that it is important to make a clear distinction between 'learning from (the other)' and 'being taught by (the other)' (which is not to suggest that the distinction is simply there but to suggest that it is important to ponder the distinction that can be made with these phrases) (see also Biesta, 2013a). While learning from the other highlights the way in which I remain in control over what I wish to learn from the other, being taught by the other indicates a different gesture, one where the other does indeed bring something radically new to me – something that, therefore, interrupts rather than that is simply confirms. It is the radical exteriority that is at stake here, the 'non-maieuticity' – to use a very ugly phrase – of teaching that highlights rupture, disconnection, and 'non-relatedness,' and thus reveals another facet of the 'non-relational' dimensions of education.

Concluding Remarks

As I have said before, the ambition of this chapter has not been to present an argument against educational relations, but rather to explore aspects of educational processes and practices that reveal gaps, interruptions, distances and disconnections – *not* in order to refute the idea of educational relations but to add a moment of hesitation to our thinking about education and about educational relations in particular. As I have nothing to argue for, I have perhaps also nothing to conclude, so let me rather try to capture what I see as some of the main insights emerging from my exploration.

One has to do with educational communication and reveals that there is always a gap between the partners in communication; a gap, or in the words of Bhabha, a third space of enunciation, in which meaning forever escapes us, is forever beyond our control. We cannot close *this* gap by trying to 'reach out' to our partners in communication, by trying to listen them, by trying to understand them, because each time that we return our understandings to them, a new gap emerges, a new third space of enunciation comes into existence. The main advantage of understanding communication in this way is that it can help us to see that any attempt to close the gap always requires force – either by forcefully putting forward a particular representation of what, in itself, is unrepresentable, or by selecting and rewarding from a wide variety of meanings and actions those that are considered to be 'right' or 'true.' The latter has been my description of the process of assessment, and while the discussion reveals that assessment in itself is always a forceful intervention, I have suggested that such an intervention is not without educational reason, if, that is, our orientation is towards qualification and socialisation. The issue does, however, become an entirely different one when our interest is in subjectification, and I would argue that education – unlike training – should always have an interest in this dimension *as well*.

The question of speech – and more specifically the question of how the child can *be* a subject of speech (and I prefer to speak in existential terms of *being* a subject of speech rather than in developmental terms of *becoming* a subject of speech) – moved the discussion more explicitly to education in a subjectification 'mode.' In addition to two relational ways of enacting the assumption that the child is a subject of speech – listening and recognition – I have put forward a third option, that of 'being addressed.' While listening and recognition reach out to the other and in precisely this way can be characterised as relational gestures, 'being addressed' reaches 'out' to the self – a gesture I have also characterised as one of 'reaching in' – and thus in a sense creates a gap or a distance, rather than a connection. But one could say that it is precisely because of this distance, because of the fact that there is no attempt to capture the other or to require that the other proves his or her ability or capacity, that educational possibilities open up. The recognition of 'being addressed' is therefore not factual but can perhaps best be understood as counterfactual, that is, as a belief – or as Schaffar (2009, p. 109) calls it: a moral demand – upon which education becomes possible.

Thirdly I have explored what it means for teaching to be possible *not* as something that is immanent, as something that is *accidental* to learning, to use Kierkegaard's phrase, but rather as something that is *essential* to learning and therefore as something that is transcendent, that is, something that radically comes from 'outside,' as rupture, interruption (Biesta, 2009c), intervention, or, with the word that we can find in both Kierkegaard and Levinas: as *revelation*. Teaching as revelation in a sense looks at the experience of being addressed from the other side, which is why I have highlighted the importance of the distinction between 'learning from' and 'being taught by.'

These insights, in sum, do not do away with the idea that to educate is to relate, but they may help us to look differently at educational relations, not only in order to see the gaps, fissures, disjunctions and disconnections that are at work, but also, and most importantly in order to appreciate why they might matter educationally.

Notes

1   An earlier version of this chapter was my presidential address for the Philosophy of Education Society of North America, subsequently published as: Biesta, G. J. J. (2012). No education without hesitation. Thinking differently about educational relations. In C. Ruitenberg et al. (Eds.), *Philosophy of education 2012* (pp. 1–13). Urbana-Champaign, IL: Philosophy of Education Society.
2   Please note that what follows is in no way meant to be a critical discussion of existing literature on listening and recognition. My point here is not to deny what has been said there but to add a slightly different perspective that perhaps may reveal a slightly different way of understanding and being.
3   I would like to thank Nina Johannesen for bringing this notion to my attention.

CHAPTER 7

Transclusion: Overcoming the Tension between Inclusion and Exclusion in the Discourse on Democracy and Democratisation

Women who seek to be equal with men lack ambition.
TIMOTHY LEARY

∴

Introduction[1]

Timothy Leary's suggestion that women who seek to be equal with men lack ambition, articulates in an interesting way one of the main tensions in the discussion about inclusion. The tension, briefly stated, is that as long as we think of inclusion as a process of bringing those who are on the 'outside' into the 'inside,' we run the risk of reproducing the very social and political structures that label some as insiders and others as outsiders in the first place. At a deeper level we therefore run the risk of keeping in place the very divisions and power relations that the agenda of inclusion seeks to expose and overcome. While this does not mean that all attempts at bringing about more inclusive ways of doing and being through the inclusion of those who are on the 'outside' are automatically bad or unhelpful, there is a risk that thinking of inclusion *only* in these terms may prevent us from addressing the more fundamental issues out of which questions about inclusion and exclusion arise.

Addressing these problems, so I wish to suggest, not only requires practical and political work, but might also benefit from theoretical and conceptual exploration, and it is to the latter task that I wish to contribute in this chapter. The concept I will put forward in what is to follow is that of 'transclusion.' With this notion I seek to articulate a double movement of 'moving position' and 'shifting the terrain.' The concept of 'transclusion' thus has an echo of inclusion (moving position) but seeks, at the very same time, to point at the need for transforming the very field where positions can be held and taken (shifting the terrain). 'Transclusion' thus seeks to articulate a movement that changes the positions (and hence identities and relationships) of *both* outsiders and insiders, rather than leaving insiders in their place (literally and metaphorically) and only requiring (or facilitating or demanding) movement from those on the outside.

Stated in this way, the idea of 'transclusion' may sound simple and perhaps even simplistic. In what follows I therefore seek to add some theoretical 'flesh' to this line of thinking. I do this through an exploration of the idea of inclusion in discussions about democracy and education for democratic citizenship. This field, as I will seek to show, not only provides a fertile ground for articulating the tension between inclusion and exclusion, but also provides a more concrete 'case' of how 'transclusion' might be understood, conceived and enacted. While I confine myself to the field of democracy and citizenship education, I hope that the theoretical and conceptual work I do in this chapter may also be relevant for engaging with the tension between inclusion and exclusion in other areas and domains.

Inclusion and Democracy

It could well be argued that inclusion is one of the core values and perhaps even *the* core value of democracy. The 'point' of democracy, after all, is the inclusion of everyone (that is, the whole *demos*) into the ruling (*kratein*) of society. This is why Pericles defined democracy as the situation in which "power is in the hands not of a minority but of the whole people" (Held, 1987, p. 16) and it is why Aristotle wrote about democracy as the "rule of all over each and of each by turns over all" (ibid., p. 19) – and similar definitions of democracy have been given up to the present day, including Abraham Lincoln's definition of democracy as government "of the people, by the people, and for the people." Inclusion also has an important role to play in the legitimacy and legitimation of democracy because, as Iris Young has pointed out, the normative legitimacy of democratic decision-making precisely depends "on the degree to which those affected by it have been included in the decision-making processes and have had the opportunity to influence the outcomes" (Young, 2000, pp. 5–6).

However, inclusion is not only the main point and purpose of democracy; it is also one of its main problems. After all, the question that has haunted democracy from day one (and in a sense already troubled democracy before it took off) is about who are to be included in the (definition of the) *demos*. This is the question of *democratic citizenship* and we know all too well that in the city-state of Athens citizenship was a highly restricted affair. Only Athenian men over the age of 20 were eligible for citizenship. Women, children, slaves (who made up about 60% of the population) and immigrants, even from families who had settled in Athens several generations earlier, were simply excluded from political participation (Held, 1987, p. 23). On the one hand the history of democracy can be written as a continuous quest for inclusion. After all, some of the most powerful and successful social movements of the last two centuries – including the women's movement and the labour movement – have precisely been organised "around demands for oppressed and marginalized people to be included as full and equal citizens" (Young, 2000, p. 6).

But the history of democracy is not only a history of inclusion but also a history of *exclusion*. In some cases, exclusion is justified in the name of democracy. This is, for example, the case with *liberal* democracy, where the democratic principle of popular rule (expressing the principle of *equality*) is qualified by a set of basic liberties that take priority over popular rule in order to make sure that popular rule does not restrain or obstruct individual freedom (thus expressing the principle of *liberty*) (Gutmann, 1993, p. 413) – a situation aptly characterised by Chantal Mouffe as the democratic paradox (see Mouffe, 2000). Whereas liberal democracy seeks to exclude certain *outcomes* of democratic decision-making (and thus would exclude those who would argue for such outcomes; discussions around the notion of freedom of speech show some of the complexities of this issue), there is also a more direct link between democracy and exclusion, one in which education plays a particular role. The argument here focuses on those who are deemed not to be 'fit' for democracy, either because they lack certain qualities that are considered to be fundamental for democratic participation – such as rationality or reasonableness (see below) – or because they do not subscribe to the ideal of democracy itself.

As Bonnie Honig has already made clear in the early 1990s, this is not only an issue for communitarians who wish to see democratic politics organised around particular political identities. It is also an issue for liberals since they tend to restrict political participation to those who are willing and able to act in a rational way and who are willing to leave their substantive conceptions of the good life behind them in the private sphere (for more detail see Honig, 1993). Such strategies not only result in the exclusion of those who are considered to be 'sub-rational' – that is, those deemed to be lacking the minimum level of rationality to act in a rational way (which, of course, raises crucial questions about what counts as rationality and who is able to define and decide). They are also used to justify the exclusion of those who we might call 'pre-rational' or, in a more general sense, 'pre-democratic' – and children are the most 'obvious' example of such a category (which again raises questions about the definitions of the child that are at stake here and questions about who has the right or the power to define and decide). It is here that there is an important link with education, because education for democratic citizenship is often seen as the process that should make individuals 'ready' for their participation in democratic decision-making, either by promoting their rationality or, more directly, by promoting their democratic knowledge, skills and dispositions – and often by doing both.

If this gives a first indication of how the question of inclusion plays a role in discussions about democracy and education for democratic citizenship, I now wish to look in more detail at a number of different ways in which, in recent discussions, the question of democratic inclusion has been addressed and how attempts have been made to expand the terms of the discussion. In a first step I will look at the so-called 'deliberative turn' in democratic theory. Through a discussion of the work of Jon Elster, John Dryzek and Iris Young I will show how different conceptions of deliberation have sought to make democracy more inclusive. In a second step I will turn to the work of Jacques Rancière who, as I will suggest, provides a more radical approach to the question of democratic inclusion – one that not only shows the problem with attempts at making existing democratic constellations more inclusive and welcoming, but that also seeks to articulate the need for the double movement I mentioned above. Rancière thus provides the building blocks for what, in the final step, I will articulate as the idea of 'transclusion.'

Making Democracy More Inclusive: The Deliberative Turn

The question of inclusion plays a central role in discussions about political decision-making. In contemporary political theory there are two main models of democratic decision-making: the *aggregative* model and the *deliberative* model. The first model sees democracy as a process of aggregating the preferences of individuals, often, but not exclusively, in choosing public officials and policies. A central assumption in this model is that the preferences of individuals should be seen as given and that politics is only concerned with the aggregation of preferences, often, but not exclusively, on the basis of majority rule. Where these preferences come from, whether they are valid or not, and whether they are held for egoistic or altruistic reasons, is considered to be irrelevant. The *aggregative* model assumes, in other words, "that ends and values are subjective, non-rational, and exogenous to the political process" and that democratic politics is basically "a competition between private interests and preferences" (Young, 2000, p. 22).

Over the past two decades an increasing number of political theorists have argued that democracy should not be confined to the simple aggregation of preferences but should involve the *deliberative transformation* of preferences. Under the deliberative model democratic decision-making is seen as a process which involves "decision making by means of arguments offered *by* and *to* participants" (Elster, 1998, p. 8) about the means *and* the ends of collective action. As Young explains, deliberative democracy is not about "determining what preferences have greatest numerical support, but [about] determining which proposals the collective agrees are supported by the best reasons" (Young, 2000, p. 23).

The reference to 'best reasons' indicates – and this is important – that deliberative democracy is based upon a particular conception of deliberation. Dryzek, for example, acknowledges that deliberation can cover a rather broad spectrum of activities but argues that for *authentic* deliberation to happen the requirement is that the reflection on preferences should take place in a *non-coercive* manner (Dryzek, 2000, p. 2). This requirement, so he explains, "rules out domination via the exercise of power, manipulation, indoctrination, propaganda, deception, expression of mere self-interest, threats ... and attempts to impose ideological conformity" (ibid.). This resonates with Elster's claim that deliberative democracy is about the giving and taking of arguments by participants "who are committed to the values of rationality and impartiality" (Elster, 1998, p. 8) and with his suggestion that deliberation must take place between "free, equal and rational agents" (ibid., p. 5).

In one respect the 'deliberative turn' (or as Dryzek has suggested: re-turn; see Dryzek, 2000, pp. 1–2) is an important step forward in democratic theory and democratic practice. First of all, it seems to be a fuller expression of the basic values of democracy, particularly the idea that democracy is about actual participation in collective decision-making. In the aggregative model there is, after all, little participation, and decision-making is mainly algorithmic. Secondly, as for example Young has argued, the deliberative approach seems to have a much stronger educational potential, because in the deliberative model "political actors not only express preferences and interests, but they engage with one another about how to balance these under circumstances of inclusive equality" (Young, 2000, p. 26). Such interaction, so Young suggests, "requires participants to be open and attentive to one another, to justify their claims and proposals in terms of [being] acceptable to all, the orientation of participants moves from self-regard to an orientation to what is publicly assertible" (ibid.).

Through this "people often gain new information, learn different experiences of their collective problems, or find that their own initial opinions are founded on prejudice and ignorance, or that they have misunderstood the relation of their own interests to others" (ibid.). As Warren (1992, p. 8) has put it, participation in deliberation can make individuals "more public-spirited, more tolerant, more knowledgeable, more attentive to the interests of others, and more probing of their own interests." A third asset of deliberative democracy lies in its potential impact on the *motivation* of political actors, in that participation in democratic decision-making is more likely to commit participants to its outcomes. This suggests that deliberative democracy is not only an intrinsically desirable way of social and political problem-solving, but probably also a more effective way for doing so (see Dryzek, 2000, p. 172).

Entry Conditions and Democratic Exclusions

The deliberative turn can be seen as an attempt to bring democracy closer to its core values and in this respect represents an important correction to the individualism and 'disconnected pluralism' (Biesta, 2006a) of the aggregative model and of liberal democracy more generally. However, by raising the stakes of democracy, deliberative democracy has also brought the difficulty of democratic inclusion into much sharper focus, and thus has generated – ironically but not surprisingly – a series of problems around the question of inclusion.

The main issue here centres on the *entry conditions for participation* in deliberation. The authors quoted above all seem to suggest that participation in democratic deliberation should be regulated and that it should be confined to those who commit themselves to a particular set of values and behaviours. Young, for example, argues that the deliberative model "entails several normative ideas for the relationships and dispositions of deliberating parties, among them inclusion, equality, reasonableness, and publicity" which, so she claims, "are all *logically* related in the deliberative model" (Young, 2000, p. 23; emphasis added). Most of the proponents of (versions of) deliberative democracy specify a set of entry conditions for participation, although what is interesting about the discussion is that most go at great pains to delineate a *minimum* set of conditions necessary for democratic deliberation rather than an ideal set (see, e.g., the contributions in Elster, 1998).

Young provides an interesting example with her distinction between reasonableness (which she sees as a necessary entry condition) and rationality (which she doesn't see as a necessary condition). For Young being reasonable doesn't entail being rational. Reasonableness refers to "a set of *dispositions* that discussion participants have [rather] than to the substance of people's contributions to debate" (Young, 2000, p. 24; emphasis added). She concedes that reasonable people "often have crazy ideas," yet "what makes them reasonable is their willingness to listen to others who want to explain to them why their ideas are incorrect or inappropriate" (ibid.). In Young's hands reasonableness thus emerges as a communicative *virtue*, and not as a criterion for the logical 'quality' of people's preferences and convictions.

This example not only shows why the issue of inclusion is so prominent in the deliberative model. It also explains why the deliberative turn has generated a whole new set of issues around inclusion. The reason for this is that deliberation is not just a form of political decision-making but first and foremost a form of political *communication*. The inclusion question in deliberative democracy is therefore not so much a question about who should be included – although this question should be asked always as well. It is first and foremost a question about who is able to participate effectively in deliberation. As Dryzek aptly summarises, the suspicion about deliberative democracy is "that its focus on a particular kind of reasonable political interaction is not in fact neutral, but systematically excludes a variety of voices from effective participation in democratic politics" (Dryzek, 2000, p. 58).

In this regard Young makes a helpful distinction between two forms of exclusion: *external exclusion*, which is about "how people are [actually] kept outside the process of discussion and decision-making," and *internal exclusion* where people are formally included in decision-making processes but where they may find, for example, "that their claims are not taken seriously and may believe that they are not treated with equal respect" (Young, 2000, p. 55). Internal exclusion, in other words, refers to those situations in which people "lack effective opportunity to influence the thinking of others even when they have access to fora and procedures of decision-making" (ibid.) which can particularly be the outcome of the emphasis of some proponents of deliberative democracy on "dispassionate, unsituated, neutral reason" (ibid., p. 63).

Overcoming Internal Exclusion: Making Democracy More Welcoming

To counteract the internal exclusion that is the product of a too narrow focus on argument, Young has suggested several other modes of political communication which should be added to the deliberative process, not only to remedy "exclusionary tendencies in deliberative practices" but also to promote "respect and trust" and to enable "understanding across structural and cultural difference" (ibid., p. 57).

The first of these is *greeting* or *public acknowledgement*. This is about "communicative political gestures through which those who have conflicts ... *recognize* others as included in the discussion, especially those with whom they differ in opinion, interest, or social location" (ibid., p. 61; emphasis in original). Young emphasises that greeting should be thought of as a starting-point for political interaction. It "*precedes* the giving and evaluating of reasons" (ibid., p. 79) and does so through the recognition of the other parties in the deliberation. The second mode of political communication is *rhetoric* and more specifically the affirmative use of rhetoric (ibid., p. 63). Although one could say that rhetoric only concerns the form of political communication and not its content, the point Young makes is that inclusive political communication should pay attention to and be inclusive about the different forms of expression and should not try to purify rational argument from rhetoric.

Rhetoric is not only important because it can help to get particular issues on the agenda for deliberation. Rhetoric can also help to articulate claims and arguments *"in ways appropriate to a particular public in a particular situation"* (ibid., p. 67; emphasis in original). Rhetoric always accompanies an argument by situating it "for a particular audience and giving it embodied style and tone" (ibid., p. 79). Young's third mode of political communication is *narrative* or *storytelling*. The main function of narrative in democratic communication lies in its potential "to foster understanding among members of a polity with very different experience or assumptions about what is important" (ibid., p. 71). Young emphasises the role of narrative in the educative dimension of political communication. "Inclusive democratic communication," so she argues, "assumes that all participants have something to teach the public about the society in which they dwell together" and also assumes "that all participants are ignorant of some aspects of the social or natural world, and that everyone comes to a political conflict with some biases, prejudices, blind spots, or stereo-types" (ibid., p. 77).

It is important to emphasise that greeting, rhetoric and narrative are not meant to *replace* argumentation. Young stresses again and again that deliberative democracy entails "that participants require reasons of one another and critically evaluate them" (ibid., p. 79). Other proponents of the deliberative model take a much narrower approach and see deliberation exclusively as a form of *rational* argumentation (e.g., Benhabib, 1996), where the only legitimate force should be the "forceless force of the better argument" (Habermas, 1975, p. 108). Similarly, Dryzek, after a discussion of Young's ideas, concludes that argument always has to be central to deliberative democracy" (Dryzek, 2000, p. 71).[2] Although he acknowledges that other modes of communication can be present and that there are good reasons to welcome them, their status is different "because they do not have to be present" (ibid.). For Dryzek at the end of the day all modes of political communication must live up to the standards of rationality. This does not mean that they must be subordinated to rational argument "but their deployment only makes sense in a context where argument about what is to be done remains central" (ibid., p. 168).

Can Democracy Reach as State of Total Inclusions? And Should It?

The foregoing shows how the discussion about democracy and inclusion has developed over the past two decades. While this can be seen as progress, this does not mean that there are no problems left. I wish to suggest that two aspects deserve further attention. The first has to do with the assumption that democracy can become 'normal' (my reasons for using this particular word will be explained in more detail below); the second has to do with the assumption that inclusion is a process that works from the inside out, so to speak.

With regard to the first assumption we can see that the ambition to make democracy more inclusive is understood as a trajectory that will ultimately lead to a situation where *everyone* is included in the democratic 'order.' After all, in the discussion about democracy and inclusion the main challenge seems to be perceived as a practical one, that is, as the question how we can make our democratic practices more inclusive (internal inclusion) and how we can include more individuals into the sphere of democratic deliberation (external inclusion). The idea here is that if we can become even more attentive to otherness and difference, we will eventually reach a situation of *total* democratic inclusion – which we could characterise as the situation where democracy has become 'normal.' While people may have different views about when and how this situation might be reached and whether or not there will always be some 'remainders' (Mouffe, 1993), the idea that democratisation means including more and more people into the sphere of democracy reveals the underlying idea that the best democracy is the most inclusive democracy, so that, ultimately, democracy is the situation where all are included.

This relates to the second assumption, which is the idea of inclusion as a process in which those who are on the outside of the sphere of democracy are being brought inside and, more importantly, are being brought inside by those who are already there. This is the idea that inclusion is a process that operates from the inside out – a process that emanates from the position of those who are already considered to be democratic (or who consider themselves to be democratic). This also implies that those on the inside are setting the terms for inclusion and that it is for those who seek to be included to meet the terms thus set.

There is, of course, no need to throw out the baby of deliberative democracy with the bathwater of theoretical purity, and this is definitely not my intention. Deliberative democracy clearly has many advantages over other political practices and processes. But the question we should ask is whether the underlying assumptions about democracy result in the best and, so we might say, most democratic way to understand and 'do' democracy. The first step in answering this question is to ask whether democracy can be understood differently. One author who has tried to approach the question of democracy in a way that is indeed different from the prevailing discourse about democracy and inclusion and who, more specifically, has done so by challenging the two assumptions mentioned here, is Jacques Rancière.

From Democracy to Democratisation

Whereas in the prevailing discourse democracy is seen as something that can be permanent and normal, Rancière argues for an understanding of democracy as *sporadic*, as something that only 'happens' from time to time and in very particular situations (see Rancière, 1995, pp. 41, 61). This point is related to an important distinction in Rancière's writings, namely between politics (which for him always means *democratic* politics; democracy as "the institution of politics itself," as he puts it – Rancière, 1999, p. 101), and what he refers to as *police* or *police order*. In a way which is reminiscent of Foucault, Rancière defines the police as "an order of bodies that defines the allocation of ways of doing, ways of being, and ways of saying, and that sees that those bodies are assigned by name to a particular place and task" (Rancière, 1999, p. 29). It as an order "of the visible and the sayable that sees that a particular activity is visible and another is not, that this speech is understood as discourse and another as noise" (ibid.).

Police should not be understood as the way in which the state structures the life of society. It is not, in Habermasian terms, the 'grip' of the system on the lifeworld, but includes *both* system and lifeworld. As Rancière explains, "the distribution of places and roles that defines a police regime stems as much from the assumed spontaneity of social relations as from the rigidity of state functions" (ibid.). One way to read this definition of police is to think of it as an order that is *all-inclusive* in that everyone has a particular place, role or position in it. This is not to say that everyone is included in the running of the order. The point simply is that no one is excluded from the order. After all, women, children, slaves and immigrants had a clear place in the democracy of Athens, namely as those who were not allowed to participate in political decision making. In precisely this respect every police order is all-inclusive.

Against this background Rancière then defines *politics* as the disruption of the police order in the name of or with reference to the idea of equality. Rancière reserves the term 'politics' "for an extremely determined activity antagonistic to policing: whatever breaks with the tangible configuration whereby parties and parts or lack of them are defined by a presupposition that, by definition, has no place in that configuration" (ibid., pp. 30–31). This break is manifest is a series of actions "that reconfigure the space where parties, parts, or lack of parts have been defined" (ibid., p. 31). Political activity so conceived is "whatever shifts a body from the place assigned to it" (ibid.). "It makes visible what had no business being seen, and makes heard a discourse where once there was only place for noise" (ibid.).

> Political activity is always a mode of expression that undoes the perceptible divisions of the police order by implementing a basically heterogenous assumption, that of a part of those who have no part, an assumption that, at the end of the day, itself demonstrates the sheer contingency of the order [and] the equality of any speaking being with any other speaking being. (ibid)

Politics thus refers to the event when two 'heterogeneous processes' meet: the police process and the process of *equality* (see ibid.).

There are two points to add to this account. The first is that for Rancière politics understood in this way is always *democratic* politics. Democracy, so he argues, "is not a regime or a social way of life" – it is not and cannot be, in other words, part of the police order – but should rather be understood "as the institution of politics itself" (ibid., p. 101). Every politics – or 'act of politics' – is democratic, therefore, *not* in the sense of a set of institutions, but in the sense of forms of expression "that confront the logic of equality with the logic of the police order" (ibid.). Democracy, so we might say, is a 'claim' for equality.

The second point concerns the question as to *who* it is that makes this claim. Who, in other words, 'does' politics or 'performs' democracy?[3] The point of asking the question in this way is not to suggest that there is no subject of politics; that there are no democratic actors involved in democracy. The point is that political actors as democratic subjects do not exist *before* the 'act' of democracy, or to be more precise: their political identity, their identity as democratic subjects only comes into being in and through the act of disruption of the police order. This is why Rancière argues that politics is itself a process of *subjectification* (see also Biesta, 2010a, 2011a, 2011b). It is a process in and through which political subjects are constituted. Rancière defines subjectification as "the production through a series of actions of a body and a capacity for enunciation not previously identifiable within a given field of experience, whose identification is thus part of the reconfiguration of the field of experience" (Rancière, 1999, p. 35).

Democracy – or to be more precise: the appearance of democracy – is therefore not simply the situation in which a group who has previously been excluded from the realm of politics steps forward to claim its place under the democratic sun. It is at the very same time the *creation* of a group as group with a particular identity that didn't exist before.[4] Democratic activity is, for example, to be found in the activity of nineteenth-century workers "who established a collective basis for work relations" that were previously seen as "the product of an infinite number of relationships between private individuals" (ibid., p. 30). Democracy thus establishes new, *political* identities. Or as Rancière puts it: "Democracy is the designation of subjects that do not coincide with the parties of the state or of society" (ibid., pp. 99–100). This means that "the place where the people appear" is the place "where a dispute is conducted" (ibid., p. 100). The political dispute is distinct from all conflicts of interest between constituted parties of the population, for it is a conflict "over the very count of those parties" (ibid.). It is a dispute between "the police logic of the distribution of places and the political logic of the egalitarian act" (ibid.). Politics is therefore "primarily a conflict over the existence of a common stage and over the existence and status of those present on it" (ibid., pp. 26–27).

For Rancière, therefore, democratisation is *not* a process that emanates from the centre and extends to the margins. It is not a process in which those who are already democratic – an impossible position from Rancière's point of view anyway – include others into their sphere. Rather democracy appears as a claim from the 'outside,' a claim based upon the perception of injustice, or of what Rancière refers to as a 'wrong' – and, moreover, a claim made in the name of and with reference to the idea of equality. And the crucial difference here is that those who make the claim do not simply want to be included in the existing order; they want to *redefine* the order in such a way that *new* identities, new ways of doing and being become possible and can be 'counted.'

This means that for Rancière democratisation is no longer a process of inclusion of excluded parties into the existing order; it rather is a transformation of that order in the name of equality. The impetus for this transformation does not come from the inside but rather from the outside. But it is important to see that, unlike in the prevailing discourse about democratic inclusion, this outside is not a 'known' outside. Democratisation is, after all, not a process that happens *within* the police order in which it is perfectly clear who are taking part in decision-making and who are not. Democratisation is a process that *disrupts* the existing order from a place that could not be expressed or articulated from within this order, which reveals another important aspect of Rancière's analysis, in that he shows that in addition to the struggle for inclusion of those who are known to be excluded there is also a need for a struggle for inclusion of those who cannot yet be conceived to be excluded, precisely because the lack an identity – and hence a way to speak and be – in the existing police order and it is here, as I will suggest below, that the concept of 'transclusion' seeks to be a marker of this difference.

It is, finally, important to see that for Rancière the purpose of democracy and the 'point' of democratisation is not to create constant chaos and disruption. Although Rancière would maintain that democratisation is basically a good thing, this does not mean that the police order is necessarily bad. Although this may not be very prominent, Rancière does argue that democratisation can have a positive effect on the police order. Democratic disputes do produce what he refers to as "inscriptions of equality" (ibid., p. 100); they leave traces behind in the (transformed) police order. This is why Rancière emphasises that "(t)here is a worse and a better police" (ibid., pp. 30–31). The better one is, however, not the one "that adheres to the supposedly natural order of society or the science of legislators" – it is the one "that all the breaking and entering perpetrated by egalitarian logic has most jolted out of its 'natural' logic" (ibid., p. 31). Rancière thus acknowledges that the police "can produce all sorts of good, and one kind of police may be infinitely preferable to another" (ibid., p. 31). But, so he concludes, whether the police is 'sweet and kind' does not make it any less the opposite of politics (see ibid.).

Discussion: Marking the Difference between Inclusion and Transclusion

Is this chapter I have used recent discussions about democracy and inclusion to highlight wider problems with the way in which the idea of inclusion has been and can be thematised. The discussion has centred on two aspects: the idea of inclusion as bringing outsiders into an existing state of affairs, and the idea that such a process should aim for the inclusion of everyone in the existing state of affairs. I have suggested that there are several problems with this understanding of democracy and democratisation. The main problem is that it is premised on the idea that we – and the key-question is of course who the 'we' here are – already know what democracy is and that inclusion is nothing more than a technical matter of bringing more people into the existing democratic order. The main problem with this way of thinking is that the political order itself, that is, the 'state of democracy' in which others are being included, is taken for granted. It appears as the starting-point and frame of reference which, in itself, cannot be questioned. This is not only a problem for international politics where this particular logic is often forcefully enacted under the premise of 'bringing democracy' to an undemocratic world. It is at the same time a problem for those forms of democratic education which operate on the assumption that it is the task of democratic education to include children and other 'newcomers' into the existing democratic order by facilitating a transition from a pre-rational and pre-democratic stage to a stage at which children have met the entry conditions for their future participation in democracy.

The importance of Rancière's work lies precisely in the fact that he puts this way of thinking about democracy and inclusion on its head. For him democracy is not a normal situation, i.e., it is not a way in which the police order exists. Democracy rather occurs in the interruption of the order in the name of equality – which is why he says that democracy is sporadic. Furthermore, democratisation for Rancière is not something that is done *to* others – bring 'them' into 'our' democratic order. He rather depicts democratisation as a process that people can only do *themselves*. Thirdly, Rancière helps us to see that we should not understand democratic inclusion in terms of adding more people to the existing order, but rather as a process that necessarily involves the transformation of that order. As long as we restrict our inclusive efforts to those who are known to be excluded, we only operate within the existing order. This, so I wish to emphasise, is definitely not *un*important because, as Rancière reminds us, there is a worse and a better police. But what Rancière provides us with is an understanding of the need for a different kind of inclusion: the inclusion of what cannot be known to be excluded in terms of the existing order; the inclusion of what I have elsewhere referred to as the 'incalculable' (see Biesta, 2001).

Rancière thus provides us with a template that at the very same time challenges some of the core assumptions of the idea of inclusion and provides us with a way to overcome the tension between inclusion and exclusion that I have discussed in this chapter. Rancière suggests the need for a double movement, where inclusion is not just about what I have termed 'moving position' – that is, moving from the place of the outsider to the place of the insider – but at the same time requires 'shifting the terrain' – that is, redefining the very 'field' where the tension between inclusion and exclusion is being played out. Crucial in this double movement is that inclusion is no longer a process of bringing in those who are known to be excluded – that is, those who already have an identity within a given (police) order – but is about a redistribution and redefinition of identities, places and spaces.

It therefore goes *beyond* the simple inclusion of those who are outside and it is for precisely this reason that I have suggested that the notion of 'transclusion' is a more appropriate way to highlight the importance of this double movement, so that our inclusive efforts are no longer just directed to those who are outside of where 'we' are, but also affect the playing field where 'we' are and thus affects the identities and subject positions of all – both those who in the logic of the conception of inclusion I have sought to challenge in this chapter – are on the 'inside' and those who according to the same logic are on the outside. 'Transclusion' this hints at an inclusive 'gesture' that goes in two directions at the same time and thus helps to see that inclusive ambitions not only require that 'we' become more open and welcoming but that, at the very same time, there is a need for a redefinition and repositioning of the very 'we' that seek to be inclusive. 'Transclusion' thus exposes the complicity of the good intentions upon which attempts at inclusion are often based – not to necessarily discredit such intentions, but to highlight that there is no safe and secure ground from which such intentions can be issued.

Notes

1 This chapter incorporates some material from Biesta, G. J. J. (2007). "Don't count me in." Democracy, education and the question of inclusion. *Nordisk Pedagogik*, 27(1), 18–31.
2 Dryzek refers to work published by Young before her *Inclusion and Democracy*. Several of the issues Dryzek raises about Young's position seem no longer to be part of the position she takes in *Inclusion and Democracy*.
3 I am aware that this is a rather clumsy way of putting the question, but it is consistent with Rancière's line of thinking. He himself writes at some point about "(t)he people through which democracy occurs" (Rancière, 1999, p. 99).
4 There is an interesting connection here with Dewey's ideas on the democratic public as articulated in his 1927 publication *The public and its problems* (Dewey, 1954), particularly with his claim that 'the public has to define itself.' For a detailed discussion see Ljunggren (2003).

CHAPTER 8

Education and Democracy Revisited: Dewey's Democratic Deficit

School education is but one educational agency out of many,
and at the best is in some respects a minor educational force.
JOHN DEWEY (1987a, p. 414)

∴

Introduction[1]

In her 2008 essay 'Speculation on a Missing Link: Dewey's democracy and schools' (Stone, 2008), Lynda Stone makes the interesting claim that despite Dewey's 'iconic status' in the field, the connection between democracy and education and, more specifically, between democracy and school education may not be as strong as representations of and references to Dewey's work assume. Based on a review of about thirty of Dewey's publications, Stone concludes that "Dewey is interested in both democracy and schools, but he does not, indeed almost never, link them, directly or conceptually" (Stone, 2008). According to Stone, Dewey's interest takes two prominent forms. "One is to focus on political democracy in times of national crisis; the other is to focus on democracy and education more broadly than with schools," mostly writing about "broad psychological and sociological processes for children's development" (Stone, 2008). In an essay on the relationships between democracy and education, Jürgen Oelkers also remarks that Dewey's views on how education should relate to democracy are actually "unexpectedly unclear" (Oelkers, 2000, p. 16), and according to him they are also insufficient because "democracy cannot be defined merely as a *form of life* and ... education cannot simply be its correlation" (Oelkers, 2000, p. 5; emphasis in original).

Stone's observations about the apparent 'missing link' between democracy and education in Dewey's work, and Oelkers' concerns about a lack of clarity in making the connection, raise some important questions about the *substance* of Dewey's ideas (which is an altogether different question than the one about Dewey's status, where I would concede that he has played a key role in putting the question of the relationship between democracy and education on

© KONINKLIJKE BRILL NV, LEIDEN, 2019 | DOI: 10.1163/9789004401105_009

the intellectual and political agenda). There is, therefore, some reconstructive work required, not least because the book where many would expect to find clear answers – Dewey's 1916 *Democracy and Education* – actually "yields rather few," as Alan Ryan has put it (Ryan, 1995, p. 81). In what follows I attempt such a reconstruction of Dewey's ideas, making a distinction between the ideas themselves and the rationale Dewey provided for them.

With regard to the ideas I will argue that there is a remarkable *continuity* in Dewey's thinking, whereas with regard to the rationale there are interesting *discontinuities,* which are particularly connected to the shift Dewey made "from absolutism to experimentalism" – or in more precise terms, the shift from idealism to cultural naturalism as he called it in an autobiographical essay from 1930 (Dewey, 1984; for the latter term also see Dewey, 1938). The key question I raise is whether the second framing of Dewey's account of the relationship between democracy and education is actually helpful. I am inclined to argue that this is not the case and that Dewey's earlier position, because it is more explicitly normative, may actually be a more desirable way to underpin education's democratic 'project' – not only in Dewey's time but also for today.

Connecting Democracy and Education: The Moral Argument

While many authors who write about Dewey's views on democracy and education turn to Chapter 7 – 'The democratic concept of education' – of *Democracy and Education,* which according to Ryan (1995, p. 183) "has always been seen as a privileged statement of Dewey's understanding of both democracy and education," I wish to follow a lead suggested by David Hansen in a chapter called 'Dewey's book of the moral self' (Hansen, 2006). In it, Hansen directs our attention to the very last sentence of *Democracy and Education.* Here Dewey writes: "Interest in learning from all the contacts of life is the essential moral interest" (Dewey, 1966, p. 360). At first sight it might seem odd that Dewey ends a book called *Democracy and Education* with a sentence like this. Hansen indeed asks:

> Why does Dewey conclude his long inquiry by underscoring the ideas of interest, learning, and the moral, especially since other concepts such as growth, experience, and democracy loom large in the book. Why does he bequeath us, as his parting act, with an image of the moral self? (Hansen, 2006, p. 167)

The answer Hansen gives to these questions is that for Dewey the "associative mode of human interaction (...) supports in every way possible each human being's growth, while it also draws from each human being the best that he or she can provide to others" (Hansen, 2006, pp. 167–168). In this concise formulation we can not only find in a nutshell Dewey's views about the relationship between self and society, to which we might refer as a social conception of the self (see Biesta, 2007c). It also hints at a particular 'quality' of the social – a quality Dewey will define as 'democratic' – and at a particular 'quality' of the self, to which Dewey will refer as 'moral.' I therefore agree with Hansen that the idea of the moral self lies at the very heart of Dewey's conception of democratic education, which is why Hansen's suggestion to refer to *Democracy and Education* as 'Dewey's book of the moral self' is actually quite appropriate.

The suggestion that Dewey's approach to the question of democracy and education is actually based on a view of the moral self – and thus, to put it briefly, that the basis for Dewey's conception of democracy is moral rather than political, a theme I will return to later in this chapter – is also put forward by Matthew Festenstein in his reconstruction of Dewey's political thought (Festenstein, 1997). Indeed, Festenstein argues that Dewey's political theory rests upon his moral philosophy and that at the core of his 'theory of the moral life' we find a "teleological conception of human self-development as intrinsically social and cooperative" (Festenstein, 1997, p. 12). This conception "points towards his political theory for its completion, as it raises the question of how the self-development of each is compatible with the self-development of all" (Festenstein, 1997, p. 12). Festenstein also shows how Dewey's "moral and psychological theory" – his social conception of the self – "shapes his account of positive freedom as the expression of disciplined and creative individuality, in the form of a social order which fosters individuality in all" (Festenstein, 1997, pp. 12–13). This demands "a more extensive scope for 'social action' than what can be found in the individualism of what Dewey takes to be 'the bankrupt tradition of laissez-faire liberalism" (Festenstein, 1997, p. 13).

The idea that "the aim of social action is the liberation of human capacities for their full development" (Festenstein, 1997, p. 72) permeates most if not all of Dewey's thinking on democracy and on the role of education in it. In the final paragraph of *Democracy and Education*, for example, he writes that "all education which develops power to share effectively in social life is moral [as it] forms a character which not only does the particular deed socially necessary but one which is interested in that continuous adjustment which is essential to growth" (Dewey, 1966, p. 360). This requires a form of education where:

> learning is the accompaniment of continuous activities or occupations which have a social aim and utilize the materials of typical social situations [for] under such conditions the school becomes itself a form of

social life, a miniature community and one in close interaction with other modes of associated experience beyond the school walls. (Dewey, 1966, p. 360)

Although Dewey thus focuses strongly on the growth of the moral self, Carr and Hartnett argue that this should not be read in an entirely individualistic way but should be understood as a "dynamic and dialectical process of self-transformation and social change" (Carr & Hartnett, 1996, p. 59). It is a process "whereby individuals, in the course of remaking their society, remake themselves," which is the reason why for Dewey the individual and society "are neither separate nor distinct [but] are both elements within a single process of growth" (Carr & Hartnett, 1996, p. 59).

Education as *Bildung*

Before I turn to a discussion of some of the 'roots' of Dewey's views in his earlier work, I wish to highlight one important point about what we might call the structural characteristics of his approach and, more specifically, his approach to and understanding of education. The suggestion I wish to make here is that Dewey's understanding of education fits within the German tradition of *Bildung* which itself goes back to the Greek idea of *paideia* – a tradition which I have discussed in more detail in Chapter 3. I make this observation in order to show that the way in which Dewey approaches the question of democracy and its connection with education does not stand on its own. Instead it fits rather well with a longstanding tradition in which education is seen as a process of the formation of the individual through interaction with society and culture.

Two points are important here. One is that once we see that Dewey's thinking about the relationship between democracy and education basically follows an *educational* logic – that is, the logic of *Bildung* – rather than a political one, it becomes easier to understand why the formation of the moral self plays such a key role in his approach. The other point – which is perhaps easier to understand by those who have knowledge of the development of education as a field in the German-speaking context (on this see also Biesta, 2011d) – is that Dewey's outlook on education is in terms of a theory of *Bildung* and not a theory of *Erziehung*. His interest, therefore, is more in the educative – or if one wishes, formative – 'quality' of culture and society than the dynamics and complexities of the relationships between educators and those being educated. This might explain why it is a bit of a challenge, for example, to find a clear account in Dewey's work of the role, position and work of the teacher (see Biesta & Stengel, 2016).

With this in mind, let me return to the reconstruction of Dewey's views on education and democracy.

From the Ethics of Democracy to Democracy and Education

Democracy and Education is not the first place where Dewey's unfolds his ideas about democracy and the role of education in it, and it is here that we touch upon the remarkable *continuity* in Dewey's ideas. In an essay from 1888 called *The Ethics of Democracy* we can already find, in outline, many of the ideas Dewey would hold throughout his career, including the framework he would use to argue for the intimate connection between democracy and education. In the essay Dewey argues, for example, that "in conception ... democracy approaches most nearly the ideal of all social organization; that in which the individual and society are organic to each other" (Dewey, 1969, p. 237).

Dewey arrives at this conclusion through a discussion of the idea of society as an organism. However, he does criticise the "German theory, which despite recognizing professedly the organic conception, rids it of its significance ... by giving a physiological sense to the term" (Dewey, 1969, pp. 235–236). Dewey argues for a conception of the organism as "a thoroughly reciprocal concep- tion" suggesting that human society "represents a more perfect organism" than the animal body, because in the animal body the parts are "absorbed in [the] whole" so that they cannot "take on the appearance of independent lives" (Dewey, 1969, p. 237). Dewey thus contrasts the idea of "an individualism of numerical character" (Dewey, 1969, p. 248) with the idea of man as "essentially a social being" (Dewey, 1969, p. 232). He connects this to his belief of democ- racy as "an ethical ideal" (Dewey, 1969, p. 248) – in other words, the ideal that expresses how our individuality comes about through our engagement with the social.

Unlike Henry Maine, whose book *Popular Government* provides the starting point for Dewey's essay, Dewey believes that democracy is *not* "merely a form of government" (Dewey, 1969, p. 239). He argues instead that democracy is a form of government "only because it is a form of moral and spiritual associa- tion" (Dewey, 1969, p. 240), one, moreover, based upon "personal responsibility [and] individual initiation" (Dewey, 1969, p. 243), upon "an individualism of freedom, of responsibility, of initiative to and for the ethical ideal" (Dewey, 1969, p. 244). Towards the end of his essay Dewey admits that his position is a form of idealism – one that he would transform over time into a form of 'cultural naturalism' (Dewey, 1938), which was more a reworking of idealist thought than a departure from it (see Dewey, 1984) – adding that "the best test of any form of society is the ideal which it proposes for the forms of its life, and the degree in which it realizes this ideal" (Dewey, 1969, p. 249).

When we move forward from here to 1916, the year *Democracy and Education* was published, we find an account of 'the democratic conception of education' that in many respects is identical to what Dewey wrote 28 years earlier. Central in the discussion of "the democratic ideal" (Dewey, 1966, p. 86) we do indeed find Dewey's contention that "democracy is more than a form of government; it is primarily a mode of associated living, of conjoint communicated experience" (Dewey, 1966, p. 87). Because Dewey characterises education itself as "a social function, securing direction and development in the immature through their participation in the life of the group to which they belong" (Dewey, 1966, p. 81) – which, as I have shown, is clearly an account of education as *Bildung*: that is, formation through engagement with society and culture – the issue that becomes central for judging the quality of education and its 'effects' is the quality of social life itself. After all, so Dewey's argument goes, not any social arrangement, not any mode of participation will have beneficial effects on those who take part – "hence the need of a measure for the *worth* of any given mode of social life' (Dewey, 1966, p. 83, emphasis added).

Dewey (1966, p. 83) suggests that in any social group, "even in a gang of thieves, we find some interest held in common, and we find a certain amount of interaction and cooperative intercourse with other groups." From this he derives two questions that form his 'standard' for judging the quality of social life: "How numerous and varied are the interests which are consciously shared?" and "How full and free is the interplay with other forms of association?" (Dewey, 1966, p. 83). Why are these aspects of social life important? Dewey's answer is simple and clear. They are important because they result in "a greater diversity of stimuli to which an individual has to respond" and thus "secure a liberation of powers which remain suppressed as long as the incitations to action are partial" (Dewey, 1969, p. 87). They result, in other words, in *growth* – or, in Dewey's words, in "a freeing of individual capacity in a progressive growth directed to social aims" (Dewey, 1966, p. 99).

For Dewey, the standard for the *educative* quality of social life is therefore at the very same time the standard for the *democratic* quality of social life. As he writes (1966, pp. 86–87):

> The two elements in our criterion both point to democracy. The first signifies not only more numerous and more varied points of shared common interest, but greater reliance upon the recognition of mutual

interests as a factor in social control. The second means not only freer interaction between social groups ... but change in social habits – its continuous readjustment through meeting the new situations produced by varied intercourse. And these two traits are precisely what characterize the democratically constituted society.

Whereas an "undesirable society" is one that "internally and externally sets up barriers to free intercourse and communication of experience," a democratic society "makes provision for participation in its good of all its members on equal terms." It also secures "flexible readjustment of its institutions through interaction of the different forms of associated life" (Dewey, 1966, p. 99).

Against this backdrop it is relatively easy to understand why Dewey makes a case for the school as an "embryonic society" – an idea he put forward for the first time in his 1899 publication *The School and Society* (Dewey, 1990, p. 18) – as it is only when the school meets the democratic 'standard' for the quality of social interaction that it will contribute to the growth of all the individuals who take part in it. It is important to see that Dewey does not conceive of this as a one-way process in which individuals are shaped by the particular qualities of the social situation they are in. Dewey's standard for the democratic quality of social life does not merely refer to plurality – that is, to the number of different interests – but to the extent to which different interests are *consciously shared* – i.e. the extent to which individuals are aware of the fact that their actions are part of the wider 'social fabric,' so that each "has to refer his own action to that of others, and to consider the action of others to give point and direction to his own" (Dewey, 1966, p. 87).

What makes such a situation simultaneously educative *and* democratic is the fact that individuals take an active part in shaping the contexts and conditions that in turn shape them (see also Festenstein, 1997, p. 70). For Dewey (1987b, p. 218) this is what democracy is about, because in a democracy:

> All those who are affected by social institutions (...) have a share in producing and managing them. The two facts that each one is influenced in what he does and enjoys and in what he becomes by the institutions under which he lives, and that therefore he shall have, in a democracy, a voice in shaping them, are the passive and active side of the same fact.

The kind of intelligence at stake in the shaping of the conditions that shape one's self is *social* intelligence. Social intelligence is at the very same time a requirement for and the outcome of participation in intelligent cooperation. As Carr and Hartnett (1996, p. 59) put it:

By participating in this process, individuals develop those intellectual dispositions which allow them to reconstruct themselves and their social institutions in ways which are conducive to the realization of their freedom and to the reshaping of their society.

A Democratic Deficit?

The foregoing passages provide an account of the main elements of Dewey's views about democracy and its relation to education, although it might be more appropriate to say that they provide an account of the main elements of Dewey's views about *education* and how they relate to democracy. After all, democracy only enters the 'scene' because it is the optimal environment for individual growth, not the other way around. What is at stake in Dewey's approach to democracy is a concern for the self and, more specifically, a concern for the *moral* self – the self who "not only does the particular deed socially necessary," but who is also "interested in that continuous adjustment which is essential to growth" (Dewey, 1966, p. 360). In *The Public and its Problems* (1954, p. 150) Dewey would refer to this as an 'individualized self.'

Starting from the assumption that "men are not isolated non-social atoms, but are men only when in intrinsic relations" (Dewey, 1969, p. 231), Dewey seeks to formulate what, in the first edition of his *Ethics*, he describes as a "moral criterion by which to try social institutions and its political measures" (Dewey, 1978, p. 431) to identify the conditions that make possible the "freeing of individual capacity in a progressive growth directed to social aims" (Dewey, 1966, p. 99). This criterion appears in *Democracy and Education* in the form of the two questions that make up the standard for judging the quality of social life. What is peculiar about this standard is that it not only denotes the *democratic* quality of social life but at the very same time denotes its *educative* quality, and the two are actually more difficult to disentangle than it might appear.

I wish to draw two conclusions from this discussion, one that raises a problem for Dewey's theory of democratic *education* and one that raises a problem for his conception of *democracy*. To begin with the first: we might say that Dewey does not so much articulate an educational programme for democracy, or a programme for democratic education, as he highlights the educative *function* of democratic life – that is, the fact that 'real' democratic life always has an educative 'impact.' Taking it one step further I would even like to suggest that the relationship in Dewey's work between democracy and education is actually not an *empirical* relationship, in which case we could ask such questions as: what kind of education we might need for democracy to flourish, or what is the impact of democratic arrangements on the education of those who take part in them? Rather it is more like a *conceptual* relationship – that is, a relationship established through definition of concepts. After all, in Dewey's way of thinking we could say that if social life is educative – which means that it makes the growth of the moral self possible – we should call it democracy, just as we can say that social life is democratic when it makes growth possible.

If we look at the relationship between democracy and education in this way, we begin to understand why there is actually relatively little in Dewey's work that engages with the question of how we should educate *for* democracy. This is one way in which we can understand Stone's idea about the 'missing link' between the two – although Dewey might perhaps contest that this is a question that does not make a lot of sense within his theoretical 'universe.' All this also helps to understand why Dewey doesn't really seem to have a theory about democratic education and its workings, as such a theory would precisely specify empirical rather than conceptual links between the domains of education and democracy.

There are, however, not only repercussions for the theory of democratic education. I also wish to suggest that my reconstruction highlights a problem with Dewey's conception of democracy itself – and more specifically, with its justification. When we ask the question why democracy is good – that is, when we ask why it is a more desirable form of human existence than others – the answer that follows from Dewey's views is that democracy is good because it makes growth possible. Democracy is, in other words, that 'mode' of social life that lends us "the power to be an individualized self, making a distinctive contribution and enjoying in its own way the fruits of association" (Dewey, 1954, p. 150). If pushed, Dewey will have to concede that the answer to the question why democracy is good can only be that democracy is good because it is good *for us*. This means, however, that for Dewey democracy does not, in itself, represent a preferred mode of political existence. It simply is that form of social life that makes individuality – and perhaps we should say 'Deweyan' individuality, which is always individuality-in-relation – possible. The conclusion to draw from this, is that Dewey's justification of democracy is *instrumental* rather than *intrinsic*. Democracy, as Festenstein (1997) also shows, does not appear in Dewey's writings as a desirable *political* project, but rather is the kind of social 'set up' that enables optimal growth for the largest number of people. And one could even argue, by way of a thought experiment, that if a different way made optimal growth for the largest number of people possible, Dewey would not really have an argument for why we would need to retain democracy.

Key in all of this is Dewey's understanding of human individuality – Dewey's theory of the moral self. Unlike classical liberalism, where engagement with others would always be seen as a possible constraint of our freedom, Dewey articulates the position that it is only through engagement with others that we can become an "individualised self." [2] It is from this starting point – which Dewey continues to defend and articulate throughout his career, for example, in such books as *The Public and its Problems* (1954), *Individualism Old and New* (1930), and *Liberalism and Social Action* (1935) – that Dewey builds up his conception of education and within it his conception of democracy. While the structure and 'logic' of his argument are therefore quite clear, the justification of Dewey's position remains more problematic because, as also Festenstein argues, Dewey ultimately expresses a "moral preference" about how we should understand human individuality, yet expressing this moral preference is "at odds with his own emphasis on the plurality of goods and ideals at large in modern societies." In this respect it expresses "simply a differing opinion" (Festenstein, 1997, p. 99).

Whereas those who share Dewey's "moral preference" – that is, his conception of individuality – might be convinced by the way he connects this with his views about education and democracy, those who do not share his views about human individuality – either because they opt for a more traditionally liberal view or, say, a religious or spiritual understanding of the self – will most likely *not* be convinced. This not only indicates a weakness in Dewey's justification. We might even conclude that it indicates a 'democratic deficit' in his conception. Before I draw my conclusions of what this might mean for our appreciation of Dewey's work today, there is one more step I would like to take. The step relates to the wider justification Dewey provides for his position, and is one that, as I conclude, provide a small but nonetheless significant 'opening' in the discussion so far.

From Absolutism to Experimentalism

I have shown how Dewey, early on in his career, expressed his ideas about democracy and education within an idealistic framework. Here democracy appears as an ethical ideal that expresses "the ideal of all social organization; that in which the individual and society are organic to each other" (Dewey, 1969, p. 237). Starting from the claim that man is "essentially a social being" (Dewey, 1969, p. 232), Dewey argues that the realisation of our individuality is the result of our engagement with social life and can never appear outside of it. The idea, to put it in more Hegelian terms, is that the realisation of freedom takes place through our engagement with social life in its ideal form. Dewey refers to this ideal form as 'democracy'; however, not only does he explicitly reject reducing democracy to 'merely a form of government,' we might even say he expands the idea of democracy so much that it becomes equivalent to social life in general, instead of denoting a particular political organisation of social life.

What Dewey is interested in is that quality of social life that makes the realisation of freedom possible. Because the realisation of freedom is also key to educational interests, it explains why for him democracy and education 'map' onto each other. While Dewey does make an effort to show that this conception of democracy as the ideal form of social life embodies the values of freedom and equality, his interest in democracy nonetheless stays at a general level and is far less concerned with the complexities of democratic politics. Festenstein (1997, p. 95) pushes this point slightly further when he writes that "Dewey attaches no particular value to political participation: his ideal of associated living aims to outline principles constitutive of social life as such, and not principles which define the political sphere."

The language Dewey uses later on in his career is remarkably similar to how he expressed his ideas earlier on. In *The Public and its Problems* (1954, p. 148), to give one more example, he writes that "regarded as an idea, democracy is not an alternative to other principles of associated life. It is the idea of community life itself." Dewey seems a bit more cautious here than he was in 1888 when he adds that this conception of democracy "is an ideal in the only intelligible sense of an ideal: namely, the tendency and movement of some thing which exists carried to its final limit, viewed as completed, perfected" (Dewey, 1952, p. 148). However, because "things do not attain such fulfilment but are in actuality distracted and interfered with, democracy in this sense is not a fact and never will be" (Dewey, 1952, p. 148).

Nonetheless, Dewey argues that the "idea or ideal of community presents ... actual phases of associated life as they are freed from restrictive and disturbing elements, and are contemplated as having attained their limit of development" (Dewey, 1952, pp. 148–149). This means that "wherever there is a conjoint activity whose consequences are appreciated as good by all singular persons who take part in it, and where the realization of the good is such as to effect an energetic desire and effort to sustain it in being just because it is a good shared by all, there is in so far a community" (Dewey, 1952, p. 149). And it is "the clear consciousness of a communal life, in all its implications [that] constitutes the idea of democracy" (Dewey, 1952, p. 149). In this context "liberty is that secure release and fulfilment of personal potentialities which take place only in rich and manifold association with others: the power to be an individualized self, making a distinctive contribution and enjoying in its own way the fruits of the association." Equality, meanwhile, "denotes the unhampered share which each individual member of the community has in the consequences of associated action" (Dewey, 1952, p. 150).

While the language remains constant, however – and to a certain extent it is rather difficult to read this passage other than through a Hegelian lens – the general framework and rationale for Dewey's philosophising had clearly moved away from his earlier 'absolutism' towards what he would characterise in his autobiographical essay from 1930 as 'experimentalism' – albeit experimentalism with a clear Hegelian 'deposit' (see Dewey, 1984). In Dewey's "cultural naturalism" (Dewey, 1938), which was based on Darwinism and strongly influenced by the ideas of William James (see Dewey, 1930), the human being (re)appears as an "acculturated organism." Acculturation is itself understood as the outcome of participation, or with a term that becomes central in Dewey's later philosophy (see Biesta, 2006b), a process of communication, where communication is understood in thoroughly practical terms – i.e. as the "making of something in common in at least two different centers of behavior" (Dewey, 1958, p. 178), something Dewey understands as the outcome of the successful coordination of action between two or more human organisms.

Mind, consciousness, thought, subjectivity, meaning, intelligence, language, rationality, logic, inference, and truth are all seen as outcomes of such participation rather than as their condition. In *Experience and Nature,* first published in 1925 and revised in 1929, Dewey writes that "the world of inner experience is dependent upon an extension of language which is a social production and operation" (Dewey, 1958, p. 173), which means that "psychic events ... have language for one of their conditions" (Dewey, 1958, p. 169). Language itself is presented as 'a natural function of human association' and its consequences 'react upon other events, physical and human, giving them meaning or significance' (Dewey, 1958, p. 173). Failure to see this, Dewey argues, has led to the "subjectivistic, solipsistic and egoistic strain in modern thought" (Dewey, 1958, p. 173). Yet for Dewey "soliloquy is the product and reflect of converse with others; social communication not an effect of soliloquy" (Dewey, 1958, p. 170). This ultimately means that "communication is a condition of consciousness" (Dewey, 1958, p. 187), just as intelligence and meaning are "natural consequences of the peculiar form which interaction sometimes assumes in the case of human beings" (Dewey, 1958[1929], p. 180).

Although the philosophical framework for Dewey's thinking is completely 'overhauled,' the new, Darwinist framework termed 'cultural naturalism' still allows Dewey to argue that we only become who we are through participation in a larger whole – to which Dewey now refers as 'culture.' In this new framework democracy is still a desirable mode of common living because it provides the human organism with the widest opportunities for growth. And it is through this that we become an individualised self.

Because Dewey's cultural naturalism allows for almost identical moves as his earlier absolute idealism, there is little change in the structure of his thinking and only, one might say, in the packaging – that is, the underlying philosophical framework. What does change, however, is the justification for the democratic form of life and the explanation of its educative function and here, I think, we encounter a further problem with Dewey's position. Whereas the idealistic framing of democracy and its educative function expressed a particular normative – or as I have suggested, with Festenstein, moral – preference, Dewey's shift from absolutism to experimentalism seems to lead to a situation where the 'case' for democracy becomes scientific – that is, based on the Darwinist view of the world. Again, for those who believe in this worldview, nothing really changes. But for those who have doubts about it, the case for democracy becomes even more difficult to accept. Democracy is no longer outlined as a moral preference with which one might disagree, but becomes tied up in a much more complicated discussion about the truth of the Darwinist worldview (on this issue see also Biesta, 2010d).

Before I come to my conclusions there is, however, one more point I wish to add to the discussion, which has to do with the question of how we should actually understand Dewey's cultural naturalism and his wider recourse to the Darwinist worldview. One reading is to say that Dewey believed in this worldview – that is, he saw it as true – and hence made it the foundation for his philosophy. On this account authors such as Max Horkheimer may well be right in accusing Dewey of scientism (see Horkheimer, 1992). However, such a reading relies on the idea that the Darwinist worldview is true, that is, that it is an adequate and correct representation of the world 'out there.' Yet such an understanding of truth is clearly at odds with Dewey's own understanding of knowledge and its relation to reality, and his wider critique of the 'spectator theory of knowledge.' This suggests that the situation might be slightly more complicated – or if one wishes: more interesting – than such an objectivist understanding of Dewey's cultural naturalism might indicate. To appreciate the opening that might emerge here, we need to take a brief look at Dewey's wider philosophical and political 'project.'

Overcoming the 'Crisis in Culture'

The point I wish to make here is one often overlooked in discussions about Dewey, both by his critics and his admirers. It has to do with what we might term the most pragmatic question of all: what is the problem, and more specifically, what is the problem to which Dewey's work is responding (see also Biesta, 2009d)? When at the age of almost 80 Dewey looked back on his career, he concluded that the main purpose of his writings always had been that of reintegrating "knowledge and activity in the general framework of reality and natural processes" (Dewey, 1991, p. 80). Dewey felt that this was required to respond effectively to what he saw as a 'crisis' in modern culture, a crisis that had arisen as a result of the impact of modern science on society.

Modern science, so Dewey observed, has completely changed our understanding of the world we live in. It has given us a view of the world as a machine or, in his words, "a scene of indifferent physical particles acting according to mathematical and mechanical laws" (Dewey, 1960, p. 33). Modern science has thus "stripped the world of the qualities which made it beautiful and congenial to men" (Dewey, 1960, p. 33). According to Dewey, the problematic impact of this shift on the world of everyday life is mainly the result of how the scientific worldview has been *interpreted*, namely as an accurate or 'true' account of reality as it really is. As soon as we take what is known as describing what is real – or more concretely, as soon as we take the knowledge produced by science as the ultimate and final account of what the world is really like – then all other dimensions of human life, such as the practical, the aesthetic, the ethical, and the religious, can only be seen as real if they can in some way be reduced or traced back to what is revealed through science.

By assuming that scientific knowledge provides the 'norm' for what is real, so Dewey argued, other aspects of our lives are relegated to the domain of the subjective. As Dewey put it: "When real objects are identified ... with knowledge-objects, all affectional and volitional objects are inevitably excluded from the 'real' world, and are compelled to find refuge in the privacy of an experiencing subject or mind" (Dewey, 1958, p. 30). The "net practical effect" of this is the belief "that science exists only in the things which are most remote from any significant human concern, so that as we approach social and moral ques tions and interests we must either surrender hope of the guidance of genuine knowledge or else purchase scientific title and authority at the expense of all that is distinctly human" (Dewey, 1991, p. 51).

Dewey's point was that our interpretation of modern science's worldview as an account of how the world really is, has resulted in two equally unattractive realities: the 'inhuman' rationality of modern science or the 'human' irrationality of everyday life. According to Dewey this predicament lies at the very heart of the crisis in modern culture, which means that for him the crisis should first and foremost be understood as a crisis of rationality.

The fact that Dewey related the crisis in modern culture to a specific *interpretation* of modern science's worldview should not be read as the suggestion that this crisis is only a theoretical problem and has nothing to do with the urgent practical problems of contemporary life. Rather Dewey wanted to stress that the hegemony of scientific rationality and the scientific worldview – that is, the situation in which it is assumed that rationality only concerns the 'hard facts' of science, and not values, morals, feelings, emotions, and so on – makes it almost impossible to find an adequate solution for these problems, since the situation we are in is one in which rationality gets restricted to facts and means, while values and ends are, by definition, excluded from rational deliberation.

What makes all of this even more urgent, so Dewey argued, is the fact that modern life is to a large extent what it is because of the "embodiment of science in the common sense world" (Dewey, 1991, p. 81). We are, after all, constantly confronted with its products and outcomes, particularly through the omnipresence of technology in our lives. This seems to 'prove' again and again the truth of the scientific knowledge upon which it is based, which is why Dewey claimed that the world of everyday experience "is a house divided against itself" (Dewey, 1991, p. 84).

The key question is whether the interpretation of the scientific worldview as an account of what reality is really like, is inevitable. According to Dewey, this is not the case. Central to his argument is the claim that the interpretation of the scientific worldview as an objective account of the world 'out there' is the result of applying an ancient epistemology, one that originated in Greek philosophy, to the findings of modern science. Whereas this was perhaps the only available option at the time when modern science arose, it was not an inevitable option. Yet the road that was not taken at the time was to ask what would happen to our understanding of knowledge and reality if, rather than applying an understanding of knowledge that predated the rise of modern science, we had based our understanding of what it means to know on the way that modern science itself engaged with the world in order to gain knowledge of it – that is, through intervention and experimentation.

The latter is what Dewey did by making the experimental method the framework within which he developed his ideas about knowledge, reality, and truth. While this might be seen on a superficial reading as a surrender of philosophy to science – which is precisely how Horkheimer defines 'scientism' – this is not where Dewey ended up. He showed that if we take the assumptions of modern science about knowledge and coming to know seriously, we have to come to the conclusion that knowledge thus generated is precisely *not* a representation of a world independent of our actions, but rather an account of the relationship between our (experimental) actions and the consequences that follow from it. This, in a nutshell, is how Dewey conceives of knowledge. Rather than science giving us the ultimate account of what reality is really like,

Dewey shows that the experimental way of generating knowledge characteristic of modern science moves knowledge from the realm of certainty to the
realm of possibility – that is, that scientific knowledge provides us with nothing more, but of course also nothing less, than possible relationships between
our actions and the consequences that follow from them. While having such
knowledge might be very useful when we seek to gain control over the world –
both in the physical and social domains – this does not mean that this is all
there is to say about our lives and the world in which we live them.

Rather than scientism, this reading actually shows that Dewey's philosophy provides one of the most effective criticisms of scientism and thus of the
hegemony of modern science. Instead of having to concede that science and
its worldview is the ultimate arbiter of everything we ought to believe about
our lives and ourselves, it becomes one of the possible ways to make sense
of relationships between actions and consequences – useful where it matters,
but utterly irrelevant in other domains. Instead of, therefore, seeing Dewey's
philosophy succumbing to the hegemony of scientific rationality, his 'project'
can in fact be understood as an attempt to restore rationality to all aspects of
human life – that is, to restore rationality – and reality – to "all that is distinctly
human" (Dewey, 1991, p. 51).

I do not wish to claim that this resolves all problems with Dewey's conception of democracy and his views on democratic education. But I do think that
it is important to approach Dewey's philosophy in a pragmatic way and not
make the mistake of reading his own philosophy in terms of the very views
about knowledge and reality he sought to challenge. When we do so, we can
see that Dewey's engagement with the scientific worldview is more complex
and more sophisticated than it may seem, and that his underlying philosophical and, as I wish to suggest, ultimately political project is precisely to overcome the hegemony of modern science and its (instrumental) rationality (for
further details on this reading see Biesta & Burbules, 2003). Perhaps we could
even say, therefore, that Dewey sought to democratise rationality itself.

Concluding Comments: The Missing Link Revisited

In the preceding pages I have tried to show that Dewey's views on the relationship between education and democracy have remained rather constant
throughout his career, even though early on in his career they were articulated in the language of absolute idealism before being reformulated within
the framework of cultural naturalism. One way the point I have tried to make
in this chapter could be summarised is by saying that Dewey's conception of

democratic education is neither about democracy nor about education. This is perhaps a little too harsh, but not entirely beside the point. With regard to education it is important to highlight that Dewey sees education mainly as a process of formation-through-engagement-with culture. In English we might refer to this as a theory of socialisation; in German, as I have suggested, as a theory of *Bildung*.

Having outlined some of the main tenets of the idea of *Bildung*, it is remarkable how closely Dewey's views about democratic education fit. To say that Dewey's theory of democratic education is actually not a theory of education, becomes possible on the basis of the distinction within the German language – and within educational thought as it has developed within the German-speaking world – between *Bildung* and *Erziehung*, where the former refers to a general theory of acculturation and the latter to intentional actions by an educator to promote a grown-up way of existence. Such a discourse is quite absent in Dewey's writings about education, including his writings about democratic education. Whereas the distinction between *Bildung* and *Erziehung* might sound a little alien to those mostly familiar with concepts and conceptualisations of education as they have evolved in the English language, the distinction nonetheless suggests two quite different approaches to education and what it means to educate. At the very least they help to show that there is more to education than the framework that informs Dewey's account.

The reason I am highlighting the influence of the tradition of *Bildung* on Dewey's thought – and the point that needs to be addressed elsewhere is how this influence might be explained; the Hegelian 'deposit' in Dewey's work is definitely a contender here – is because it shows in quite an elegant way how democracy emerges in Dewey's thinking. For Dewey, democracy simply is the description of the kind of social environment that provides the optimal conditions for acculturation or, in Dewey's vocabulary of cultural naturalism, the optimal conditions for growth. Putting it in this way we can see that, in this particular sense, what emerges as 'democracy' in Dewey's work has little to do with democracy as an explicitly *political* project. One way to make the point is that Dewey's account of democracy is functionalist. Another, which actually connects better with where Dewey's thinking started, is to think of it as moral, since democracy is the context for the emergence of the moral self, which later on in Dewey's work becomes the 'individualized self.'

While this should not be read as a condemnation of all that Dewey has said about democracy throughout his long career, it does highlight that where it concerns the relationship between democracy and education, there is a conception of democracy at play that is social and moral rather than political (see also Biesta, 2007c). In this regard I tend to agree with Stone that there is a 'missing link,' although I would suggest that it is not so much the link between democracy and education as the link between how democracy is theorised within the context of education understood as formation-through-engage-ment-with-culture and how democracy is theorised in Dewey's other writings, outside the confines of education. Whether Dewey has something to contrib-ute to contemporary discussions about democracy and education if we explore this 'other' connection, remains to be seen. His own account of the connection is, in my view, too limited – both as an account of education and an account of democracy – to be significant for education for democracy in the 21st century.

Notes

1   This chapter is based on ideas previously published as Biesta, G. J. J. (2010). "The most influential theory of the century." Dewey, democratic education and the limits of pragmatism. In D. Troehler, T. Schlag, & F. Osterwalder (Eds.), *Pragmatism and modernities* (pp. 197–213). Rotterdam, The Netherlands: Sense Publishers.

2   Festenstein (1997, p. 67) shows that there are three aspects to Dewey's notion of "freedom as individuality." The first is that freedom consists in intelligent self-control. This refers to "the capacity and willingness of an agent to reflect on her own goals, aims and purposes, and to revise them as a result of this reflection" (Festenstein, 1997, p. 67). As Dewey put it: "to foresee future objective alternatives and to be able by deliberation to choose one of them and thereby weigh its changes in the struggle for future existence, measures our freedom" (quoted in Festenstein, 1997, p. 67). The second aspect is articulated in the idea that individuality in this strong sense "is not a given faculty but depends on the appropriate social environ-ment for its realization" (Festenstein, 1997, p. 69). Here Dewey clearly differs from classical liberalism, which thought that "all that is necessary to secure freedom is the removal of external impediments" (Festenstein, 1997, p. 69). Thirdly, Dewey's view of freedom as individuality implies "participation in shaping the social condi-tions of individuality" (Festenstein, 1997, p. 70).

CHAPTER 9

Making Pedagogy Public: For the Public, of the Public, or in the Interest of Publicness?

Introduction[1]

Within a still growing body of literature, the idea of public pedagogy is often used as an *analytical* concept aimed at theorising and researching the educative 'force' of media, popular culture and society more generally (see Sandlin, Schultz, & Burdick, 2010). Henry Giroux (2004, p. 77), for example, describes his interest in public pedagogy as being concerned with "the diverse ways in which culture functions as a contested sphere over the production, distribution and regulation of power and how and where it operates both symbolically and institutionally as an educational, political and economic force." We can find this interpretation of public pedagogy reflected in at least two of the five main areas of research and scholarship identified by Sandlin, O'Malley and Burdick (2011, pp. 343, 351) in their review of the field, one being "popular culture and everyday life as public pedagogy" and the other being "dominant discourses as public pedagogy."

Within the North-American discussion there is explicit recognition of more activist and political strands of "education and learning beyond schooling" (Sandlin, Schultz, & Burdick, 2010), something which Sandlin, O'Malley and Burdick locate in research and scholarship on "public intellectualism" (Sandlin, O'Malley, & Burdick, 2011, p. 354) and in emerging work that explores "the performative and activist dimensions of public pedagogy as possibilities for advancing democratic projects" (ibid., p. 357). What is less present in the discussion is the rich history of adult, community, and popular education (see, for example, Fieldhouse, 1998; Knowles, 1962; Welton, 1995; Wildemeersch, Finger, & Jansen, 1998) and also the Continental tradition of what, with a rather limited translation of the German word 'Sozialpädagogik,' might be referred to as 'social pedagogy.' This is pedagogy that operates outside of the confines of educational institutions such as schools, colleges, and universities but that nonetheless conceives of itself as *pedagogy* (in German: *Pädagogik*), that is, as intentional educational 'work' (see, for example, Füssenhäuser, 2005; Kommission Sozialpädagogik, 2010).

The idea that society may not only be is a educative *force* but may also have an educational *responsibility* (see Perquin, 1966) – an idea which underlies

© KONINKLIJKE BRILL NV, LEIDEN, 2019 | DOI: 10.1163/9789004401105_010

much adult, community and popular education and also informs 'social pedagogy' – thus hints at a more *programmatic* reading of the idea of public pedagogy, and it is this reading that I wish to explore in more detail in this chapter.
What I have in mind here is an understanding of public pedagogy as a specific
'form' of pedagogy, a specific form of doing educational 'work,' one in which
pedagogy 'operates' in a public way, so to speak, and in what follows I will distinguish between three different ways in which such a public mode of pedagogical operation might be understood. My ambition here is to articulate a
notion of public pedagogy that (re)connects the educational and the political
and locates both firmly in the public sphere.

The need for this not only stems from the ongoing privatisation and de-
politicisation of public spaces and places (see below), but also comes from
the ongoing privatisation of education itself, where education is increasingly
positioned and perceived as a private good, that is, a means for private (economic) advantage, rather than as a public good orientated towards democracy
and social justice (see Biesta, 2006a). This chapter is therefore an attempt to
characterise what it might mean to enact pedagogy in the interest of the public
quality of human togetherness. Doing so allows me to respond to two challenges put by Sandlin, O'Malley, and Burdick (2011) in their review of the field,
one being the question why public pedagogy is actually conceived as *pedagogy*
rather than as curriculum or as a form of cultural studies, and the other having to do with the observation that the issue of what 'public' means "is almost
unexplored in the literature" (ibid., p. 365; on this issue see also Savage, 2010).

In what follows, I start with a brief overview of discussions about the decline
of the public sphere. Against this background, and in conversation with the
work of Hannah Arendt, I develop an understanding of the public character
of public spaces and places in terms of a space "where freedom can appear"
(Arendt, 1955, p. 4). In a third step I explore how we might think of public
pedagogy in relation to this, by making a distinction between three modes or
modalities of public pedagogy, that is, as a pedagogy *for* the public, a pedagogy
of the public, and a pedagogy *for publicness*, that is, a pedagogy enacting an
interest in the public quality of human togetherness.

The Decline of the Public Sphere

Over the past decades there has been a steady stream of work in which concerns have been raised about the transformation of the public sphere. Such
work, which comes from a range of different disciplines and fields, tends to
depict the transformation of the public sphere as a process of decline or loss,

one in which essential qualities of the public sphere are under pressure, are at the brink of extinction, or have already disappeared (see, for example, Sennett, 1992). David Marquand (2004), in his book *Decline of the Public*, argues that the public sphere is being threatened from two sides, one being the (logic of the) *market* and the other being (the logic of) *private interest*.

Marquand shows how the neoliberal shift from a public logic to a market logic has led to a situation where citizens are less and less involved in democratic contestation about the public good and have instead been turned into consumers of public services. Such 'citizen-consumers' are being offered 'choice,' 'quality' and 'value for money' from a set menu of 'public services,' rather than being involved in deliberations about what goes on such a menu in the first place. With regard to the threat from the side of the private sphere, Marquand sees two problems. One has to do with what he calls the "revenge of the private" (Marquand, 2004, p. 79). What he has in mind here is a perceived decrease in the willingness of citizens to take up the "hard, demanding, 'unnatural' austerities of public duty and public engagement" (ibid., p. 79). The other problem has to do with the rise of identity politics, that is, with the idea that identity – either individual identity or group identity – is the non-negotiable 'currency' of democratic politics. Here Marquand observes that that the idea that "the private self should be omni-competent and omnipresent" has made deliberative politics of any sort "virtually impossible" (ibid., pp. 80–82; see also Biesta, 2010a).

Marquand's evaluation of the decline of the public sphere stems from what Mitchell (1995, p. 116) correctly characterises as a *normative* conception of public space in which "the public sphere is best imagined as the suite of institutions and activities that mediate the relations between society and the state." Marquand (2004, p. 27) does indeed define what he refers to as the public domain[2] as "a space, protected from the adjacent market and private domains, where strangers encounter each other as equal partners in the common life of the society" (ibid., p. 27). In this conception the key functions of the public domain are to define the public interest and to produce public goods. This, so Marquand argues, implies that the values "that sustain, and are sustained by, the public domain" are not the values of self-interest but of collective interest (ibid., p. 57). Given that collective interest may sometimes go against one's immediate self-interest – one's immediate wants and preferences – engagement with and commitment to the public domain thus implies "a certain discipline" and "a certain self-restraint" (ibid., p. 57). Marquand argues that this does not come naturally but has to be "learned and then internalized, sometimes painfully" (ibid., p. 57).

In the eyes of authors such as Marquand the public domain – or, the term favoured by Habermas (1989), the public sphere – is not to be understood as a physical location, but as a certain 'quality' of social interaction. Marquand (2004, p. 4) thus refers to the public domain as a "set of activities" with its own norms and decision rules, and emphasises that relationships in the public domain are both different from the relationships "of love, friendship and personal connection" that characterise the private sphere, and from relationships of "buying and selling [and] interest and incentive" that characterise the domain of the market. So how might we understand the "norms and decision rules" that characterise the public sphere and what kind of activities are proper to this sphere? For an answer to these questions I turn to the work of Hannah Arendt, continuing ideas presented in Chapter 5.

Arendt on Action, Plurality, and Freedom

Arendt's philosophy centers on an understanding of human beings as *active* beings, that is, as beings whose humanity is not simply defined by their capacity to think and reflect but where being human has to do with what one *does*. Arendt (1958) distinguishes between three modalities of the active life (the '*vita activa*'): labour, work, and action. While labour is the activity that corresponds to the biological processes of the human body and is therefore exclusively focused on the maintenance of life, work has to do with the ways in which human beings actively transform their environments and through this create a world that is characterised by durability. Work is concerned with making and therefore "entirely determined by the categories of means and end" (Arendt, 1958, p. 143). Action, on the other hand, is an end in itself and its defining quality, so Arendt argues, is *freedom*.

For Arendt to act first of all means to take initiative, to begin something new, to bring something new into the world. Arendt (1977) characterises the human being as an *initium*: a "beginning and a beginner" (p. 170). Arendt (1958, p. 178) likens action to the fact of birth, since with each birth something 'uniquely new' comes into the world. Through what we do and say we actually *continuously* bring new beginnings into the world. "With word and deed," Arendt (1958, p. 176–177) writes, "we insert ourselves into the human world and this insertion is like a second birth." For Arendt action is intimately connected with freedom. She emphasises, however, that freedom should not be understood as a phenomenon of the will, that is, as the freedom to do whatever we choose to do, but that we should conceive of it as the freedom "to call something into being which did not exist before" (Arendt, 1977, p. 151). The subtle difference between "freedom as sovereignty" and "freedom as beginning" implies that freedom is not an 'inner feeling' or a private experience but something that is by necessity a public and hence a political phenomenon. That is why Arendt (1977, p. 146) writes that "the rasion d'etre of politics is freedom" and that "its field of experience is action."

Arendt (1977, p. 149) stresses again and again that freedom needs a "public realm" to make its appearance. Moreover, freedom only exists *in* action, which means that human beings are free – as distinguished from their "possessing the gift of freedom" – as long as they act, "neither before nor after" (ibid., p. 153). How can freedom appear? In order to understand Arendt's answer to this question it is crucial to see that 'beginning' is only half of what action is about, as everything depends on how others take up our initiatives. This is why Arendt writes that the agent is not an author or a producer, but a subject in the two-fold sense of the word, namely one who began an action and the one who suffers from and is literally subjected to its consequences. The basic idea of Arendt's understanding of action is therefore very simple: *we cannot act in isolation.* If I were to begin something but no one would respond, nothing would follow from my initiative and, as a result, my beginnings would not come into the world. *I* would not appear in the world. But if I begin something and others do take up my beginnings, I *do* come into the world, and in precisely this moment – but not before or after – I *am* free.

The 'problem,' however, is that others respond to our initiatives in ways that are unpredictable. We are, after all, always acting upon beings "who are capable of their own actions" (Arendt, 1958, p. 190). Although this frustrates our beginnings, Arendt (1958, p. 244) emphasises again and again that the "impossibility to remain unique masters of what [we] do" is at the very condition – and the *only* condition – under which our beginnings can come into the world. We can of course try to control the ways in which others respond to our beginnings, and Arendt acknowledges that it is tempting to do so. But if we were to do so, we would deprive other human beings of their opportunities to begin. We would deprive them of their opportunities to act, and hence we would deprive them of their freedom.

This means first of all that action in the Arendtian sense is therefore never possible in isolation. Arendt even goes so far as to argue that "to be isolated is to be deprived of the capacity to act" (Arendt, 1958, p. 188). In order to be able to act we therefore need others – others who respond to our initiatives and take up our beginnings. It also means that action is never possible without plurality. As soon as we erase plurality – as soon as we erase the otherness of others by attempting to control how they respond to our initiatives –we deprive others of their actions and their freedom, and as a result we deprive ourselves of our possibility to act, and hence of our freedom. This is why Arendt (1958, p. 8) concludes that plurality, that is, the situation in which difference is *not* reduced to sameness, "is the condition of human action."

"The Space Where Freedom Can Appear"

Along these lines Arendt provides us with a highly political understanding of freedom. This is not only because she sees freedom in terms of our appearance in the public realm – the *polis* – and not, as is the case in liberal political theory, as something that is ultimately private. It is also, and more importantly, because she shows that our freedom is fundamentally interconnected with the freedom of others, so that it is only under the condition of plurality that action becomes possible – unlike in the case of communitarian political theory where the assumption is that action is only possible on the basis of an underlying sameness, and underlying commonality. The suggestion that my freedom is contingent upon the freedom of everyone else, is not to be understood as an empirical observation, but is the normative 'core' of Arendt's philosophy. This is because Arendt is committed to a world in which *everyone* has the opportunity to act, to appear, and to be free.

One implication of this line of thinking is that for Arendt the public domain as the domain "in which freedom can appear" (Arendt, 1955, p. 4), should not be understood in physical terms, that is, as a certain *location*, but rather denotes a particular *quality* of human interaction. She writes:

> The *polis*, properly speaking, is not the city-state in its physical location; it is the organization of the people as it arises out of acting and speaking together, and its true space lies between people living together for this purpose, no matter where they happen to be. (...) It is the space of appearance in the widest sense of the word, namely, the space where I appear to others as others appear to me, where men [sic] exist not merely like other living or inanimate things but make their appearance explicitly. (Arendt, 1958, pp. 198–199)

Given that this "space of appearance" comes into being "when men [sic] are together in the manner of speech and action" (ibid., p. 199), it means that "unlike the spaces which are the work of our hands," that is, the spaces created through *work*, "it [the public sphere] does not survive the actuality of the movement which brought it into being, but disappears (...) with the disappearance or arrest of the activities themselves" (ibid., p. 199).

Arendt's explorations of the interrelationships between action, freedom, and plurality contain an important lesson for our understanding of the public sphere, as she shows that it is only under the condition of *plurality* that action is possible and freedom – that is, *democratic* freedom-as-beginning, not *liberal* freedom-as-sovereignty or communitarian freedom-as-sameness – can appear. She shows that as soon as we begin to reduce plurality, as soon as we begin to 'homogenise' and 'purify' public spaces by prescribing and policing what can be done and said in such spaces, by prescribing and policing what is 'proper' and what is 'deviant,' we begin to eradicate the very conditions under which action is possible and freedom can appear.

It is important to bear in mind, however, that a concern for the public quality of human togetherness, is not about the promotion of *any* plurality. For Arendt the question of public action – of acting-in-public, of acting in the presence of others – is not about a sheer plurality of individual initiatives but about what she refers to as 'acting in concert' (see also Benhabib, 1993). The question this raises is how acting in concert is possible "given the simultaneous presence of innumerable perspectives and aspects in which the common world presents itself and for which no common measurement or denominator can ever be devised" (Arendt, 1958, p. 57). While Arendt strongly rejects the (communitarian) idea that common action is only possible on the basis of total agreement, total consensus, or total sameness – that would, after all, destroy the very plurality that is the condition for action – she also maintains that common action is not possible on the basis of mere plurality. Common action, acting in concert, requires decision and hence deliberation and judgement about what is to be done. It requires, in other words, an orientation towards the common good rather than towards the pursuit of private agendas. But just as Arendt rejects what we might call pluralism-without-judgement, she also rejects judgement-without-plurality.

Arendt (1994) tries to capture what is at stake in keeping plurality in our common judgements with the idea of 'understanding.' Understanding, however, is not to be understood as "correct information and scientific knowledge" but is "an unending activity by which, in constant change and variation, we come to terms with, reconcile ourselves to reality, that is, try to be at home in the world" (Arendt, 1994, pp. 307–308). Common action under the condition of plurality is therefore not made possible through 'fraternity' – a common identity, or a cosmopolitan sense of sameness – but relies on the preservation of distance and strangeness. This requires the promotion of forms of human togetherness which are not after the establishment of a common ground but rather have an interest in the ongoing challenge of the 'achievement' of a common *world* (on this distinction see Gordon, 2001).

For the Public, of the Public, or in the Interest of Publicness?

If this gives an idea of how we might understand the idea of the public and, more specifically, the public quality of human togetherness, I turn, in a final step, to the question of pedagogy in order to ask what kind of educational 'work' can be done, what kind of pedagogy can be enacted in the interest of the public quality of our ways of acting and being together. Here I would like to suggest a distinction between three possible readings of the idea of public pedagogy. Each provides a different conception of what it means to make pedagogy public, so to speak, that is, to conduct intentional educational work 'in' the public sphere. (I put the word 'in' in quotation marks because the three conceptions of public pedagogy that I will distinguish think differently about this 'location' and thus about the connection between 'pedagogy' and 'public.') As I will make clear, in each case there is a pedagogue – someone who conducts intentional educational 'work' – but what distinguishes the three modes of public pedagogy lies precisely in what the public pedagogue *does*. Yet, this matters crucially for what public pedagogy as intentional educational work is able to achieve. Let me try to explain what I have in mind.

One way to think of public pedagogy is as a pedagogy *for* the public, that is, a pedagogy *aimed at* the public. The pedagogical form here is that of *instruction*. In this conception the world appears as a giant school and the main role of educational agents – of public pedagogues – is to *instruct* the citizenry. This involves telling them what to think, how to act and, perhaps most importantly, what to be. Such a form of public pedagogy is therefore ultimately orientated towards the erasure of plurality, and thus towards the erasure of the conditions for politics and freedom. We can see such a form of public pedagogy enacted whenever the state instructs its citizens to be something, for example, law-abiding, tolerant, respectful, or active – which the state either does directly or through its educational agents (for a critical discussion see Biesta, 2011e). In this mode of public pedagogy, we could say the pedagogue is teaching the citizenry a lesson, and putting it this way helps to see the moralistic undertones of this conception of public pedagogy, as it is ultimately aimed at the telling the citizenry how to behave. The problem with this form of public pedagogy has to do with the fundamental difference between the 'logic' of schooling and the 'logic' of democratic politics. From a democratic angle it is therefore important to remind ourselves that the world is not a school and also should not become a school (see Bingham & Biesta, 2010).

If the idea of public pedagogy as a form of instruction runs the risk of erasing the very plurality that is the condition for forms of human togetherness in which freedom can appear, then perhaps we need to approach the idea of public pedagogy in terms of learning rather than instruction. This is indeed a second interpretation of the idea of public pedagogy that can be reconstructed from the literature – an approach I wish to characterise as a pedagogy *of* the public, that is, done *by* the public itself. Here the pedagogical work is not done from the 'outside' so to speak – that is, by educational agents who instruct – but is located *within* democratic processes and practices (thus leading to an interest in the learning opportunities provided by such practices; see Van der Veen et al., 2007). The pedagogical 'mode' in this interpretation is that of collective *learning* or of what Paulo Freire has referred to as 'conscientization,' a process aimed at the generation of critical awareness and 'critical consciousness' (Freire, 1970). Here the world appears as a giant adult education class in which educational agents perform the role of facilitator. Unlike in the first interpretation of public pedagogy, the direction in which such processes move is not determined from the outset, but is part of what is 'at stake' in such processes of collective political learning.

While this interpretation of public pedagogy therefore connects much better to the idea of plurality, one limitation of this view is that it brings democracy under a 'regime' of learning and in the Freirean version this is a very particular kind of learning aimed at overcoming alienation from the world or restoring the mode of being in the world that Freire calls 'praxis' (see Freire, 1972; Galloway, 2012). Unlike what is often assumed, I wish to suggest that learning is not some kind of open and natural process that can go in any direction, but is rather a very particular and specific regime; a regime that demands a particular relation of the self to the self, that is, a relation of awareness, reflection and of drawing conclusions and acting upon them. In this sense one might say that the learning regime remains an educational regime, even if it occurs in anomalous places or in anomalous forms (Elsworth, 2004), because it comes with a demand that citizens learn. With regard to this there is not only the question whether there is anything to learn about democratic citizenship or whether the very point of democracy is that it is radically open towards the future. (I have explored this problem in more detail through the figure of the ignorant citizen; see Biesta, 2011b.) The demand for learning also makes visible the 'politics of learning' (Biesta, 2012, 2013b) at work in this understanding of public pedagogy, which is the tendency to turn social and political problems into learning problems so that, through this, they become the responsibility of *individuals* rather than that they are seen as the concern for and remain a responsibility of the collective.

The main motivation for the third reading of public pedagogy that I wish to offer here, is to move beyond such a regime so that public pedagogy can work at the *intersection* of education and politics, that is in the interest of the public's 'condition of plurality,' rather than that it works towards erasing the very conditions under which action is possible and freedom can appear. Instead of seeing public pedagogy as a pedagogy *for* the public or *of* the public, there is therefore a different interpretation possible and necessary, one where public pedagogy appears as an enactment of a concern for 'publicness,' that is, a concern for the public *quality* of human togetherness and thus for the possibility of actors and events to *become public*. Becoming public is not about a physical relocation from the home to the street or from the *oikos* to the *polis,* but about the achievement of forms of human togetherness – or, as I have put it elsewhere, forms of political *existence* (Biesta, 2010c) – in which action is possible and freedom can appear.

In this third 'mode' of public pedagogy, the educational 'work' does not take the form of instruction of the public or the facilitation of learning by the public, but becomes more activist, more experimental, and more demonstrative. It becomes more *activist* in that it is aimed at the creation of real alternatives, that is, alternative ways of being and doing – of 'acting in concert' – that reclaim opportunities for public relationships-in-plurality. It is, therefore, about the creation of ways of being and doing that, on the one hand, resist and 'push back' the logic of the market and that, on the other hand, resist and 'push back' incursions from the private sphere. Such work is always *experimental* as it is about the invention of new ways of being and doing – new ways of 'doing' economy, for example, not based on profit maximisation and exploitation but on solidarity and sustainability; new ways of 'doing' schooling, for example, not focused on individual advantage, competition and excellence, but orientated towards cooperation and the hard work of living together in plurality and difference – so as to reclaim public ways of acting in concert. That such forms of experimental activism in the interest of the public quality of human togetherness can be understood as forms of pedagogy is, so I wish to suggest, because they *demonstrate* that it is possible to do things differently; they demonstrate, against the often heard claim from politicians and policy makers that 'there is no alternative,' that there is *always* an alternative, that things not only *should* be done differently but actually *can* be done differently. It is in this sense that this third 'mode' of public pedagogy is a form of pedagogy – a pedagogy of demonstration – and not a curriculum that has to be taught or has to be learned. And it is a form of pedagogy that is entirely public, both in its orientation and in its execution.

Conclusion

In this chapter I have explored what it might mean for pedagogy to operate in the interest of the public quality of human togetherness. I have situated this question within a wider set of concerns about the erosion of the public sphere, and have, with the help Hannah Arendt, highlighted the connection between plurality, action and freedom. Against this background I have presented three possible interpretations of the idea of public pedagogy. The key issue with regard to each of them is whether they result in modes of educational work that *reduce* plurality or *promote* plurality. Whereas public pedagogy as a pedagogy *for* the public and as a pedagogy *of* the public tend to work towards reduction of plurality – either through instruction or through a demand for learning – the third form of public pedagogy works in the opposite direction, that is, towards pluralisation, and thus towards the promotion of the very conditions under which action is possible and freedom can appear.

Notes

1   An earlier version of this chapter was published as Biesta, G. J. J. (2014). Making pedagogy public: For the public, of the public, or in the interest of publicness? In J. Burdick, J. A. Sandlinm, & M. P. O'Malley (Eds.), *Problematizing public pedagogy* (pp. 15–25). New York, NY: Routledge.
2   The discussion is not helped by the fact that different authors use different concepts. I treat the notions of 'public domain' and 'public sphere' as equivalent. The idea of 'public space,' on the other hand, refers to physical locations and should therefore be distinguished from notions of public domain and public sphere also because one of the key questions in the discussion is to what extent public spaces can (still) be locations where public ways of human togetherness are possible.

Looking Back and Looking Forward

There is relatively little I would want to add to the preceding chapters. As clarified in the introduction, they contain ideas that were developed and published over the past fifteen years or so, and although I have since sharpened up my thinking, have added new themes and interests and have engaged in new areas of policy and practice, I still feel confident that the lines of thought brought together in this book speak to more enduring concerns and issues in education. Contemporary education has become even more entangled in global networks, particularly the networks of the global education measurement industry. This creates an ongoing pressure for education to adapt and perform, which makes it even more important for education not to just slip into a responsive mode, but to remain responsible for the educational interest in helping and encouraging the new generation to find a grown-up way of living their lives – in the world but not in the centre of it.

The globalisation of education also continues to impact on the curriculum, with an ongoing push towards the 'basics' and increasingly in many countries also to so-called 'powerful knowledge.' This is where a healthy scepticism about epistemological arguments around the curriculum is important, not in order to suggest that knowledge is 'just' a social construction and that, therefore, all knowledge is 'just' relative, but to see that what is presented as 'general' and therefore is often also presented as important and powerful, is in most cases an asymmetrical expansion of a particular local context. This doesn't diminish the value of knowledge, but keeps the wider societal picture into focus without succumbing to accusations of relativism that actually miss the point of what is going on. All this suggests that education has an important role to play in making the next generation wise, albeit that this is not just about becoming symbol-wise, that is, gaining an understanding of the connection between understanding, language and the world, but that there is an ongoing need for becoming world-wise, that is not just being able to navigate the world 'as it is' or (re)presents itself, but always remaining at a (critical) distance, always seeking for different ways of presenting, representing, and ordering the world.

Critique, critical thinking and being critical therefore remain important orientation points for education, though what I have tried to do in Chapter 4 is to scrutinise in detail what 'criticality' actually is, how it can manifest itself, how it can be enacted, and what would 'drive' all this. It is after all quite easy to say that students need to be critical or should develop critical thinking skills, but quite difficult to figure out what this exactly entails and how it can be justified. The distinction between three 'forms' of critique – critical dogmatism, transcendental critique and deconstruction – is in my view still a helpful 'frame' for ensuring that critique and critical thinking in education keep their critical 'edge' and are not made entirely 'safe' by being listed as, for example, just useful (21st century) skills. Philosophy, as I have explored in Chapter 5, can definitely contribute to this, but here again there is a danger that philosophy is made 'safe,' that it is turned into an instrument that can be applied 'at will.'

While philosophy can be used in this way, there is a danger that it doesn't really bring children and young people into contact with the world – a world that is not just there for them as an object for critical analysis, but perhaps first of all as a world that speaks, that addresses them and to which they are exposed, whether they want it or not. This is also important with respect to the relational dimensions of education – the topic of Chapter 6. Next to the fact that it is important that education doesn't become too relational, so to speak, but always keeps a place for that which limits or interrupts educational relations, I tend to think that the distinction between listening, recognition and being addressed as three ways in which students can get 'in touch' with the world, remains important, particularly if it is agreed that education ultimately needs to have a worldly orientation – world-centred rather than child-centred, student-centred or curriculum centred.

The notion of 'transclusion' is one of the ideas that has not been presented in published form before, although the underlying argument has been developed in related discussions. I am inclined to think that transclusion as a concept provides an interesting corrective to the work on inclusion which, although tremendously important, may sometimes forget that inclusion always requires a double move – not just including those who are 'outside' into an existing societal order, but always also working on the transformation of such orders so that inclusion is not just about acquiring existing identities but can truly be a process of subjectification.

The latter connects educational inclusion directly to questions of democracy, and what I've tried to do in Chapter 8 is to argue that despite its fame, Dewey's book *Democracy and Education*, and the wider theory he has developed about this, actually has little to offer where it concerns democracy as a *political* project. This is not to suggest that Dewey was not interested in democracy and democratisation but, as I have suggested, Dewey's real contribution here lies in his attempts at democratising rationality, reconnecting it to the broad spectrum of human endeavours and thus reclaiming it from the hegemony of modern science. This connects quite nicely with the main point made in the final chapter, where I have argued that if pedagogy wishes to be 'public,' it needs to keep an orientation on and a connection with the struggle for democracy, against attempts to domesticate it or replace it with scientism.

There are two points where my views have changed or where I would at least use a different vocabulary and would be more nuanced and perhaps also more precise in my writing. One, as already mentioned earlier on in this book, concerns the use of the idea of *Bildung*. I have increasingly come to the insight that *Bildung* belongs to the line of thinking that sees education as a process of the cultivation of the individual – which, in itself, is a useful and worthy dimension of education as cultivation equips individuals with cultural 'tools' (language, concepts, orientations, traditions, practices, and so on). But what I think is missing in the 'paradigm' of *Bildung* are the existential and political dimension, that is, the question how the self 'emerges' out of these processes, not as an 'acculturated organism' (Dewey), and also not as an individual with an identity, not even a self-identity, but as a subject – as some *one* who is not just responsive, to put it in the language of the first chapter, but can take on a responsibility or, to be more precise, can take on a responsibility for his or her responsibility, for the responsibility where the self 'encounters' himself or herself.

Here lies the difference between becoming symbol-wise and becoming-world wise; here lies the difference between empowerment and emancipation; here lies the difference between the human being as an identifiable 'thing,' and the being of the human being; here lies, in short, the difference between essence and existence. Whereas the 'paradigm' of *Bildung* is thus interested in the cultivation of the individual, the 'paradigm' of *Erziehung* is interested in how education can call, encourage, seduce the (cultivated) individual to be a subject in its own right, rather than remain an object of cultivation. Although there are many traces of the distinction between these two educational 'paradigms' throughout the chapters in this book, I probably needed to work my way through the discussions presented in them in order to gain clarity about the importance of this distinction – not just theoretically or philosophically, but first and foremost at the practical level of education itself. I would now see this as the existential 'turn' which I document more autobiographically in the appendix of this book.

The existential argument is most likely also how I would respond to recent discussions about posthumanism in education – and this is the second point – emphasising that the work of education is fundamentally *existential*. This existential orientation remains worth fighting for, particularly against all the attempts to deny that our existence as human beings is ultimately an existential matter that can never be replaced by knowledge about our genes, the brain, or anything else that may be offered as an 'escape' from the inescapable fact that each of us has his or her own life to live. To be obstinate about this very point, to resist all 'solutions' that distract from this inescapable fact, is the proper position for education to take – now more perhaps than ever.

From Experimentalism to Existentialism: Writing in the Margins of Philosophy of Education

Early Years: 1957–1990[1]

I was born in Rotterdam, the Netherlands, in 1957, twelve years after the end of the Second World War, and grew up in a city centre that was still largely empty as a result of the May 1940 bombings. My daily walk to school thus took me along many building sites and the sound of pile drivers was constantly in the background for many years to come. I cannot deny that I had an early fascination for education. As a child one of the first jobs I imagined I wanted to have, was that of an architect in order then to become a teacher of architects. While my (Montessori) kindergarten and (regular) primary school were rather easy and uneventful, secondary school turned out to be more challenging, so I only just managed to get through. As economics was one of the very few subjects in which I had done well, I decided to study it at university. I soon found out, however, that it was not really 'my' subject, so after a year I switched to theology. This was a much more enjoyable experience, but a rather serious car accident two years into my studies put an abrupt end to it. This put me in a position where I had to reconsider my options, and I decided to look for work rather than continuing at university. I found a job in a hospital and took courses to become a radiographer.

After I had obtained my diploma I had the good fortune of being asked to contribute to the teaching of radiographers. For the next 10 years I taught physics to student radiographers. In the first years I did this alongside my job as a radiographer, but after having completed a two year part-time teacher certification programme, I was eager to deepen my knowledge of education, so I decided to return to university, now to study education. Whereas in most English speaking countries the study of education tends to happen in the context of teacher education, in the Netherlands education – in Dutch: *pedagogiek* – exists as an academic discipline in its own right and it was this discipline that I focused on for the next four years at the University of Leiden. My initial plan was to specialise in curriculum and instruction, but I became increasingly interested in the theoretical and historical aspects of education, and thus decided to focus on this area instead.

It was here that I became interested in philosophy, first and foremost through the work of Ben Spiecker, Professor at the Free University Amsterdam, who had written a number of exciting essays on Wittgenstein and education. In the second year of my studies I followed an additional one year programme in philosophy. This covered the philosophical 'basics,' and I particularly enjoyed logic, epistemology, philosophy of science, and Greek philosophy, including a superb course on Aristotle. The third year in Leiden was devoted again to *pedagogiek*, although I was able to make connections with my developing interest in philosophy. Through courses from Vygotskij-specialist René van der Veer I became interested in Piaget's genetic epistemology, while Rien van IJzendoorn, stimulated my interested in the philosophy of educational and social research. Courses from Siebren Miedema not only fuelled my interest in critical theory (Habermas), critical pedagogy (both the German and the North American variety), and the theory and philosophy of educational and social research, but also brought me into contact with the work of John Dewey. Dewey's work had been largely absent from the educational conversation in the Netherlands since the early 1950s and had only received sporadic attention from Dutch philosophers. I eventually decided to write a Master's thesis on Dewey under Siebren's supervision.

I further pursued my interest in philosophy through a newly established programme in the philosophy of the social sciences at Erasmus University Rotterdam, which I started in my final year as a *pedagogiek* student, and finished successfully three years later. My studies not only allowed me to deepen my understanding of logic, epistemology and the philosophy of science, but also brought me into contact with analytic philosophy, phenomenology, existentialism, postmodern and post-structural philosophy (particularly the work of Foucault), and – just emerging at the time – the neo-pragmatism of Richard Rorty. Rorty's *Philosophy and the Mirror of Nature* (Rorty, 1979) formed the framework for the thesis I wrote, which focused on paradigmatic pluralism in educational research in the Netherlands. Whilst still studying philosophy, I was fortunate to receive a four year studentship to conduct PhD research on Dewey, focusing on his views about the relationship between knowledge and action and the implications for educational and social research. I conducted my PhD research at Leiden University under the supervision of Siebren Miedema and Rien van IJzendoorn. I worked closely with Siebren, particularly on the study of Dewey, and many of my early publications were co-authored with him, including a joint book (Miedema & Biesta, 1989). I obtained my PhD in 1992 (Biesta, 1992), but again was lucky in having been selected for a lectureship in education at the University of Groningen before I had finished my PhD. I thus started my academic career there in the summer of 1990, teaching courses in *pedagogiek* and in the philosophy of educational and social research.

An important aspect of the early years of my career was the fact that I did not develop my intellectual and academic identity within philosophy or philosophy of education, but within *pedagogiek*. That is why up to the present day I prefer to refer to myself as an educationalist (or in Dutch: a *pedagoog*) with a particular interest and expertise in philosophy, and not as a philosopher and only hesitantly as a philosopher of education – my hesitation having to do with the fact that 'philosopher of education' remains a rather imperfect translation of my identity as a *pedagoog* and my commitment to *pedagogiek*. The question of the differences between *pedagogiek* and philosophy of education has continued to intrigue me, and became even more of an issue when I moved from the Netherlands to the UK (in 1999) and was faced in very concrete ways with the differences between the Continental and the Anglo-American 'construction' of the field – something I have explored since in a number of publications (for example, Biesta, 2011a). This is why I have always felt to be working more in the margins of Anglo-American philosophy of education – and perhaps even more so with regard to the British variety than the one in North America – rather than at its centre.

The context in which I was a student of *pedagogiek* and philosophy was one of a rapid and radical transformation of the field of Dutch educational research and scholarship. If there was a 'Positivismusstreit' in educational research in the 1980s in the Netherlands – and I think there was – it was between two fundamentally different conceptions of empirical research, one that made a case for quantitative-explanatory research as the only properly scientific mode of research and one that tried to make a case for qualitative-interpretative research. The fact that quantitative-explanatory research – in the Dutch context often referred to as 'empirical-analytical' research – 'won,' is particularly significant when compared to developments in the English-speaking world. There the debate between 'quantitative' and 'qualitative' approaches was mainly about attempts from the side of qualitative approaches to overcome the hegemony of quantitative research so as to make a case for methodological pluralism. In the Netherlands, in contrast, there had actually been a long and flourishing tradition of interpretative research, particularly the phenomenology of the Utrecht School where, in the areas of education and developmental psychology, M.J. Langeveld was for a long time the leading figure.[2] In the Netherlands the debate thus went in the opposite direction, that is, of quantitative-explanatory research trying to replace qualitative-interpretative research. The 'Streit' that was going on in the Netherlands was not only a battle about the 'right' or 'proper' form of *empirical* research, but was also directed against non-empirical forms of inquiry. It was as a result of this that theoretical and philosophical traditions became increasingly marginalised. Over time this led to what, in hindsight and from a distance, I would characterise as an academic mono-culture that, unlike what I was going to experience in the UK, left little room for other forms of empirical research and for non-empirical modes of inquiry and scholarship.

The transformation of educational research in the Netherlands also brought with it a strong push towards internationalisation. This definitely had an impact on my own formation as a researcher since I was encouraged early on to make connections with researchers and scholars in other countries and, given my interest in Dewey, particularly in North America. In 1988, the first year of my PhD, I attended the AERA conference in New Orleans and visited the Centre for Dewey Studies in Carbondale, then under the directorship of Jo-Ann Boydston, who was extremely helpful in the early stages of my PhD research. Since Dewey's collected works had not yet all been published, and since this was well before the age of the internet, my visits to Carbondale, and also to archives at Teachers College Columbia University and the University of Chicago, provided me with access to unique materials for my PhD. They also formed the beginning of my networks in North America, a process in which the John Dewey Society was particularly important.

The Netherlands: 1990–1999

The years in Groningen were stimulating and enjoyable, not only because there was a group of supportive colleagues who were willing to put trust in a relatively inexperienced lecturer, but also because in my teaching I could focus on 'my' subject, that of *pedagogiek*. This allowed me to deepen my understanding of Continental educational theory (and here I would particularly highlight the work of Dutch educationalists such as M.J. Langeveld, Nic. Perquin, Ben Spiecker and Jan Dirk Imelman, and of German theorists such as Klaus Mollenhauer and Klaus Schaller), and also of the forerunners of North American critical pedagogy, particularly the 'social reconstructionism' of authors such as George Counts. My main task during the first two years in Groningen was the completion of my PhD. Part of the work I did was a more or less straightforward reconstruction of Dewey's views on the relationship between knowledge and action. Yet I did not want to present Dewey's ideas as 'just another philosophical position' that either could be adopted or rejected. There was much in Dewey that I considered to be important for the discussion about the status of social and educational research – a discussion that, at the time, was still strongly influenced by the work of Karl Popper. Yet what troubled me about Dewey was the metaphysical framework that seemed to come with his ideas, a framework that was clearly rooted in secular naturalism and ultimately went back to Darwinism (something which Dewey explicitly acknowledged in his autobiographical essay *From Absolutism to Experimentalism*; Dewey, 1984[1930]).

My concerns partly had to do with Darwinism itself, which I saw as a rather limited and ultimately limiting understanding of the human condition, and partly with the scientism it seemed to bring in through the backdoor, something which Max Horkheimer in his book *Eclipse of Reason* indeed had identified as the main problem of Deweyan pragmatism (Horkheimer, 1947). I eventually found a way to resolve these issues through a paper Dewey had written relatively late in his career – called Experience, Knowledge and Value: A Rejoinder (Dewey, 1991[1939]) – which was a response to essays written about his work published in *The Philosophy of John Dewey*, edited by Paul A. Schilpp. This paper helped me to identify the problem that had motivated Dewey's intellectual and political 'project,' and thus allowed me to provide a *pragmatic* reading of Dewey's work, that is, to see it as an attempt to address a problem rather than as the articulation of a philosophical position (see also Biesta, 2009a). I could show that Dewey's philosophy was actually motivated by a critique of scientism – that is, a critique of the idea that science is the only valid kind of knowledge – and a critique of a cognitive worldview in which it is assumed that knowledge is the only 'real' way in which we are connected to the world. That is why, in my reconstruction of Dewey's work, I made the case that 'crisis in culture' to which he was responding had to be understood as a crisis in *rationality*, and that his ultimate project was aimed at restoring rationality to all domains of human experience rather than to confine it to the domain of cognition or, even worse, to the domain of scientific knowledge.

What was particularly interesting about Dewey's work was that he was able to criticise the hegemony of scientific rationality without having to reject the technological and practical 'fruits' of what goes on under the name of 'science.' Dewey thus opened up a third way between a wholesale *rejection* of science on the one hand and a wholesale *acceptance* of science on the other. This became an important theme in my own thinking as it allowed for a much more precise critique of the hegemony of the scientific worldview and scientific rationality, and also a much more mature engagement with the possibilities and limitations of what goes on under the name of 'science.' This line of thought was further reinforced through my reading of Bruno Latour's *Science in Action* (Latour, 1987), an author whose work has continued to play an important role in my work on knowledge and the curriculum (for example Biesta & Miedema, 1990; Biesta, 2002, 2012a), well before a rather watered-down version of his ideas became fashionable as 'actor-network theory.' While over the years I have become increasingly critical of key-aspects of Dewey's work – particularly his views on democracy, which I have characterised as social more than as political (see Biesta, 2007a, 2010a), and the totalising tendencies in his conception of communication (see Biesta, 2010b) – I find Dewey's wider project still very valuable for an effective critique of contemporary forms of scientism (for example, Biesta, 2009b, 2011b).

During my work on the PhD I had increasingly become interested in the educational dimensions of pragmatism, particularly with regard to the theory of communication in Dewey's work, and this topic became a central interest in the years following my PhD. In the first paper I wrote on the topic (Biesta, 1994) I explored the relationships between critical theory (Habermas) and pragmatism (Dewey, Mead) around the idea of 'practical intersubjectivity.' Inspiration for this partly came from my own readings of Dewey, partly from the work of Hans Joas on Mead (see Joas, 1985), and also from Jan Masschelein's PhD thesis on Habermas, communication and education (Masschelein, 1987). I presented a first version at AERA in 1993. It was here that I met Jim Garrison – a meeting that formed the start of many important conversations about Dewey and pragmatism in the years to come. The paper was accepted for publication in *Educational Theory*, my first journal article in English. Jim Garrison subsequently invited me to contribute to a book he was editing on the new scholarship on Dewey, and in my contribution I further pursued my interests in the implications of Dewey's understanding of communication for education (Biesta, 1995a).

In 1993 I had moved from Groningen to the University of Leiden to take up a lectureship in the department where I had studied *pedagogiek* and done my PhD. Fairly soon after I had started the opportunity arose to apply for a senior lectureship in *pedagogiek* at the University of Utrecht. As this would allow me to focus more strongly on *pedagogiek* and work more closely with Jan Dirk Imelman in the theory of education and Brita Rang in the history of education, I decided to apply. My application was successful so I moved to Utrecht in the spring of 1995 (unfortunately Imelman took early retirement soon after I had arrived, and Rang left for a Professorship in Frankfurt). In the autumn of 1994 I had submitted an application for a Spencer Postdoctoral Fellowship with the National Academy of Education USA – encouraged and endorsed by Jim Garrison and Ben Spiecker – and early in 1995 I learned that I had been selected. For the next two academic years I was therefore able to spend a considerable amount of time on research. In hindsight I would say that these years were truly formative for the development of my academic 'habitus.' The project I had submitted extended my explorations of pragmatism to the work of George Herbert Mead. I spent part of the time in the Netherlands but also at

Virginia Tech with Jim Garrison. I also was able to study the George Herbert Mead papers at the University of Chicago. Here I discovered an unpublished set of lecture notes of a course Mead had given on the philosophy of education. I eventually managed to publish the lectures in English and in German translation, co-edited with Daniel Tröhler (Mead, 2008a, 2008b). The Spencer project led to the publication of a number of articles on Mead (Biesta, 1998, 1999) – who I actually found a stronger theorist than Dewey. 1994 was also the first year that I attended the annual conference of the Philosophy of Education Society USA, and I have returned almost every year up to the present day.

Perhaps the most significant event during my time as a Spencer postdoc was the invitation I received from Jim Marshall in New Zealand to contribute a chapter on Derrida in a collection he was editing. At the time I had only heard of Derrida, but never had had a chance to read his work properly. I told Jim that although I had no special knowledge of Derrida I would be very happy to take on the challenge. Jim took the risk and this set me off on a sustained period of reading. The encounter with Derrida's work had a profound impact on my thinking. Whereas up that point I had hoped that pragmatism could provide an 'answer' to the postmodern critique of the modern 'philosophy of consciousness' (Habermas) by replacing a consciousness-centred philosophy with a communication-centred philosophy, Derrida helped me to realise that the point was not to find a new and better starting-point or foundation for philosophy, but rather to question the very possibility of articulating and identifying such a foundation. Derrida also showed me, however, that the way out of this predicament was not to become anti-foundational – the route taken by Rorty and other anti-foundational (neo)pragmatists – as such a rejection of foundations would end up with the same problem, namely that it also had to rely on some fixed and secure place from which foundations could be rejected. What I found in Derrida was the suggestion that as soon as we go near a foundation – either to accept it or reject it or to use it as a criterion to identify performative contradictions – we find a strange oscillation between the foundation and its rejection; an oscillation that cannot be stopped. It is this oscillation that Derrida referred to as 'deconstruction,' thus highlighting that deconstruction isn't a method and cannot be transformed into one (Derrida, 1991, p. 273), but that it is something that occurs or, as he put it, "cannot manage to occur ... wherever there is something rather than nothing" (Derrida & Ewald, 2001, p. 67).

The work of Derrida not only helped me to put pragmatism in perspective but also made it possible to articulate more clearly some of the problems I always had had with metaphysical readings of pragmatism that would just end up as another form of foundationalism. I thus started to argue that we needed a more radical understanding of intersubjectivity (Biesta, 1999) and eventually came to the conclusion that the only possible pragmatism would thus be a deconstructive pragmatism, one that acknowledges that communication is always 'in deconstruction' (Biesta, 2010b). The encounter with Derrida also allowed me to create an opening in the discussion about critique – both in philosophy and in education – showing both the problem with dogmatic forms of critique that relied on a (fixed) criterion or a (fixed) truth about the human being, and with transcendental forms of critique that relied on a similar foundational gesture by highlighting the occurrence of performative contradictions, that is, contradictions between utterances and their conditions of possibility. With Derrida I could show that the latter form of critique – quite prominent in the educational literature on critical thinking – relied on the assumption that it is possible to identify conditions of possibility, whereas Derrida would argue that such a gesture would at the same time reveal conditions of *im*possibility and can therefore not achieve what it intends (and pretends) to achieve (see Biesta & Stams, 2001). The shift from critique to deconstruction was particularly significant in light of my interest in North American critical pedagogy. I had been following the important work of its main proponents – Henry Giroux and Peter McLaren – for a good number of years, and was now able to raise some more precise concerns about the question as to what it actually means to be critical in and 'for' education (see Biesta, 1998).

Derrida's work also helped me to see that the point of deconstruction was not negative or destructive, but thoroughly affirmative, not just of what is excluded but more importantly from what is excluded from a particular 'system' or 'order' and yet makes such a 'system' or 'order' possible. That meant that deconstruction is not just affirmative of what is known to be excluded, but also of what lies outside of what is (currently) conceptualisable – something to which Derrida in some of his writings referred to as the 'incalculable.' I slowly began to see that to prepare for the arrival of the incalculable could be seen as a thoroughly educational gesture (Biesta, 2001) and also began to connect Derrida's suggestion that the affirmative 'nature' of deconstruction means that deconstruction is (driven by) justice with educational concerns and themes (Biesta, 2003).

The final way in which the encounter with Derrida was important for my further trajectory had to do with the fact that Derrida did not position deconstruction in epistemological terms but rather put ethico-political considerations at the (de)centre of his writings. This helped me to articulate more clearly what I had always thought that the postmodern turn was after (see Biesta, 1995b), namely that it did not want to replace epistemological objectivism with epistemological relativism – a misreading of postmodern thought that goes on until the present day – but rather wanted to call for a shift from an epistemological worldview where knowledge of the world is the first and final 'thing,' towards an ethico-political 'attitude' that puts ethical and political concerns at the centre of our being-in-the-world and sees knowledge always in relation to and derivative of it, rather than that it founds ethics and politics on some deeper knowledge about the world and/or the human being. Derrida thus helped me to achieve (or perhaps I should say: complete) an ethico-political 'turn' that, in a sense, had always already been waiting in the wings of my writings. With regard to this 'turn' two other philosophers became increasingly important and influential, one being Hannah Arendt and the other – who I had already encountered early on in my career but whose thought needed time to 'arrive' – being Emmanuel Levinas.

Looking back, the seven years after finishing my PhD in 1992 allowed me to explore a number of different themes and issues and engage with a number of different theorists and philosophers, so as to eventually arrive at a position where I felt that I was beginning to find my own voice and my own trajectory. The next period of about seven years – culminating in the publication in 2006 of my first monograph, *Beyond Learning* (Biesta, 2006; to date published in Swedish, Danish and Portuguese) – allowed me to pursue a number of these lines more confidently. Whereas in the 1990s my interest had been more strongly philosophical, educational themes, issues and concerns began to become more central in my reading, writing and research. Two further important events happened during this period. One was meeting Bill Doll who introduced me to complexity theory and provided generous enthusiasm for my work during a period where I was still searching for its direction. Through Bill I met Denise Egéa-Kuehne. Our shared interest in Derrida let to the publication of the first book length study on his work and education, simply titled *Derrida & Education* (Biesta & Egéa-Kuehne, 2001). The other was the invitation from Jim Garrison to take over as editor-in-chief of *Studies in Philosophy and Education*. I started to work on this behind the scenes in 1999 and became the journal's next editor in 2001.

Although my job in Utrecht provided me with interesting opportunities and interesting colleagues – including Bas Levering who, at the time was one of the few people in the country who continued to work within a much broader tradition of educational research and scholarship with clear connections back to the Utrecht School – I increasingly felt the need for a different, more plural intellectual context. Having briefly considered a move to North America, I was lucky to find a job in England. In the autumn of 1999 I thus took up a senior lectureship at the University of Exeter.

England and Scotland: 1999–2012

My job in Exeter was designated as a senior lectureship in post-16 education, and thus had a clear focus on vocational and adult education. My teaching was partly connected to teacher education in those fields and partly involved working with teachers on masters and doctoral programmes. Unlike in the Netherlands, where universities are hierarchically structured and much time is spent making sure that everything has its 'proper' place – which creates difficulties for those individuals or areas of research that do not fit in such a system – what I encountered in Exeter was a much more open and much more horizontal academic culture where there was far less eagerness to tell others what they should do or be. This not only created a much greater degree of intellectual freedom but also made my own academic identity less fixed, which allowed me to pursue both theoretical-philosophical and empirical lines of work. I had the good fortune to work with Martin Bloomer, who eventually became Professor of Post-16 Education, and Rob Lawy, who had just started in Exeter as a postdoc. With Rob I began to develop my work on citizenship and democracy, resulting in a number of empirical studies on young people's citizenship (see, for example, Biesta, Lawy, & Kelly, 2009; Lawy et al., 2010) and more theoretical work on education, democracy and citizenship (for example Biesta, & Lawy, 2006; Lawy, & Biesta, 2006). The work on theory and policy of citizenship education and civic learning eventually ended up in a short book, published in 2011 (Biesta, 2011c – to date translated into Danish and Japanese).

Martin was key in developing my research interests in vocational education and adult education and generously involved me in a research proposal on learning and the life-course. The project was originally conceived as one on learning and identity; I suggested adding the theme of 'agency,' as I was interested in what people can do with their learning, rather than just who they become. Martin very sadly died in 2002, just after he had completed and submitted the proposal for what was to become the *Learning Lives* project (Biesta et al., 2011), still the first large-scale longitudinal study into learning, identity and agency in the life-course. At the time of his death, Martin was also co-directing a large scale study into the Further Education sector, called *Transforming Learning Cultures in Further Education* (see James & Biesta, 2007). I was asked to replace Martin on the project team. This not only meant that for the next 6 years I was strongly involved in major empirical projects working closely with a range of interesting and highly committed colleagues. It also brought me in touch with the overarching national research programme within which both projects were funded, the Teaching and Learning Research Programme (TLRP). All this work taught me a lot about the joys and the complexities of large-scale collaborative research, and provided a unique opportunity to connect with many educational researchers in the UK. Given my own predilections for theory and philosophy, these projects also convinced me of the need for the closer communication between empirical and theoretical work, rather than to think that theoretical – and perhaps even more so: philosophical – work should be conducted from the sideline, only referring to itself. My experiences not only showed me that such connections were *possible*, but also that they were *necessary* for the healthy development of the field of educational research.

In 2002 the University of Exeter promoted me to Professor of Educational Theory and soon afterwards I became Director of Research of the School of Education – a position that provided me with valuable insights in the running of higher education institutions and the more political dimension of higher education policy in the UK. Under the leadership of vice-chancellor Steve Smith Exeter developed a clear sense of direction, and it was enjoyable and instructive to experience the transformation of the university at a close distance. Although administration, empirical research and research management took a significant amount of my time, I was able to continue my theoretical and philosophical work as well. *Derrida & Education* (Biesta & Egéa-Kuehne, 2001) appeared in 2001 and *Pragmatism and Educational Research,* co-authored with Nick Burbules, in 2003 (Biesta & Burbules, 2003). For the development of my more theoretical work I benefitted tremendously from a visiting professorship at Örebro University, Sweden (from 2001 until 2008) followed by a similar post at Mälardalen University, Sweden (from 2006 until 2013). The focus of the work was on education and democratic citizenship and the many courses for doctoral students I taught there allowed me to explore key aspects of the discussion in detail with great students and great colleagues, particularly Tomas Englund and Carsten Ljunggren. The collaboration with Carl Anders Säfström had already started in the 1990s, and his move to Mälardalen University made it possible to establish an institutional basis for our collaboration. I had met Tomas and Carl Anders in the early 1990s when Siebren Miedema and I organised a small conference on pragmatism in Europe. Lars Løvlie, from Oslo University, was one of the other participants and he has been an ongoing source of support and inspiration throughout my career. Also significant were my yearly visits to the annual conference of the USA Philosophy of Education Society and the American Educational Research Association, particularly to participate in activities of the Philosophical Studies SIG, of which I became programme chair and, after that, chair, and the John Dewey Society (of which I was a board member).

Publication-wise, I was particularly pleased with the appearance of *Beyond Learning: Democratic Education for a Human Future* (Biesta, 2006), which I consider to be my first 'real' single-authored book. Theoretically the book took up a theme I had already been working on in the 1990s, namely the postmodern critique of humanism, often referred to as the issue of the 'death of the subject' (see Biesta, 1998). While in popular readings of postmodernism the theme of the death of the subject is often seen as a critique of the very idea of human subjectivity, the point I tried to convey in the book was that the critique was actually aimed at philosophical humanism, that is, at the idea that it is possible and desirable to identify the essence of the human being and use this knowledge as the foundation for a range of theoretical and practical 'projects,' including education and politics. In the book I not only showed the ways in which humanism had influenced modern educational thought and practice, but also argued how it had put limits on what education could achieve by basing education on a 'template' about what the human being is and thus of what the child should become.

In *Beyond Learning* I developed an alternative set of educational concepts that did not focus on the nature or essence of human beings but rather on their existence. More specifically I focused on the question how 'newcomers' might come 'into presence.' With the help of Hannah Arendt I suggested that coming into presence is ultimately a public and hence a political process in the literal sense of the word political, that is, as 'occurring in the polis,' in the presence of others who are not like us. That is why I eventually suggested that we should think of education in terms of how newcomers come 'into the world.' Education as 'coming into the world' not only gives educators a responsibility for the new beginnings, but also for the plural or 'worldly' quality of the world, as it is only 'under the condition of plurality' (Arendt) that everyone has a possibility to bring their beginnings into the world.

The other concept I put forward was that of 'uniqueness.' Taking inspiration from the work of Emmanuel Levinas and his translator Alphonso Lingis, I developed a distinction between *uniqueness-as-difference* – which is about our identity or essence, that is, about how I differ from others – and *uniqueness-as-irreplaceability*. The latter approach – which can be characterised as existential rather than essential – moves from the question as to what *makes* me unique to the question when my uniqueness *matters*, that is, the question when it matters that I am I and no one else. Such situations, so I suggested with the help of Lingis's idea of the community of those who have nothing in common (Lingis, 1994), are situations where an appeal is made to me, where I am being addressed by another human being, and where I cannot be replaced because the appeal is made to *me* – not just to anyone. These are situations where I am literally 'singled out' by a question, by a request, by an appeal. It is then still up to me whether I respond or not, that is, whether I take up the responsibility that is waiting for me, so to speak, and thus 'realise' my unique singularity, my singular existence in that particular moment.

My hope with thinking about education in existential terms was to make it possible again (that is, after the death of the subject), to make a distinction between education as socialisation and education orientated towards freedom, a dimension to which in later publications – particularly my 2010 book *Good Education in an Age of Measurement* (Biesta, 2010c) – I started to refer to as 'subjectification.' In a sense *Beyond Learning* became a 'turning point' in my career, not only because it brought together much of the work I had been doing in previous years but also because it set the agenda for much that was to follow, particularly an increasing focus on educational questions and issues and an ambition to engage with such questions in an educational way, that is, through the development of educational forms of theory and theorising.

In the next period of about seven years I thus turned increasingly to what I saw as key educational questions and issues, particularly questions concerning education, freedom and emancipation. Here – but only here (see Biesta, 2013a) – I found the work of Jacques Rancière helpful, as it made it possible to (re)turn to the question of emancipation in a way that was significantly different from how it had been engaged with in critical theory and critical pedagogy (see Biesta, 2010d). Together with Charles Bingham I published a book on Rancière's work (Bingham & Biesta, 2010) in which the question of emancipation was a central theme. Questions concerning the nexus of education, freedom and emancipation also were central in a short text I wrote with Carl Anders Säfström, which we published under the title A Manifesto for Education (Biesta & Säfström, 2011a). The Manifesto attracted a lot of attention in many countries, not only from academics but also from students and teacher. The first translation was actually published by a Norwegian teacher union (Biesta & Säfström, 2011b).

The other line that emerged during these years focused on educational policy and practice, particularly in order to show the extent to which and the ways in which educational issues were increasingly being sidelined, either by replacing an educational language with a language of learning – which was one of my reasons for arguing that in order to bring educational questions back into view we needed to go 'beyond learning' (see also Biesta, 2004, 2013b) – or by pushing education into a logic of production, that is, of predictable connections between educational 'inputs' and outputs.' One paper I published in relation to these tendencies focused on the shift from professional-democratic responsibility to technical-managerial accountability in education (Biesta, 2004). Another paper focused on the calls to turn education into an evidence-based profession (Biesta, 2007b – to date my most cited paper – and also Biesta, 2010e). The fact that both papers attracted quite a lot of attention,[3] gave me an indication that the topics were important and that some of my reflections were seen as relevant and helpful. This gave me the motivation to focus more explicitly and more 'positively' (rather than just critically) on questions of good education, that is, questions about what education should be like and aim for. I brought a number of the papers I wrote on this together in *Good Education in an Age of Measurement* (Biesta, 2010). In the book I continued with some of the main themes from *Beyond Learning*, but I put them in a wider perspective – partly by connecting them to developments in educational policy (accountability; evidence) and partly by taking a broader view on the functions and purposes of education, through a distinction between three domains of educational purpose: qualification, socialisation and subjectification (Biesta, 2010, chapter 1). While the distinction itself was simple, it proved to be a useful heuristic device for making discussions about what education is *for* more precise and concrete – which was also recognised by the fact that the book was rather quickly translated into a number of languages (to date into Swedish, Danish and Dutch).

The stronger focus on educational theory and policy was also supported by my move, in 2007, to the University of Stirling in Scotland. In the Teaching and Learning Research Programme projects I had worked closely and productively with two professors from Stirling, John Field and Richard Edwards, and when a position opened up in Stirling I decided to try my luck. I had five wonderful years in Stirling. Together with Julie Allan and other colleagues from the Institute of Education we tried to further the case for theory in education through the establishment of the Laboratory for Educational Theory. This was an exciting adventure albeit not without difficulties, partly because we were doing something new for which there was little (research) expertise available. We nonetheless managed to stir the discussion about theory a little, both nationally and internationally, through seminars and symposia, a number of international conferences and a doctoral summer school. We also managed to give the question of theory some prominence in ongoing discussions in the UK about research capacity building (Biesta, Allan, & Edwards, 2011) and brought together a group of international scholars in an edited volume on the theory question in education and the education question in theory (Biesta, Allen, & Edwards, 2014). Another fruitful collaboration in Stirling was with Mark Priestley and focused on curriculum research and theory, a field that particularly in England had led a marginal status since the introduction of the National Curriculum in the 1990s. The work with Mark resulted, amongst other things, in an edited collection on the new curriculum, analysing curriculum trends in Scotland against the background of wider international developments (Priestley & Biesta, 2013).

Three significant other events during my time in Scotland were the publication of a short, edited book on complexity and education (Osberg & Biesta, 2010), on which I worked with Deborah Osberg, with whom I had already published a number of papers on the topic. Unlike much literature on complexity and education we particularly tried to highlight the political dimensions, potential and implications of thinking education through complexity. Through the efforts of Maria de Bie of the University of Ghent and Danny Wildemeersch at the University of Leuven I was, in 2011, awarded the International Interuniversity Francqui Professorship by the Francqui Foundation in Belgium. This allowed me to spend about half a year at the University of Ghent in the spring of 2011 to work with colleagues from Ghent and Leuven on questions concerning education, social work, democracy and citizenship. This was another project that proved the importance of connecting theoretical and empirical work and really helped to push my own thinking on the topics forward, and probably did the same with many of the people involved in the activities around the chair (see Biesta, De Bie, & Wildemeersch, 2013). The greatest recognition I received from my peers was my election as president of the USA Philosophy of Education Society for 2011–2012 – the first president of the society from outside of North America. One of the prerogatives of the president is to invite the speaker for the Kneller Lecture (a lecture at the society's annual conference sponsored by an endowment from George F. Kneller). I was extremely grateful that John D. Caputo accepted my invitation, not only because of his standing as a philosopher but also because his scholarship has had a significant impact on my own work. Caputo also provided inspiration for the title and some of the content of the book in which I brought together much of my most recent work on education, namely *The Beautiful Risk of Education* (Biesta, 2013c – with a translation in Danish on its way).

Luxembourg: 2013 and Beyond

At the time of writing, my latest – and quite likely to be last – job move is still in its initial stages.[4] After working for nearly 14 years in the UK I felt a need to (re)turn to the continent, partly because over the years I had come to realise how strongly my work and my academic identity has been shaped by Continental philosophy and educational theory, and partly out of curiosity for a very different institutional, intellectual and linguistic environment. I was lucky to be selected for the post of Professor of Educational Theory and Policy at the University of Luxembourg (a tri-lingual university), which will allow me to concentre on two areas that, over the years, have indeed become central in my work. What Luxembourg will bring lies in the future, but there are still a number of issues I wish to pursue, not only because they are important for me but also because I sense that they can be important for the direction in which educational research and practice seem to be moving internationally.

I see myself not only getting further away from the discourse of learning, but also turning increasingly towards teaching. An essay I recently published – Giving teaching back to education (Biesta, 2012b) – provides an indication of work that still needs to be done here. The distinction I operate with in the essay – between 'learning from' and 'being taught by' – not only has important practical implications for how we think about teaching and how we might do it, but also has a wider theoretical potential as it provides two very different ways of thinking about the way we are in the world with others: one where we see others as resources for our own growth and development and one where others are addressing us and where this address (literally) 'opens up' opportunities for a very different way of being human. The distinction between 'learning from' and 'being taught by' is therefore not just a micro-matter for how teachers and students might conduct themselves in the classroom, but hints at much wider ethical, political, existential and educational themes and issues. My more recent collaborations with Herner Sæverot from the University of Bergen and with colleagues from NLA University College in Bergen are particularly important in the exploration of the existential dimensions of these challenges.

There are two further aspects of the 'turn' towards teaching that require further work. One has to do with the educational significance of the experience of resistance – the resistance of the material world and the resistance of the social world – and suggests a need to return to the rather old educational theme of the education of the will, that is, the question how the will can come to a 'worldly' form (Biesta, 2012c; see also Meirieu, 2007). The other concerns the need for the development of an informed critique of constructivism and the articulation of a viable alternative, so that we can understand what it means to know no longer just in terms of (our own) constructions but also, and perhaps first of all, in terms of reception, that is, as something that is given to us. This is a line with many theoretical, philosophical and political challenges, but nonetheless important in order to challenge what seems to have become a new 'dogma' of contemporary education. A further theme has to do with developing a critical understanding of the transformation of the field of educational research and scholarship, also in order to be able to interrupt the ongoing rise of an Anglo-American definition of educational research and scholarship – one that is increasingly marginalising other, what we might call 'indigenous' forms of theory and research in education. And if I can find the time, I would also like to explore in more depth the educational significance of the idea of 'metamorphosis,' particularly to challenge the dominance of linear modes of thinking and doing that seem to suggest that we just need to start earlier and earlier with our educational 'interventions' – a way of thinking that puts an enormous amount of unwarranted pressure on (young) children and their teachers.

What might emerge from all this (and in a sense is already emerging from it) is a conception of education that is thoroughly 'world-centred' – an education for 'earthlings' (Lingis, 1994, p. 117), we might say – which is focused on the possibilities for 'newcomers' to exist in the world with others who are not like them. Questions about subjectivity, freedom, emancipation, and democracy are likely to play an important role in this wider ambition, as will be the question of the education of teachers in a world that seems to want to take all that matters educationally out of education in order to turn it into the risk-free production of pre-specified identities and learning outcomes.

Finally: the title of this chapter is an attempt to capture my intellectual and scholarly trajectory. This trajectory started with pragmatism, and I have indicated the ways in which I am still indebted to pragmatism. But the encounter with philosophers such as Derrida, Arendt, and Levinas and with educational thinkers such as Langeveld, Mollenhauer, and Meirieu, has convinced me that the most important challenge for education today lies in the question how we can be 'at home in the world,' as Arendt so beautifully has put it. This, as I have come to realise, is ultimately not a matter of theory or philosophy but a matter of existence, so that there is the ongoing challenge not to let theory and philosophy get in the way of life, not to let it get in the way of what matters and what should matter most in our existence as 'earthlings.'

Acknowledgement

This chapter is dedicated to my wife and children. They have without doubt taught me most about what education is and what it ought to be about.

Notes

1   This appendix previously appeared as Biesta, G. J. J. (2014). From experimentalism to existentialism: Writing from the margins of philosophy of education. In L. Waks (Ed.), *Leaders in philosophy of education. Volume II* (pp. 13–30). Rotterdam, The Netherlands: Sense Publishers.

2 While it is too much to say that the Utrecht School went into exile, it is interesting to note that, particularly through the efforts of Max van Manen in Canada, the
   phenomenological tradition of the Utrecht School is still alive in North America but
   definitely not in its country of origin.

3 At the time of writing (June 2013) they appear as the 1st and 3rd most quoted paper
   of the journal Educational Theory over the last 10 years – see Harzing's Publish or
   Perish.

4 Unfortunately, the time in Luxembourg turned out to be rather short. Although I
   was keen to get closer to the continent *intellectually*, I was ill-prepared for the very
   different academic culture I encountered there – an academic culture, moreover, that was still in the process of inventing itself through an amalgamation of
   German, French, Anglo-American and indigenous traditions, cultures, ways of working, doing and communicating. Form a distance, it was a remarkable experience to
   see how difficult the meeting of (academic) cultures can be. Personally, I can only say
   that it took me many years to recover from what I encountered there. I was fortunate
   to find employment in England (at Brunel University London), an academic culture
   I could 'read' and navigate. In addition I ended up with an endowed chair for one day
   a week at the University of Humanistic Studies in the Netherlands, which did allow
   me to focus more explicitly on continental traditions of educational thought and
   practice. In 2014 I was also invited to join the Education Council of The Netherlands
   (Onderwijsraad) as associate member which meant that from 2014 until 2018 I was
   closely involved in advising the Dutch government and parliament on educational
   matters. My own perception of this work was that theory and history are actually
   of crucial importance for policy, not least because they help to keep a wider and
   longer-term perspective. In addition to becoming associate editor of the journal *Educational Theory*, I also became co-editor, in 2018, of the *British Educational Research
   Journal*, the 'flagship' journal of the British Educational Research Association. At the
   time of writing these sentences I am in the process of consolidating my 'portfolio' of
   activities which, in addition to the editorships, will include a new part-time appoint-
   ment as Professor of Public Education at Maynooth University Ireland, a Professorial
   Fellowship at the University of Edinburgh, and a visiting professorship (Professor
   II) at the University of Agder, Norway. I will not make any further predictions about
   what the future will hold, but hope to be able to use the coming years for some further contributions in the domain of educational theory, broadly conceived.

Publications That Have Been Important for My Own Work

Arendt, H. (1958). *The human condition.* Chicago, IL: The University of Chicago Press.
Bauman, Z. (1993). *Postmodern ethics.* Cambridge, MA: Basil Blackwell.

Caputo, J. D. (2006). *The weakness of God: A theology of the event*. Bloomington, IN: Indiana University Press.

Derrida, J. (1976). *Of grammatology*. Baltimore, MD & London: Johns Hopkins University Press.

Dewey, J. (1929). *The quest for certainty: A study of the relation of knowledge and action*. New York, NY: Minton Balch & Company.

Latour, B. (1987). *Science in action*. Cambridge, MA: Harvard University Press.

Levinas, E. (1981). *Otherwise than being or beyond essence*. The Hague: Martinus Nijhoff.

Meirieu, P. (2007). *Pédagogie: Le devoir de résister*. Issy-les-Moulineaux: ESF éditeur.

Mollenhauer, K. (1964). *Erziehung und Emanzipation* [Education and emancipation.] Weinheim: Juventa.

Mollenhauer, K. (1983). *Vergessene Zusammenhänge. Über Kultur und Erziehung* [Forgotten connections: On culture and education]. München: Juventa.

Rorty, R. (1979). *Philosophy and the mirror of nature*. Princeton, NJ: Princeton University Press.

Some Key Publications

Biesta, G. J. J. (2006). *Beyond learning. Democratic education for a human future*. Boulder, CO: Paradigm Publishers.

Biesta, G. J. J. (2007). Why 'what works' won't work. Evidence-based practice and the democratic deficit of educational research. *Educational Theory, 57*(1), 1–22.

Biesta, G. J. J. (2010). *Good education in an age of measurement: Ethics, politics, democracy*. Boulder, CO: Paradigm Publishers.

Biesta, G. J. J. (2012). Giving teaching back to education. *Phenomenology and Practice, 6*(2), 35–49.

Biesta. G. J. J. (2014). *The beautiful risk of education*. Boulder, CO: Paradigm Publishers.

References

Biesta, G. J. J. (1992). *John Dewey: Theory & Praktijk*. Delft: Eburon.

Biesta, G. J. J. (1994). Education as practical intersubjectivity. Towards a critical-pragmatic understanding of education. *Educational Theory, 44*(3), 299–317.

Biesta, G. J. J. (1995a). Pragmatism as a pedagogy of communicative action. In J. Garrison (Ed.), *The new scholarship on John Dewey* (pp. 105–122). Dordrecht/Boston/London: Kluwer Academic Publishers.

Biesta, G. J. J. (1995b). Postmodernism and the repoliticization of education. *Interchange, 26*, 161–183.

Biesta, G. J. J. (1998). Pedagogy without humanism. Foucault and the subject of education. *Interchange, 29*(1), 1–16.

Biesta, G. J. J. (1999). Radical intersubjectivity. Reflections on the "different" foundation of education. *Studies in Philosophy and Education, 18*(4), 203–220.

Biesta, G. J. J. (2001). "Preparing for the incalculable." Deconstruction, justice and the question of education. In G. J. J. Biesta & D. Egéa-Kuehne (Eds.), *Derrida & education* (pp. 32–54). London & New York, NY: Routledge.

Biesta, G. J. J. (2002). How general can Bildung be? Reflections on the future of a modern educational ideal. *British Journal of Philosophy of Education, 36*(3), 377–390.

Biesta, G. J. J. (2003). Jacques Derrida. Deconstruction = Justice. In M. Peters, M. Olssen, & C. Lankshear (Eds.), *Futures of critical theory: Dreams of difference* (pp. 141–154). Lanham, MD: Rowman and Littlefield.

Biesta, G. J. J. (2004). Against learning. Reclaiming a language for education in an age of learning. *Nordisk Pedagogik, 23*, 70–82.

Biesta, G. J. J. (2006). *Beyond learning. Democratic education for a human future.* Boulder, CO: Paradigm Publishers.

Biesta, G. J. J. (2007a). Education and the democratic person: Towards a political understanding of democratic education. *Teachers College Record, 109*(3), 740–769.

Biesta, G. J. J. (2007b). Why 'what works' won't work. Evidence-based practice and the democratic deficit of educational research. *Educational Theory, 57*(1), 1–22.

Biesta, G. J. J. (2009a). How to use pragmatism pragmatically: Suggestions for the 21st century. In A. G. Rud, J. Garrison, & L. Stone (Eds.), *John Dewey at 150. Reflections for a new century* (pp. 30–39). Lafayette, IN: Purdue University Press.

Biesta, G. J. J. (2009b). What kind of citizenship for European Higher Education? Beyond the competent active citizen. *European Educational Research Journal, 8*(2), 146–157.

Biesta, G. J. J. (2010a). "The most influential theory of the century." Dewey, democratic education and the limits of pragmatism. In D. Troehler, T. Schlag, & F. Osterwalder (Eds.), *Pragmatism and modernities* (pp. 197–213). Rotterdam, The Netherlands: Sense Publishers.

Biesta, G. J. J. (2010b). "This is my truth, tell me yours." Deconstructive pragmatism as a philosophy for education. *Educational Philosophy and Theory, 42*(7), 710–727.

Biesta, G. J. J. (2010c). *Good education in an age of measurement: Ethics, politics, democracy.* Boulder, CO: Paradigm Publishers.

Biesta, G. J. J. (2010d). A new 'logic' of emancipation: The methodology of Jacques Rancière. *Educational Theory, 60*(1), 39–59.

Biesta, G. J. J. (2010e). Why 'what works' still won't work. From evidence-based education to value-based education. *Studies in Philosophy and Education, 29*(5), 491–503.

Biesta, G. J. J. (2011a). Disciplines and theory in the academic study of education: A comparative analysis of the Anglo-American and continental construction of the field. *Pedagogy, Culture and Society, 19*(2), 175–192.

Biesta, G. J. J. (2011b). How useful should the university be? On the rise of the global university and the crisis in higher education. *Qui Parle: Critical Humanities and Social Sciences, 20*(1), 35–47.

Biesta, G. J. J. (2011c). *Learning democracy in school and society: Education, lifelong learning and the politics of citizenship.* Rotterdam, The Netherlands: Sense Publishers.

Biesta, G. J. J. (2012a). Knowledge/Democracy. Notes on the political economy of academic publishing. *International Journal of Leadership in Education, 15*(4), 407–420.

Biesta, G. J. J. (2012b). Giving teaching back to education. *Phenomenology and Practice, 6*(2), 35–49.

Biesta, G. J. J. (2012c). The educational significance of the experience of resistance: Schooling and the dialogue between child and world. *Other Education, 1*(1), 92–103.

Biesta, G. J. J. (2013a, April 9–11). *Don't be fooled by ignorant schoolmasters.* Presentation at the Discourse, Power and Resistance 2013 Conference, London.

Biesta, G. J. J. (2013b). Interrupting the politics of learning. *Power and Education, 5*(1), 4–15.

Biesta. G. J. J. (2014). *The beautiful risk of education.* Boulder, CO: Paradigm Publishers.

Biesta, G. J. J., Allan, J., & Edwards, R. G. (2011). The theory question in research capacity building in education: Towards an agenda for research and practice. *British Journal of Educational Studies, 59*(3), 225–239.

Biesta, G. J. J., Allan, J., & Edwards, R. G. (Eds.). (2014). *Making a difference in theory: The theory question in education and the education question in theory.* London & New York, NY: Routledge.

Biesta, G. J. J., De Bie, M., & Wildemeersch, D. (Eds.). (2013). *Civic learning, democratic citizenship and the public sphere.* Dordrecht & Boston, MA: Springer Science+Business Media.

Biesta, G. J. J., & Burbules, N. (2003). *Pragmatism and educational research.* Lanham, MD: Rowman and Littlefield.

Biesta, G. J. J., & Egéa-Kuehne, D. (Eds.). (2001). *Derrida & Education.* London & New York, NY: Routledge.

Biesta, G. J. J., Field, J., Hodkinson, P., Macleod, F. J., & Goodson, I. F. (2011). *Improving learning through the lifecourse: Learning lives.* London & New York, NY: Routledge.

Biesta, G. J. J., & Lawy, R. S. (2006). From teaching citizenship to learning democracy. Overcoming individualism in research, policy and practice. *Cambridge Journal of Education, 36*(1), 63–79.

Biesta, G. J. J., Lawy, R. S., & Kelly N. (2009). Understanding young people's citizenship learning in everyday life: The role of contexts, relationships and dispositions. *Education, Citizenship and Social Justice, 4*(1), 5–24.

Biesta, G. J. J., & Miedema, S. (1990). Pedagogy of science: The contribution of pedagogy to the philosophy of science. *Phenomenology and Pedagogy, 8*, 118–129.

Biesta, G. J. J., & Säfström, C. A. (2011a). A manifesto for education. *Policy Futures in Education, 9*(5), 540–547.

Biesta, G. J. J., & Säfström, C. A. (2011b). Et manifest for utdanning. *Første Steg, 3*, i–iv.

Bingham, C., & Biesta, G. J. J. (2010). *Jacques Rancière: Education, truth, emancipation.* London & New York, NY: Continuum.

Biesta, G. J. J., & Stams, G. J. J. M. (2001). Critical thinking and the question of critique. Some lessons from deconstruction. *Studies in Philosophy and Education, 20*(1), 57–74.

Derrida, J. (1991). Letter to a Japanese friend. In P. Kamuf (Ed.), *A Derrida reader* (pp. 270–276). New York, NY: Columbia University Press.

Derrida, J., & Ewald, F. (2001). "A certain 'madness' must watch over thinking." Jacques Derrida's interview with François Ewald, trans. Denise Egéa-Kuehne. In G. J. J. Biesta, & D. Egéa-Kuehne (Eds.), *Derrida & education* (pp. 55–76). London & New York, NY: Routledge.

Dewey, J. (1984[1930]). From absolutism to experimentalism. In J. A. Boydston (Ed.), *John Dewey. The later works, 1925–1953. Volume 5: 1929–1930* (pp. 147–160). Carbondale & Edwardsville, IL: Southern Illinois University Press.

Dewey, J. (1991[1939]). Experience, knowledge, and value: A rejoinder. In J.-A. Boydston (Ed.), *John Dewey. The later works* (1925–1953), *Volume 14: 1939–1941* (pp. 3–90). Carbondale & Edwardsville, IL: Southern Illinois University Press.

Horkheimer, M. (1947). *Eclipse of reason.* New York, NY: Oxford University Press.

James, D., & Biesta, G. J. J. (2007). *Improving learning cultures in Further Education.* London: Routledge.

Joas, H. (1985). *George Herbert Mead: A contemporary re-examination of his thought.* Cambridge: Polity Press.

Latour, B. (1987). *Science in action.* Cambridge, MA: Harvard University Press.

Lawy, R. S., & Biesta, G. J. J. (2006). Citizenship-as-practice: the educational implications of an inclusive and relational understanding of citizenship. *British Journal of Educational Studies, 54*(1), 34–50.

Lawy, R. S., Biesta, G. J. J., McDonnell, J., Lawy, H., & Reeves, H. (2010). The art of democracy. *British Educational Research Journal, 36*(3), 351–365.

Lingis, A. (1994). *The community of those who have nothing in common.* Bloomington, IN: Indiana University Press.

Masschelein, J. (1987). *Communicatief handelen en pedagogisch handelen* [Communicative action and educational action] (PhD thesis). KU Leuven, Leuven.

Mead, G. H. (2008a). *Philosophie der Erziehung* (Herasugegeben und eingeleitet von Daniel Tröhler und Gert Biesta). Bad Heilbrunn: Verlag Julius Klinkhardt.

Mead, G. H. (2008b). *The philosophy of education* (Edited and introduced by Gert Biesta and Daniel Tröhler). Boulder, CO: Paradigm Publishers.

Meirieu, P. (2007). *Pédagogie: Le devoir de résister.* Issy-les-Moulineaux: ESF éditeur.

Miedema, S., & Biesta, G. J. J. (1989). *Filosofie van de Pedagogische Wetenschappen* [Philosophy of the educational sciences]. Leiden: Martinus Nijhoff.

Osberg, D. C., & Biesta, G. J. J. (Eds.). (2010). *Complexity theory and the politics of education*. Rotterdam, The Netherlands: Sense Publishers.

Priestley, M., & Biesta, G. J. J. (Eds.). (2013). *Reinventing the curriculum. New trends in curriculum policy and practice*. London: Bloomsbury.

Rorty, R. (1979). *Philosophy and the mirror of nature*. Princeton, NJ: Princeton University Press.

References

Albert, H. (1985). *Treatise on critical reason.* Princeton, NJ: Princeton University Press.

Alston, K. (1995). Begging the question: Is critical thinking biased? *Educational Theory,* 45(2), 225–233.

Andreotti, V. (2011). *Actionable postcolonial theory in education.* New York, NY: Palgrave MacMillan.

Apel, K.-O. (1973). *Transformation der Philosophie.* Frankfurt am Main: Suhrkamp.

Apel, K.-O. (1976). The transcendental conception of language-communication and the idea of a first philosophy: Towards a critical reconstruction of the history of philosophy in the light of language philosophy. In H. Parret (Ed.), *History of linguistic thought and contemporary linguistics* (pp. 32–61). Berlin: De Gruyter.

Apel, K.-O. (1980). *Towards a transformation of philosophy.* London: Routledge & Kegan Paul.

Apel, K.-O. (1987a). The problem of philosophical foundations in light of a transcendental pragmatics of language. In K. Baynes, J. Bohman, & T. McCarthy (Eds.), *After philosophy. End or transformation?* (pp. 250–290). Cambridge, MA: MIT Press.

Apel, K.-O. (1987b). Falllibilismus, Konsenstheorie der Wahrheit und Letztbegündung. In Forum für Philosophie (Eds.), *Philosophie und Begründung* (pp. 116–211). Frankfurt am Main: Suhrkamp.

Apple, M. (1979). *Ideology and curriculum.* London: Routledge Kegan Paul.

Apple, M. W. (1986). *Cultural politics and education.* New York, NY: Teachers College Press.

Apple, M. (1993). *Official knowledge: Democratic education in a conservative age.* London & New York, NY: Routledge.

Apple, M. (2004). *Ideology and the curriculum* (3rd ed.). New York, NY & London: RoutledgeFalmer.

Arcilla, R. V. (1995). *For the love of perfection.* London & New York, NY: Routledge.

Arendt, H. (1955). *Men in dark times.* New York, NY: Harcourt, Brace, Jovanovich.

Arendt, H. (1958). *The human condition.* Chicago, IL: The University of Chicago Press.

Arendt, H. (1977). *Between past and future: Eight exercises in political thought.* Harmondsworth: Penguin Books.

Arendt, H. (1994). Understanding and politics (the difficulties of understanding). In H. Arendt & J. Kohn (Eds.), *Essays in understanding 1930–1954* (pp. 307–327). New York, NY: Harcourt, Brace and Company.

Bailey, C. (1984). *Beyond the present and the particular: A theory of liberal education.* London: Routledge & Kegan Paul.

Ballauff, T., & Schaller, K. (1970). *Pädagogik: Eine Geschichte der Bildung und Erziehung, Band II: Vom 16. Jahrhundert bis zum 19. Jahrhundert.* Freiburg im Breisgau: Alber.

Bauman, Z. (1992). *Intimations of postmodernity.* London & New York, NY: Routledge.

Bauman, Z. (1993). *Postmodern ethics*. Cambridge, MA: Basil Blackwell.

Bauman, Z. (1998). De risico's van de 'Risikogesellschaft.' In R. Munters (Ed.), *Zygmunt Bauman: Leven met veranderlijkheid, verscheidenheid en onzekerheid* (pp. 48–72). Amsterdam: Boom.

Bauman, Z. (2000). *Liquid modernity.* Cambridge: Polity Press.

Benhabib, S. (1993). Feminist theory and Hannah Arendt's concept of public space. *History of the Human Sciences, 6*(2), 97–114.

Benhabib, S. (1996). Toward a deliberative model of democratic legitimacy. In S. Benhabib (Ed.), *Democracy and difference* (pp. 67–94). Princeton, NJ: Princeton University Press.

Bennington, G. (1993). Derridabase. In G. Bennington & J. Derrida (Eds.), *Jacques Derrida.* Chicago, IL & London: The University of Chicago Press.

Bhabha, H. (1994). *The location of culture.* London & New York, NY: Routledge.

Biesta, G. J. J. (1995a). Opvoeding en intersubjectiviteit: Over de structuur en identiteit van de pedagogiek van John Dewey. *Comenius, 15*(2), 21–36.

Biesta, G. J. J. (1995b). Postmodernism and the re-politicisation of education. *Interchange, 26*(2), 161–183.

Biesta, G. J. J. (1998a). Say you want a revolution ... Suggestions for the impossible future of critical pedagogy. *Educational Theory, 48*(4), 499–510.

Biesta, G. J. J. (1998b). Pedagogy without humanism: Foucault and the subject of education. *Interchange, 29*(1), 1–16.

Biesta, G. J. J. (1999a). The right to philosophy of education. From critique to deconstruction. In S. Tozer (Ed.), *Philosophy of education 1998* (pp. 76–484). Urbana-Champaign, IL: Philosophy of Education Society.

Biesta, G. J. J. (1999b). Radical intersubjectivity. Reflections on the "different" foundation of education. *Studies in Philosophy and Education, 18*(4), 203–220.

Biesta, G. J. J. (2001). "Preparing for the incalculable." Deconstruction, justice and the question of education. In G. J. J. Biesta & D. Egéa-Kuehne (Eds.), *Derrida & education* (pp. 32–54). London & New York, NY: Routledge.

Biesta, G. J. J. (2004). "Mind the gap!" Communication and the educational relation. In C. Bingham & A. M. Sidorkin (Eds.), *No education without relation* (pp. 11–22). New York, NY: Peter Lang.

Biesta, G. J. J. (2005). What can critical pedagogy learn from postmodernism? Further reflections on the impossible future of critical pedagogy. In I. Gur Ze'ev (Ed.), *Critical Theory and critical pedagogy today. Toward a new critical language in education* (pp. 13–159). Haifa: Haifa Studies in Education/University of Haifa.

Biesta, G. J. J. (2006a). *Beyond learning: Democratic education for a human future.* Boulder, CO: Paradigm Publishers.

Biesta, G. J. J. (2006b). "Of all affairs, communication is the most wonderful." Education as communicative praxis. In D. T. Hansen (Ed.), *John Dewey and our educational prospect. A critical engagement with Dewey's democracy and education* (pp. 23–37). Albany, NY: SUNY Press.

Biesta, G. J. J. (2007a). The education-socialisation conundrum. Or: 'Who is afraid of education?' *Utbildning och demokrati, 16*(3), 25–36.

Biesta, G. J. J. (2007b). Why 'what works' won't work. Evidence-based practice and the democratic deficit of educational research. *Educational Theory, 57*(1), 1–22.

Biesta, G. J. J. (2007c). Education and the democratic person: Towards a political understanding of democratic education. *Teachers College Record, 109*(3), 740–769.

Biesta, G. J. J. (2009a). Good education in an age of measurement: On the need to reconnect with the question of purpose in education. *Educational Assessment, Evaluation and Accountability, 21*(1), 33–46.

Biesta, G. J. J. (2009b). Witnessing deconstruction in education. Why quasi-transcendentalism matters. *Journal of Philosophy of Education, 43*(3), 391–404.

Biesta, G. J. J. (2009c). What is at stake in a pedagogy of interruption? In T. E. Lewis, J. G. A. Grinberg, & M. Laverty (Eds.), *Philosophy of education: Modern and contemporary ideas at play* (pp. 785–807). Dubuque, IA: Kendall/Hunt.

Biesta, G. J. J. (2009d). How to use pragmatism pragmatically: Suggestions for the 21st century. In A. G. Rud, J. Garrison, & L. Stone (Eds.), *John Dewey at 150. Reflections for a new century* (pp. 30–39). Lafayette, IN: Purdue University Press.

Biesta, G. J. J. (2010a). *Good education in an age of measurement: Ethics, politics, democracy.* Boulder, CO: Paradigm Publishers.

Biesta, G. J. J. (2010b). A new 'logic' of emancipation: The methodology of Jacques Rancière. *Educational Theory, 60*(1), 39–59.

Biesta, G. J. J. (2010c). How to exist politically and learn from it: Hannah Arendt and the problem of democratic education. *Teachers College Record, 112*(2), 558–577.

Biesta, G. J. J. (2010d). 'This is my truth, tell me yours.' Deconstructive pragmatism as a philosophy for education. *Educational Philosophy and Theory, 42*(7), 710–727.

Biesta, G. J. J. (2010e). Why 'what works' still won't work. From evidence-based education to value-based education. *Studies in Philosophy and Education, 29*(5), 491–503.

Biesta, G. J. J. (2010f). Learner, student, speaker. Why it matters how we call those we teach. *Educational Philosophy and Theory, 42*(4), 540–552.

Biesta, G. J. J. (2010g). Five theses on complexity reduction and its politics. In D. C. Osberg & G. J. J. Biesta (Eds.), *Complexity theory and the politics of education* (pp. 5–13). Rotterdam, The Netherlands: Sense Publishers.

Biesta, G. J. J. (2011a). *Learning democracy in school and society: Education, lifelong learning and the politics of citizenship.* Rotterdam, The Netherlands: Sense Publishers.

Biesta, G. J. J. (2011b). The ignorant citizen: Mouffe, Rancière, and the subject of democratic education. *Studies in Philosophy and Education, 30*(2), 141–153.

Biesta, G. J. J. (2011c). Transcendence, revelation and the constructivist classroom; or: In praise of teaching. In R. Kunzman (Ed.), *Philosophy of education 2011* (pp. 358–365). Urbana-Champaign, IL: Philosophy of Education Society.

Biesta, G. J. J. (2011d). Disciplines and theory in the academic study of education: A comparative analysis of the Anglo-American and continental construction of the field. *Pedagogy, Culture and Society, 19*(2), 175–192.

Biesta, G. J. J. (2011e). Citizenship education reconsidered: Socialisation, subjectification, and the desire for democracy. *Bildungsgeschichte. International Journal for the Historiography of Education, 1*(1), 58–67.

Biesta, G. J. J. (2012). Have lifelong learning and emancipation still something to say to each other? *Studies in the Education of Adults, 44*(1), 5–20.

Biesta, G. J. J. (2013a). Receiving the gift of teaching: From 'learning from' to 'being taught by.' *Studies in Philosophy and Education* (Special Issue).

Biesta, G. J. J. (2013b). Interrupting the politics of learning. *Power and Education, 5*(1), 4–15.

Biesta, G. J. J. (2014a). *The beautiful risk of education.* Boulder, CO: Paradigm Publishers.

Biesta, G. J. J. (2014b). You can't always get what you want: An an-archic view on education, democracy and civic learning. In I. Braendholt Lundegaard & J. Thorek Jensen (Eds.), *Museums: Knowledge, democracy, transformation* (pp. 110–119). Copenhagen: Danish Agency for Culture.

Biesta, G. J. J. (2017). *The rediscovery of teaching.* London & New York, NY: Routledge.

Biesta, G. J. J., & Burbules, N. (2003). *Pragmatism and educational research.* Lanham, MD: Rowman and Littlefield.

Biesta, G. J. J., & Säfström, C. A. (2011). A manifesto for education. *Policy Futures in Education, 9*(5), 540–547.

Biesta, G. J. J., & Stams, G. J. J. M. (2001). Critical thinking and the question of critique. Some lessons from deconstruction. *Studies in Philosophy and Education, 20*(1), 57–74.

Biesta, G. J. J., & Stengel, B. (2016). Thinking philosophically about teaching. In D. H. Gittomer & C. A. Bell (Eds.), *Handbook of research on teaching* (5th ed., pp. 7–68). Washington, DC: AERA.

Bingham, C. (2001). *Schools of recognition: Identity politics and classroom practices.* Lanham, MD: Rowman and Littlefield.

Bingham, C., & Biesta, G. J. J. (2010). *Jacques Rancière: Education, truth, emancipation.* London & New York, NY: Continuum.

Bingham, C., & Sidorkin, A. M. (Eds.). (2004). *No education without relation.* New York, NY: Peter Lang.

Black, P., Harrison, C., Lee, C., Marshall, B., & William, D. (2003). *Assessment for learning: Putting it into practice.* Maidenhead: Open University Press.

Bloom, A. (1987). *The closing of the American mind.* Harmondsworth: Penguin Books.

Bloor, D. (1991). *Knowledge and social imagery* (2nd ed.). Chicago, IL: Chicago University Press.

Böhme, G., Daele, W., Hohlfeld, R., Krohn, W., & Schäfer, W. (1978). *Die gesellschaftliche Orientierung des wissenschaftlichen Fortschrits*. Frankfurt am Main: Suhrkamp.

Bonnett, M. (2009). Education and selfhood: A phenomenological investigation. *Journal of Philosophy of Education, 43*(3), 357–370.

Brummett, B. (2012). Taking a metaperspective on rhetorical education. *Journal of Curriculum Studies, 44*(6), 809–814.

Burbules, N. C. (1990). Modes of criticality as modes of teaching. In S. Tozer (Ed.), *Philosophy of education 1998* (pp. 485–489). Urbana-Champaign, IL: Philosophy of Education Society.

Burke, K. (1951). Rhetoric – Old and new. *The Journal of General Education, 5*(3), 202–209.

Burke, K. (1955). Linguistic approaches to problems of education. In B. H. Nelson (Ed.), *Modern philosophies and education: The fifty-fourth yearbook of the National Society for the Study of Education* (pp. 259–303). Chicago, IL: University of Chicago Press.

Burke, K. (1966). *Language as symbolic action*. Los Angeles, CA: University of California Press.

Caputo, J. D. (Ed.). (1997). *Deconstruction in a nutshell. A Conversation with Jacques Derrida*. New York, NY: Fordham University Press.

Caputo, J. D. (2012). Teaching the event: Deconstruction, hauntology and the scene of pedagogy. In C. W. Ruitenberg (Ed.), *Philosophy of education 2012* (pp. 23–34). Urbana-Champaign, IL: Philosophy of Education Society.

Carr, W., & Hartnett, A. (1996). *Education and the struggle for democracy: The politics of educational ideas*. Buckingham: Open University Press.

Cipolla, C. M. (1976). *Before the industrial revolution: European society and economy, 1000–1700*. London: Methuen.

Cleary, J., & Hogan, P. (2001). The reciprocal character of self-education: Introductory comments on Hans-Georg Gadamer's address 'Education is self-education.' *Journal of Philosophy of Education, 35*(4), 519–528.

Critchley, S. (1999). *The ethics of deconstruction: Derrida and Levinas (Expanded Second Edition)*. Edinburgh: Edinburgh University Press.

Davidson, D. (1974). On the very idea of a conceptual scheme. *Proceedings and Addresses of the American Philosophical Association, 47*, 5–20.

Derrida, J. (1978). *Writing and difference*. Chicago, IL: The University of Chicago Press.

Derrida, J. (1981). *Positions*. Chicago, IL: The University of Chicago Press.

Derrida, J. (1982). *Margins of philosophy*. Chicago, IL: The University of Chicago Press.

Derrida, J. (1987). Some questions and responses. In N. Fabb et al. (Eds.), *The linguistics of writing. Arguments between language and literature* (pp. 252–264). Manchester: Manchester University Press.

Derrida, J. (1988). *Limited Inc*. Evanston, IL: Northwestern University Press.

Derrida, J. (1991). Letter to a Japanese friend. In P. Kamuf (Ed.), *A Derrida reader: Between the blinds* (pp. 270–276). New York, NY: Columbia University Press.

Derrida, J. (1992). Force of law: The 'mystical foundation of authority. In D. Cornell, M. Rosenfeld, & D. Carlson (Eds.), *Deconstruction and the possibility of justice* (pp. 3–67). New York, NY & London: Routledge.

Derrida, J. (1995a). *Points ... Interviews, 1974–1994*. Stanford, CA: Stanford University Press.

Derrida, J. (1995b). Honoris Causa: This is also extremely funny. In E. Weber (Ed.), *Points ... Interviews, 1974–1994* (pp. 399–421). Stanford, CA: Stanford University Press.

Derrida, J. (1986). Remarks on deconstruction and pragmatism. In C. Mouffe (Ed.), *Deconstruction and pragmatism* (pp. 77–88). New York, NY & London: Routledge.

Derrida, J. (1999). Hospitality, justice, and responsibility: A dialogue with Jacques Derrida. In R. Kearney & M. Dooley (Eds.), *Questioning ethics. Contemporary debates in philosophy* (pp. 65–83). New York, NY & London: Routledge.

Derrida, J., & Ewald, F. (1995). A certain 'madness" must watch our thinking. An interview with Jacques Derrida. *Educational Theory, 45*(3), 273–291.

Dewey, J. (1930). *Individualism old and new*. New York, NY: Milton Balch.

Dewey, J. (1935). *Liberalism and social action*. New York, NY: G.P. Putnam's.

Dewey, J. (1938). *Logic: The theory of inquiry*. New York, NY: Henry Holt.

Dewey, J. (1954[1927]). *The public and its problems*. Chicago, IL: The Swallow Press.

Dewey, J. (1958[1925]). *Experience and nature*. New York, NY: Dover.

Dewey, J. (1960). *The quest for certainty* (Originally 1929). New York, NY: Putnam.

Dewey, J. (1966[1916]). *Democracy and education*. New York, NY: The Free Press.

Dewey, J. (1969[1888]). The ethics of democracy. In J. A. Boydston (Ed.), *John Dewey: The early works, 1882–1898. Volume 1: 1882–1888* (pp. 227–252). Carbondale & Edwardsville, IL: Southern Illinois University Press.

Dewey, J. (1978[1908]). Ethics. In J. A. Boydston (Ed.), *John Dewey: The middle works, 1899–1924. Volume 5: 1908*. Carbondale & Edwardsville, IL: Southern Illinois University Press.

Dewey, J. (1984[1930]). From absolutism to experimentalism. In J. A. Boydston (Ed.), *John Dewey: The later works, 1925–1953. Volume 5: 1929–1930* (pp. 147–160). Carbondale & Edwardsville, IL: Southern Illinois University Press.

Dewey, J. (1987a[1937]). Education and social change. Originally 1937. In J. A. Boydston (Ed.), *John Dewey: The later works 1925–1953. Volume 11: 1935* (pp. 408–418). Carbondale & Edwardsville, IL: Southern Illinois University Press.

Dewey, J. (1987b[1937]). Democracy and educational administration. In J. A. Boydston (Ed.), *John Dewey: The later works, 1925–1953. Volume 11: 1935–1937* (pp. 217–225). Carbondale & Edwardsville, IL: Southern Illinois University Press.

Dewey, J. (1990[1899]). *The school and society; The child and the curriculum. An expanded edition with a new introduction by Philip W. Jackson*. Chicago, IL: University of Chicago Press.

Dewey, J. (1991[1939]). *Experience, knowledge, and value: A rejoinder.* In J. A. Boydston (Ed.), *John Dewey: The later works, 1925–1953. Volume 14: 1939–1941* (pp. 3–90). Carbondale & Edwardsville, IL: Southern Illinois University Press.

Dilthey, W. (1961). *Pädagogik. Geschichte und Grundlinien des Systems. Gesammelte schriften, Bd. IX. 3. Aufl.* Göttingen: Vandenhoeck & Ruprecht.

Dryzek, J. (2000). *Deliberative democracy and beyond. Liberals, critics, contestations.* Oxford: Oxford University Press.

Dryzek, J. (2010). *Foundations and frontiers of deliberative governance.* Oxford: Oxford University Press.

Ellsworth, E. (2004). *Places of learning: Media, architecture, pedagogy.* London & New York, NY: Routledge.

Elster, J. (Ed.). (1998). *Deliberative democracy.* Cambridge: Cambridge University Press.

Ennis, R. (1962). A concept of critical thinking. *Harvard Educational Review, 32*(1), 81–111.

Ennis, R. (1987). A taxonomy of critical thinking dispositions and abilities. In J. Baron & R. Sternberg (Eds.), *Teaching for thinking* (pp. 9–26). New York, NY: Freeman.

Enoch, J. (2004). Becoming symbol-wise: Kenneth Burke's pedagogy of critical reflection. *College Composition and Communication, 56*(2), 272–296.

Enoch, J. (2012). Claiming access to elite curriculum: Identification and division at the Harvard Annex. *Journal of Curriculum Studies, 44*(6), 787–808.

Feifer, G. (2006). *Breaking open Japan: Commodore Perry, Lord Abe, and American imperialism in 1853.* New York, NY: Smithsonian Books.

Festenstein, M. (1997). *Pragmatism and political theory.* Chicago, IL: University of Chicago Press.

Fieldhouse, R. (1998). *A history of modern British adult education.* Leicester: NIACE.

Foucault, M. (1970). *The order of things. An archaeology of the human sciences.* New York, NY: Random House.

Freire, P. (1970). *Pedagogy of the oppressed.* New York, NY: Continuum.

Freire, P., & Macedo, D. P. (1987). *Literacy: Reading the word & the world.* South Hadley, MA: Bergin & Garvey Publishers.

Füssenhaüser, C. (2005). *Wirkungsgeschichte(n) der Sozialpädagogik.* Baltmannsweiler: Schneider Verlag.

Galloway, S. (2012). Reconsidering emancipatory education: Staging a conversation between Paulo Freire and Jacques Rancière. *Educational Theory, 62*(2), 163–184.

Garrison, J. (1999). Reclaiming the lógos, considering the consequences, and restoring context. *Educational Theory, 49*(3), 317–337.

Garrison, J., & Phelan, A. (1990). Toward a feminist poetic of critical thinking. In R. Page (Ed.), *Philosophy of education 1989* (pp. 304–314). Normal, IL: Philosophy of Education Society.

Gasché, R. (1986). *The tain of the mirror. Derrida and the philosophy of reflection.* Cambridge, MA: Harvard University Press.

Gasché, R. (1994). *Inventions of difference. On Jacques Derrida.* Cambridge, MA: Harvard University Press.

Geissler, E. E. (1970). *Herbarts Lehre vom erziehenden Unterricht.* Heidelberg: Quelle & Meyer.

Gellner, E. (1992). *Postmodernism, reason and religion.* London & New York, NY: Routledge.

Giroux, H. (2004). Cultural studies and the politics of public pedagogy: Making the political more pedagogical. *Parallax, 10*(2), 73–89.

Gordon, M. (Ed.). (2001). *Hannah Arendt and education: Renewing our common world.* New York, NY: Westview Press.

Groothoff, H.-H. (Ed.). (1978). *Das Fischer Lexicon: Pädagogik. Neuausgabe.* Frankfurt am Main: Fischer Taschenbuch.

Gutmann, A. (1993). Democracy. In R. Goodin & P. Pettit (Eds.), *A companion to contemporary political philosophy* (pp. 411–421). Oxford: Blackwell.

Habermas, J. (1989). *The structural transformation of the public sphere: An inquiry into a category.* Cambridge, MA: MIT Press.

Habermas, J. (1975). *Legitimation crisis.* Boston, MA: Beacon Press.

Hannam, P., & Echeverria, E. (2009). *Philosophy with teenagers.* London & New York, NY: Continuum.

Hansen, D. T. (2006). Dewey's book of the moral self. In D.T. Hansen (Ed.), *John Dewey and our educational prospect* (pp. 165–187). Albany, NY: SUNY Press.

Haroutunian-Gordon, S. (1998). Some issues in the critical thinking debate: Dead horses and red herrings, anyone? *Educational Theory, 48*(3), 411–425.

Haroutunian-Gordon, S. (2004). Listening – In a democratic society. In K. Alston (Ed.), *Philosophy of education 2003* (pp. 1–18). Urbana-Champaign, IL: Philosophy of Education Society.

Held, D. (1987). *Models of democracy.* Cambridge: Polity Press.

Heydorn, H. J. (1972). *Zu einer Neufassung des Bildungsbegriffs.* Frankfurt am Main: Suhrkamp.

Hill, D., McLaren, P., Cole, M., & Rikowski, G. (Eds.). (1999). *Postmodernism in educational theory. Education and the politics of human resistance.* London: The Tufnell Press.

Hirsch Jr., E. D. (1987). *Cultural literacy: What every American needs to know.* Boston, MA: Houghton-Mifflin.

Hirsch Jr., E. D. (1989). *A first dictionary of cultural literacy: What our children need to know.* Boston, MA: Houghton-Mifflin.

Honig, B. (1993). *Political theory and the displacement of politics.* Ithaca, NY & London: Cornell University Press.

Horkheimer, M. (1992[1947]). *Eclipse of reason.* New York, NY: Continuum.

Hudak, G. (2011). Alone in the presence of others: Autistic sexuality and intimacy reconsidered. In D. Carlson & D. Roseboro (Eds.), *The sexuality curriculum and youth culture* (pp. 57–70). New York, NY: Peter Lang.

Hughes, T. (1979). The electrification of America: The system builders. *Technology and Culture, 20*(1), 124–162.

Jaeger, W. (1945). *Paideia: The ideals of Greek culture.* New York, NY: Oxford University Press.

Johnson, R. (1979). Really useful knowledge: Radical education and working-class culture. In J. Clarke, C. Critcher, & R. Johnson (Eds.), *Working class culture: Studies in history and theory* (pp. 75–102). London: Hutchinson.

Kant, I. (1784). Beantwortung der Frage: Was ist Aufklarung? *Berlinische Monatsschrift December, 1784,* 481–494.

Kant, I. (1929). *Critique of pure reason.* New York, NY: St. Martin's Press.

Kant, I. (1956). *Kritik der reinen Vernunft. Nach den ersten und zweiten Original-Ausgabe neu herausgegeben von Raymund Schmidt.* Hamburg: Felix Meiner.

Kant, I. (1982). Über Pädagogik. In I. Kant (Ed.), *Schriften zur Anthropologie, Geschichtsphilosophie, Politik und Pädagogik* (pp. 695–761). Frankfurt am Main: Insel Verlag.

Kant, I. (1992). An answer to the question 'What is Enlightenment?.' In P. Waugh (Ed.), *Postmodernism. A reader* (pp. 89–95). London: Edward Arnold.

Kierkegaard, S. (1985). *Philosophical fragments* (Edited and translated with introduction and notes by H. V. Hong & E. H. Hong). Princeton, NJ: Princeton University Press.

Klafki, W. (1964). *Studien zur Bildungstheorie und Didaktik.* Weinheim & Basel: Beltz.

Klafki, W. (1969). Zur Theorie der kategoriale Bildung. In E. Weber (Ed.), *Der Erziehungs-und Bildungsbegriff im 20. Jahrhunderts* (pp. 54–85). Bad Beilbrunnn: Klinkhardt.

Klafki, W. (1986). Die Bedeutung der klassischen Bildungstheorien für eine zeitgemäßes Konzept von allgemeiner Bildung. *Zeitschrift für Pädagogik, 32*(4), 455–476.

Kliebard, H. (1986). *The struggle for the American curriculum 1893–1958.* New York, NY & London: Routledge.

Knowles, M. S. (1962). *The adult education movement in the United States.* New York, NY: Holt, Rinehart and Winston.

Kommision Sozialpädagogik. (Eds.). (2010). *Bildung des effective citizen. Sozialpädagogik auf dem Weg zu einem neuen Sozialentwurf.* Weinheim & München: Juventa.

Koring, B. (1990). *Einführung in die moderne Erziehungswissenschaft und Bildungstheorie.* Weinheim: Deutschen Studien Verlag.

Kron, F. W. (1989). *Grundwissen Pädagogik: Zweite, verbesserte Auflage.* München & Basel: Ernst Reinhardt.

Lankshear, C., & Lawler, M. (1988). *Schooling, literacy and revolution.* Philadelphia, PA: Falmer.

Latour, B. (1983). Give me a laboratory and I will raise the world. In K. D. Knorr-Cetina & M. Mulkay (Eds.), *Science observed* (pp. 141–170). London: Sage Publications.

Latour, B. (1987). *Science in action.* Cambridge, MA: Harvard University Press.

Latour, B. (1988). *The pasteurization of France.* Cambridge, MA: Harvard University Press.

Latour, B., & Woolgar, S. (1986). *Laboratory life: The construction of scientific facts* (2nd ed.). Princeton, NJ: Princeton University Press.

Levinas, E. (1969). *Totality and infinity: An essay on exteriority.* Pittsburgh, PA: Duquesne University Press.

Levinas, E. (1981). *Otherwise than being or beyond essence.* The Hague: Martinus Nijhoff.

Levinas, E. (1985). *Ethics and infinity.* Pittsburgh, PA: Duquesne University Press.

Levinas, E. (1987). Phenomenon and Enigma. In E. Levinas (Ed.), *Collected philosophical papers* (pp. 61–74). Dordrecht: Martinus Nijhoff.

Levinas, E. (1990). *Difficult freedom. Essays on Judaism.* Baltimore, MD: The Johns Hopkins University Press.

Levinas, E. (1998). *Of God who comes to mind.* Stanford, CA: Stanford University Press.

Lingis, A. (1994). *The community of those who have nothing in common.* Bloomington, IN: Indiana University Press.

Lipman, M. (2003). *Thinking in education* (2nd rev. ed.). Cambridge, MA: Cambridge University Press.

Ljunggren, C. (2003). The public has to define itself. *Studies in Philosophy and Education, 22*(5), 351–370.

Long, F. (2005). Thomas Reid and philosophy with children. *Journal of Philosophy of Education, 39*(4), 599–615.

Marquand, D. (2004). *Decline of the public: The hollowing-out of citizenship.* Cambridge: Policy Press.

Masschelein, J. (1996). Individualization, singularization and e-ducation (between indifference and responsibility). *Studies in Philosophy and Education, 15*(1–2), 97–105.

Masschelein, J., & Simons, M. (2004). Globale immuniteit. Leuven: Acco.

Masschelein, J., & Simons, M. (2010). The hatred of public schooling: The school as the mark of democracy. *Educational Philosophy and Theory, 42*(5–6), 666–682.

Masschelein, J., & Wimmer, M. (1996). *Alterität, Pluralität, Gerechtigkeit. Randgänge der Pädagogik.* Sankt Augustin & Leuven: Academia/Leuven University Press.

McLaren, P. (1995). *Critical pedagogy and predatory culture. Oppositional politics in a postmodern era.* London & New York, NY: Routledge.

McLaren, P. (1997). *Revolutionary multiculturalism: Pedagogies of dissent for the new millennium.* Boulder, CO: Westview Press.

McPeck, J. (1981). *Critical thinking and education.* New York, NY: St. Martin's.

McPeck, J. (1990). *Teaching critical thinking.* New York, NY: Routledge.

Meirieu, P. (2007). *Pédagogie: Le devoir de résister.* Issy-les-Moulineaux: ESF éditeur.

Merton, R. K. (1942). *The sociology of science: Theoretical and empirical investigations.* Chicago, IL: University of Chicago Press.

Miller, A. (2007). Rhetoric, paideia and the old idea of a liberal education. *Journal of Philosophy of Education, 41*(2), 183–206.

Mitchell, D. (1995). The end of public space? People's park, definitions of the public, and democracy. *Annals of the Association of American Geographers, 85*(1), 108–133.

Mollenhauer, K. (1973). *Erziehung und Emanzipation.* München: Juventa.

Mollenhauer, K. (1982). *Theorien zum Erziehungsprozess.* München: Juventa.

Mollenhauer, K. (1983). *Vergessene Zusammenhänge: Über Kultur und Erziehung.* München: Juventa.

Mortensen, P. (2012). The work of illiteracy in the rhetorical curriculum. *Journal of Curriculum Studies, 44*(6), 761–786.

Mouffe, C. (1993). *The return of the political.* London & New York, NY: Verso.

Mouffe, C. (2000). *The democratic paradox.* London & New York, NY: Verso.

Mouffe, C. (2005). *On the political.* London & New York, NY: Routledge.

Murris, K. S. (2008). Philosophy with children, the stingray and the educative value of disequilibrium. *Journal of Philosophy of Education, 42*(3–4), 667–685.

Nietzsche, F. (1964). *Der Wille zur Macht: Versuch einer Umwertung aller Werte.* Stuttgart: Alfred Kröner.

Nohl, H. (1935). *Die pädagogische Bewegung in Deutschland und ihre Theorie.* Frankfurt am Main: Gerhard Schulte-Bulmke.

Norris, C. (1987). *Derrida.* Cambridge, MA: Harvard University Press.

Norris, S. (Ed.). (1992). *The Generalizability of Critical Thinking.* New York, NY: Teachers College Press.

Oelkers, J. (1996). *Reformpädagogik. Eine kritische Dogmengeschichte.* München: Juventa.

Oelkers, J. (2000). Democracy and education: About the future of a problem. *Studies in Philosophy and Education, 19*(3), 3–19.

Orr, D. (1989). Just the facts ma'am: Informal logic, gender and pedagogy. *Informal Logic, 9*, 1–10.

Osberg, D. C., & Biesta, G. J. J. (Eds.). (2010). *Complexity theory and the politics of education.* Rotterdam, The Netherlands: Sense Publishers.

Paul, R. W. (1992). *Critical thinking.* Santa Rosa, CA: Foundation for Critical Thinking.

Peters, R. (1966). *Ethics and education.* London: George Allen & Unwin, Ltd.

Perelman, C., & Olbrechts-Tyteca, L. (1958). *Traite de l'argumentation: La nouvelle rhétorique.* Paris: Presses Universitaires de France.

Perelman, C., & Olbrechts-Tyteca, L. (1969). *The new rhetoric: A treatise on argumentation.* Notre Dame, IN: University of Notre Dame Press.

Perquin, N. C. A. (1966). *De pedagogische verantwoordelijkheid van de samenleving.* Roermond: Romen.

Pickering, A. (Ed.). (1992). *Science as practice and culture.* Chicago, IL: Chicago University Press.

Portelli, S. P., & Bailin, S. (Eds.). (1993). *Reason and values: New essays in philosophy of education.* Calgary: Detselig Enterprises.

Rancière, J. (1991). *The ignorant schoolmaster. Five lessons in intellectual emancipation.* Stanford, CA: Stanford University Press.

Rancière, J. (1995). *On the shores of politics.* London & New York, NY: Verso.

Rancière, J. (1999). *Dis-agreement. Politics and philosophy.* Minneapolis, MN & London: University of Minnesota Press.

Rancière, J. (2004). *The politics of aesthetics.* London: Continuum.

Rang, A. (1987). Over de betekenis van het element 'algemeen' in het concept van de algemene vorming. *Comenius, 7*(1), 49–62.

Rorty, R. (1978). Philosophy as a kind of writing: An essay on Derrida. *New Literary History, 10*(1), 141–160.

Rorty, R. (1980). *Philosophy and the mirror of nature.* Oxford: Blackwell.

Roth, H. (1963). Die realistische Wendung in der pädagogische Forschung. *Die Deutsche Schule, 55,* 109–119.

Röttgers, K. (1990). Kritik. In J. J. Sandkühler (Ed.), *Europäische Enzyklopädie zu Philosophie und Wissenschaften. Band 2* (pp. 889–898). Hamburg: Felix Meiner Verlag.

Rutten, K., & Soetaert, R. (2012). Revisiting the rhetorical curriculum. *Journal of Curriculum Studies, 44*(6), 727–743.

Ryan, A. (1995). *John Dewey and the high tide of American liberalism.* New York, NY & London: W.W. Norton.

Sandlin, J. A., O'Malley, M. P., & Burdick, J. (2011). Mapping the complexity of public pedagogy scholarship: 1894–2010. *Review of Educational Research, 81*(3), 338–375.

Sandlin, J. A., Schultz, B. D., & Burdick, J. (Eds.). (2010). *Handbook of public pedagogy: Education and learning beyond schooling.* New York, NY: Routledge.

Sas, P. (1995). Het geweten van de transcendentaalfilosofie: Karl-Otto Apel en de mogelijkheid van strikte reflectie. *Tijdschrift voor Filosofie, 57,* 505–525.

Savage, G. (2010). Problematizing 'public pedagogy' in educational research. In J. A. Sandlin, B. D. Schultz, & J. Burdick (Eds.), *Handbook of public pedagogy: Education and learning beyond schooling* (pp. 103–115). New York, NY: Routledge.

Schaffar, B. (2009). *Allgemeine Pädagogik im Zwiespalt: Zwischen epistemologische Neutralität und moralischer Einsicht.* Würzburg: Ergon Verlag.

Sennett, R. (1992). *The fall of public man.* New York, NY: W.W. Norton.

Siegel, H. (1987). *Relativism refuted. A critique of contemporary epistemological relativism.* Dordrecht: Reidel.

Siegel, H. (1988). *Educating reason. Rationality, critical thinking and education.* New York, NY & London: Routledge.

Siegel, H. (1990). Why be rational? On thinking critically about critical thinking. In R. Page (Ed.), *Philosophy of education 1989* (pp. 392–401). Normal, IL: Philosophy of Education Society.

Siegel, H. (1992). The generalizability of critical thinking skills, dispositions and epistemology. In S. P. Norris (Ed.), *The generalizability of critical thinking* (pp. 97–108). New York, NY: Teachers College Press.

Siegel, H. (1995). What price inclusion? *Teachers College Record, 97*, 6–31.

Siegel, H. (1997). *Rationality redeemed? Further dialogues on an educational ideal.* New York, NY & London: Routledge.

Simmons, J., & Biddle, G. (1997). *The Oxford companion to British railway history: From 1603 to the 1990s.* Oxford: Oxford University Press.

Sloterdijk, P. (1996). *Selbstversuch. Ein Gespräch mit Carlos Oliveira.* München: Hanser.

Sloterdijk, P. (2009). Rules for the human zoo: A response to the 'Letter on humanism.' *Environment and Planning D: Society and Space, 27*(1), 12–28.

Snik, G. L. M., & Zevenbergen, J. K. (1995). Kritisch leren denken: Posities en problemen. *Pedagogisch Tijdschrift, 20*, 101–116.

Spencer, H. W. (1909). *Education: Intellectual, moral, and physical.* New York, NY: Appleton.

Spivak, G. C. (2004). Righting the wrongs. *South Atlantic Quarterly, 103*(2–3), 523–581.

Stojanov, K. (2006). *Bildung und Anerkennung. Soziale Voraussetzungen von Selbst-Entwicklung und Welt-Erschließung.* Wiesbaden: Verlag für Sozialwissenschaften.

Stone, L. (2008). Speculation on a missing link: Dewey's democracy and schools. *Journal of Educational Controversy, 3*(1). (Online) Retrieved from http://cedar.wwu.edu/jec/vol3/iss1/3

Sünker, H. (1989). Bildungstheorie als Gesellschaftskritik. In O. Hansmann & W. Marotzki (Eds.), *Diskurs Bildungstheorie II.* Weinheim: Deutscher Studien Verlag.

Sünker, H. (1994). Pedagogy and politics: Heydorn's 'survival through education' and its challenge to contemporary theories of education (Bildung). In S. Miedema, G. Biesta, B. Boog, A. Smaling, W. Wardekker, & B. Levering (Eds.), *The politics of human science* (pp. 113–128). Brussels: VUB Press.

Tenorth, H.-E. (Ed.). (1986). *Allgemeine Bildung. Analysen zur ihrer Wirklichkeit, Versuch über ihre Zukunft.* Weinheim: Juventa.

Thayer-Bacon, B. (1992). Is modern critical thinking sexist? *Inquiry: Critical Thinking Across the Disciplines*, 323–340.

Thayer-Bacon, B. (1993). Caring and its relationship to critical thinking. *Educational Theory, 43*(3), 323–340.

Thayer-Bacon, B. (1998). Transforming and redescribing critical thinking: Constructive thinking. *Studies in Philosophy and Education, 17*(2–3), 123–148.

Thayer-Bacon, B. (2000). *Transforming critical thinking: Constructive thinking.* New York, NY: Teachers College Press.

Thompson, A. (2011). Listening at an angle. In G. J. J. Biesta (Ed.), *Philosophy of education 2010* (pp. 1–10). Urbana, IL: Philosophy of Education Society.

Todd, S. (2003). *Learning from the other.* Albany, NY: SUNY Press.

Usher, R., & Edwards, R. (1994). *Postmodernism and education.* London & New York, NY: Routledge.

Vanderstraeten, R. (1995). *Leren voor het leven.* Leuven & Apeldoorn: Garant.

van der Veen, R., Wildemeersch, D., Youngblood, J., & Marsick, V. (Eds.). (2007). *Democratic practices as learning opportunities.* Rotterdam, The Netherlands: Sense Publishers.

Vansieleghem, N. (2005). Philosophy for children as the wind of thinking. *Journal of Philosophy of Education, 39*(1), 19–37.

van Woudenberg, R. (1991). *Transcendentale reflecties. Een onderzoek naar transcendentale argumenten in de contemporaine filosofie, met bijzondere aandacht voor de transcendentale pragmatiek van Karl-Otto Apel.* Amsterdam: Vrije Universiteit.

Waks, L. J. (2010). Two types of interpersonal listening. *Teachers College Record, 112*(11), 2743–2762.

Walters, K. S. (Ed.). (1994). *Re-thinking reason: New perspectives on critical thinking.* Albany, NY: SUNY Press.

Warren, M. (1992). Democratic theory and self-transformation. *American Political Science Review, 86*(1), 8–23.

Welton, M. R. (1995). *In defense of the lifeworld: Critical perspectives on adult learning.* Albany, NY: SUNY Press.

Westbrook, R. (1991). *John Dewey and American democracy.* Ithaca, NY: Cornell University Press.

Westphal, M. (2008). *Levinas and Kierkegaard in dialogue.* Bloomington, IN: Indiana University Press.

Wildemeersch, D., Finger, M., & Jansen, T. (1998). *Adult education and social responsibility.* New York, NY: Peter Lang.

Winter, P. (2011). Coming into the world, uniqueness, and the beautiful risk of education: AN interview with Gert Biesta by Philip Winter. *Studies in Philosophy and Education, 30*(5), 537–542.

Woolgar, S. (1988). *Science: The very idea.* London & New York, NY: Tavistock Publications.

Young, I. M. (2000). *Inclusion and democracy.* Oxford: Oxford University Press.

Zappen, J. P. (2012). US and Russian traditions in rhetoric, education and culture. *Journal of Curriculum Studies, 44*(6), 745–760.

Zevenbergen, J. K. (1997). Twee rechtvaardigingen van kritisch denken en rationaliteit: Siegel en Apel. *Pedagogisch Tijdschrift, 22,* 289–308.

Zijderveld, A. (1974). *De relativiteit van kennis en werkelijkheid: Inleiding tot de kennissociologie.* Meppel: Boom.